UpDrafts

UpDrafts

Case Studies in Teacher Renewal

Edited by

ROY F. FOX
University of Missouri–Columbia

National Council of Teachers of English
1111 W. Kenyon Road, Urbana, Illinois 61801-1096

"The Lost Son," copyright 1947 by Theodore Roethke, from *Collected Poems of Theodore Roethke* by Theodore Roethke. Used by permission of Doubleday, a division of Random House, Inc.

Staff Editor: Bonny Graham
Interior Design: Jenny Jensen Greenleaf
Cover Design: Diana Coe/ko Design Studio
Author Photo: Beverly Fox

NCTE Stock Number: 55758-3050

It is the policy of NCTE in its journals and other publications to provide a forum for the open discussion of ideas concerning the content and the teaching of English and the language arts. Publicity accorded to any particular point of view does not imply endorsement by the Executive Committee, the Board of Directors, or the membership at large, except in announcements of policy, where such endorsement is clearly specified.

Library of Congress Cataloging-in-Publication Data

UpDrafts: case studies in teacher renewal/edited by Roy F. Fox.
    p. cm.
   Includes bibliographical references and index.
   ISBN 0-8141-5575-8 (pbk.)
    1. Teachers—United States—Psychology—Case studies. 2. Teachers—In-service training—United States—Case studies. I. Fox, Roy F. II. National Council of Teachers of English. III. Title.
LB1775.2.U63 2000
371.1'001'9—dc21

                              00-037974

For Ben F. Nelms

A lively understandable spirit
Once entertained you.
It will come again.

THEODORE ROETHKE, "The Lost Son"

Contents

FOREWORD xi
   Mihaly Csikszentmihalyi

ACKNOWLEDGMENTS xv

INTRODUCTION: BIOGRAPHIES OF PASSION AND SELF-EXILE xvii
   Roy F. Fox

I **Tailwinds** 1

1 *Making Myself Visible: Voice as Renewal*
  Lucy Stanovick 5

2 *The Woman Who Resurrected Words:*
  Writing as Renewal
  Susan Baruffi 24

3 *Collecting Dreams: Imagination as Renewal*
  Jill Weisner 43

II **Crosswinds** 61

4 *Washing Dishes or Doing Schoolwork?*
  Reflective Action as Renewal
  Janet Alsup 65

5 *"Miss White Will Not Be Here Today":*
  Feedback as Renewal
  Marilyn Schultz 85

6 *"Logic and Sermons Never Convince":*
  Maternal Thinking as Renewal
  Marilyn Richardson 107

Contents

III Whirlwinds 123

7 *Finding Her Way: Searching as Renewal*
Patrick Shaw.................................... 127

8 *Chaos and Renewal*
Roy F. Fox 148

9 *Toward a New Model for Teacher Renewal*
Roy F. Fox 164

WORKS CITED 179

INDEX 185

EDITOR 191

CONTRIBUTORS 193

FOREWORD

MIHALY CSIKSZENTMIHALYI
Claremont Graduate University

Human beings more or less like you and me have lived on this planet for roughly two million years. During this period about 100,000 generations have followed each other—an unbroken chain throughout which elders had to pass on to youth everything they knew. If even a single generation fell short, thousands of years' worth of learning would be lost, and have to be painstakingly retrieved. Thus teaching was considered an almost sacred task that involved the entire community and was held in high esteem.

But teaching children how to become adult men and women is not easy. The problem with the notion that "It takes a whole village to bring up a child" is that the village must do many other things besides. So communities, in an effort to save time and effort, have always tried to find ways to cut corners in educating their children. With the advent of literacy, it became possible to imagine that most learning could be accomplished through the vicarious medium of reading. By the time of the Roman Empire, wealthy parents were delegating the task of teaching to slaves armed with rolls of papyrus manuscripts.

A more recent stride in education was taken in the past two centuries, when advances in mass production that had proven so effective in industry and the armed forces were applied to schooling. If you could stamp out steel gaskets to a tolerance of a thousandth of an inch by following rationally planned and rigidly implemented steps, surely you could turn out young men and women who knew everything they needed to know by following a well-thought-out curriculum rigorously implemented by competent instructors. And if that didn't work, perhaps smart machines—computer-assisted teaching—would. Or if these also fail, we can always place our hopes in drugs that enhance learning, or in genetic engineering. . . . Unfortunately, however, technological solutions, while they may be saving time and effort, don't quite do the job. In order to realize their potential as human beings, children need attention and care from adults who have their well-being at heart. In other words, they need teachers.

They need teachers who are not just enforcers of discipline and transmitters of information, but real people who can laugh and cry, individuals with personal beliefs, idiosyncrasies, and passions. Persons who through example show young people that growing up is worth it, that becoming an adult is not a total loss, that the life of the mind can be an exciting adventure. Of course, it is not easy to accomplish this when teachers have to work in factorylike conditions entangled in increasingly stifling red tape, while at the same time they are expected to compensate for all the deficiencies in children's lives caused by families in free fall, or by the mind-numbing molasses of the media.

Yet as we all know, wonderful people still keep entering the teaching profession. For them, the importance of the task justifies the often miserable conditions of the job. Many of them struggle in isolation, too busy trying to live up to the standards they set for themselves to wonder how education might be changed.

For such teachers who care about their mission, *UpDrafts* will be a breath of fresh air. It is a collection of case studies that shows with stark honesty the pressures teachers are likely to confront on their job, from prejudice to conformity, from lack of understanding to lack of time. They are expected to perform miracles under conditions that are little better than slavery. Yet, as these moving vignettes of renewal illustrate, somehow it is possible to break through the bonds and create careers that support the freshness of personal ideals while nurturing personal growth.

UpDrafts provides hope and inspiration to every teacher who is toiling against great odds in a noble cause. But it does more than that: through the careful selection, analysis, and presentation of these life stories within a theoretical framework, this book suggests a method for renewing one's life, no matter what the external circumstances. And by renewal the authors don't mean just healing and restoration, but progression toward greater complexity—a creative evolution toward a more fulfilling life. Who could not benefit from such an effort? But be reassured that the book is never technical or preachy—the theory emerges organically from the vivid lives of the teachers portrayed.

In closing, I should mention that as I finished the manuscript I could not help wondering what an anthropologist from Mars would think of it. Wouldn't he, she, or it be surprised, for instance, that of the eight valiant teachers presented here, seven are of the same gender? Why is it, the Martian anthropologist might ask itself, that Americans believe that it makes no difference whether or not grown men are involved in the education of their children? This is just one of many puzzles that a naive observer might encounter in trying to make sense of what we do in our schools. But any reader, whether Martian or terrestrial, would be reassured that as long as creative teachers such as those described in these pages are willing to take on the job, there is hope for the future.

Claremont, California, March 2000

ACKNOWLEDGMENTS

Many good people helped with this book. I thank the National Writing Project for providing an initial small grant to document the work of one of its sites, the Missouri Writing Project. We especially thank Jo Fyfe, Mary Ann Smith, and Mark St. John for their encouragement, as well as Pete Feely of NCTE for steering a manuscript that resisted traditional categories.

I thank the reviewers of these updrafts for their intelligent, sincere responses, as well as Bonny Graham of NCTE for her expert editing. I am grateful to my own family, Bev Fox, Emma Fox, and Joel Fox, for tolerating all the absences and lapses (memory, judgment, tolerance, etc.) which afflict people who mess around with words. I especially thank Bev Fox for her editing acumen and unfailing support.

Most of all, I thank the veteran teachers who agreed to be "subjects" for these chapters—for taking time out of their strenuous schedules to help us try to gauge a few of the changeable currents which keep us all airborne.

Introduction:
Biographies of Passion and Self-Exile

ROY F. FOX
University of Missouri–Columbia

What the teacher "teaches" is by no means chiefly in the words he speaks. It is at least in part in what he is, in what he does, in what he seems to wish to be. The secret curriculum is the teachers' own lived values and convictions, in the lineaments of his expressions and in the biography of passion or self-exile which is written in his eyes.

JONATHAN KOZOL, *The Night Is Dark and I Am Far from Home*

Demands upon teachers have multiplied as quickly as cellular phones. Our demands have increased not just in number but also in type. We now expect teachers to be surrogate parents, offering love, support, moral values, and discipline. We expect them to be psychologists, career counselors, and health and wellness educators who focus on nutrition, exercise, substance abuse, teen pregnancy, sexually transmitted diseases, and legal issues. Of course, the list of roles is even longer than this. None of the roles, however, includes that for which teachers are primarily trained—being experts in an academic discipline and its pedagogy. At the same time that such demands on teachers proliferate, so do demands for greater student achievement and teacher accountability, as well as requirements for teachers to continue their professional development. In this overheated work environment, teachers must not merely survive but thrive—not just this year, but next year, and the years after that. This book explores how excellent teachers renew themselves, professionally as well as personally. Hence, we employ a broad definition of teacher renewal: the teacher's overall personal, emotional, and psychological rejuvenation, in and out of the classroom, including specific instances of renewal that occur within a classroom, discipline, or community.

Many forces influence teacher renewal: (1) the teacher's (and each student's) multiple roles and identities; (2) the established curriculum, the ideal curriculum, and all points in between—each viewed from multiple perspectives; (3) the teacher's disciplinary knowledge and instructional theories, processes, and strategies; (4) the contexts in which each of these elements occurs, from the school's administration, to parents, to "standards-bearing" organizations, to ever-larger communities; (5) the intense, direct experiences of everyday life, including those which involve symbols; (6) the teacher's family and financial circumstances; (7) current educational movements; and (8) the larger culture, especially our electronic media environment.

But this is not all. Daily, teachers face pressures in addition to their professional ones. I think of Andy, a young teacher who taught in a school without a separate restroom for adults. "The only stall in the 'boy's bathroom' doesn't have a door on it," he told me. "Whenever I was there, kids came in and pointed at me and laughed and yelled—'Hey, look, everyone—there's Mr. Jamison!'" Andy's only solution was to drive to the closest gas station.

And I think of Kate, profiled in Lucy Stanovick's "Making Myself Visible: Voice as Renewal." Every day after school, she drove to a hospital in another town to be at the bedside of her brother, who was dying of AIDS, a secret which she felt compelled to hide from her disapproving family and her generally antigay colleagues at school. I think of Eleanor, a veteran teacher at an urban school who, to prepare for the coming year, devoted three full days to fasting and praying. I think of Tish, described in Patrick Shaw's "Finding Her Way: Searching as Renewal." After Tish gave every ounce of her time and energy to teaching, she opened a book one evening to find a note addressed to her from one of her students. It read, "Ms. Spenser's a dyke." The best teachers—like Andy, Kate, Eleanor, and Tish—are driven by passion for what they do. But often this very passion brings on periods of self-exile or other phases during which a teaching life does not go so well. Then that passion must be rekindled. Such periods of passion and self-exile ebb and flow in a teaching life, and teachers seldom travel the same route.

Despite such problems, this study focuses on people who succeeded, who overcame obstacles, and relates how they flourished regardless of external constraints. That is why this book is called *UpDrafts*—the teachers' experiences described here constitute an upward current of air, a fresh gust of change, a collection of stories that are "uppers." This book is intended for teachers, teachers-in-training, administrators, students, and parents—for anyone concerned about teaching and learning and the future.

How This Study Was Designed

For this project, each of seven researchers developed a case study of one highly successful teacher, while I constructed a first-person account. We were all experienced (and successful) teachers in our own right, currently teaching in public schools and universities. Most researchers were also pursuing doctoral degrees in English education. Because we had been long engaged in the teaching and learning of literacy, we were dedicated to the powers of language and other representations that not only reflect reality, but create it, as well.

We hoped that sharing stories of renewal would help other teachers reflect on and construct (or reconstruct) their own paths to renewal. Therefore, this study's design integrates teacher lore (e.g., Ayers and Schubert 1994) and case-study approaches (e.g., Stake 1995). The subjects of our case studies varied in age, personal and academic background, and instructional style. They especially differed in approach to renewal. As is common in qualitative research, we employed an "emergent design" approach, making adjustments as the study unfolded. We met twice a month to discuss questions and to examine the same set of readings, as well as to keep our procedures uniform and to link our discussions back to teaching and learning. Our research focused on two questions:

1. How do successful teachers rejuvenate or renew themselves for their teaching—what common, everyday things do they do (on or off the job) to generate energy and interest in teaching?
2. How do successful teachers describe their passions for activities which are both related and unrelated to their profession?

Theoretical Framework

Because of the highly interdisciplinary nature of teacher renewal, this study's theoretical framework includes concepts from several areas of psychology (especially teachers' commitment or passion for teaching, "flow" experiences, and the development of "voice" and identity), as well as from professional development, teacher lore, and literacy. Initially, the research team reviewed these areas to identify concepts relevant to teacher renewal, whether they focused on professional or personal elements. I will provide a brief overview here, since theory and research are explored more fully in a later section of this introduction (Four Processes of Teacher Renewal).

Several sources helped us understand the larger contexts of teacher renewal. In addition to Lieberman and Miller's (1992) *Teachers—Their World and Their Work*, Cohen and Scheer's (1997) collection of first-person narratives, *The Work of Teachers in America: A Social History Through Stories*, provides a vivid history of teaching. For example, writings by Emma Hart Willard, Anne Sullivan, Walt Whitman, W. E. B. Du Bois, Jesse Stuart, and Eric Rofes remind us of teaching's rich legacy and the fact that many of our values and struggles have remained the same, regardless of time, place, and culture.

Mihaly Csikszentmihalyi's *Flow: The Psychology of Optimal Experience* (1991) was crucial for our understanding of one consistent pattern of teacher renewal: the experience of becoming deeply absorbed in challenging yet pleasurable activities. Csikszentmihalyi's theories on psychological development have grown from his own research (e.g., Csikszentmihalyi, Getzels, and Kahn 1984; Csikszentmihalyi and Getzels 1988), as well as the earlier work of Maslow (1954), Frankl (1963), Bateson (1978), and others. Csikszentmihalyi believes that flow experiences are necessary for growth of the self to occur. The self grows by becoming more complex through experiencing the broad psychological processes of differentiation and integration. For instance, if we are immersed within a pleasurable challenge and succeed, we feel more in control, more articulated than others, and hence more differentiated. On the other hand, flow experiences also lead to integration of the self. That is, when we are in deep concentration, our "thoughts, intentions, feelings, and all the senses are focused on the same goal" (1991, 41). During flow, then, our consciousness is more ordered, more integrated. The notion that the self must constantly grow by becoming increasingly complex by means of differentiation and integration seems especially true for teachers.

Fried's (1995) work helped us understand how flow experiences in a teacher's personal and professional life (as well as the development of a teacher's oral and written "voice") may link to passion or commitment to teaching. Also, the work of Lindley (1993), heavily influenced by the psychoanalytic theories of Carl Jung (1976), and Britzman's (1994) work on the psychology of teaching helped us hypothesize that flow, passion, and voice are evolving, socially constructed, and integral parts of a teacher's identity.

Selection of Teachers for Case Studies

During our first meeting, I warned the other researchers that we were embarking on "true research," in that we had no way of telling what we would learn or how we might most effectively discover it. After all, we were each studying a unique individual. We read and talked at length about what constitutes a highly successful teacher. Although we resisted precise and narrow definitions of "renewal" and "successful teacher," we selected only teachers who met the following criteria:

- ◆ Communicates clearly and effectively
- ◆ Connects material to students' lives in interesting, relevant ways

- ◆ Inspires or motivates students in creative ways
- ◆ Avoids reliance on number crunching when evaluating students
- ◆ Engages in plentiful and rich language and values the artifacts that students create
- ◆ Communicates with students as one human being to another about nonschool topics as well as school topics
- ◆ Values learning processes as much as products, providing choices for students
- ◆ Demonstrates self-awareness by articulating what they do, how they do it, and why
- ◆ Demonstrates teaching success in documented ways, such as teaching full time for at least ten years; winning teaching awards, grants, and other forms of public recognition; being recognized by their administrators, colleagues, students, parents, and community; participating in professional organizations
- ◆ Navigates major career shifts and transitions

Every meeting, researchers brought questions, confusions, and contradictions to the table. Our discussions often crackled with the energy of trying to understand a teacher's actions or words within the context of her personal and professional lives. Our interest was acute because, in a way, we were connecting these teachers' lives to our own. Because we wanted to make certain that we studied the most effective and creative teachers, many researchers interviewed their own mentors and role models—colleagues who had not only positively influenced legions of students over time, but also deeply touched their own lives. This closeness helped us unravel the teachers' stories. And because we often explored private, sensitive topics, we hoped that such key informants would feel safe enough to tell us how they survived and thrived in the teaching profession.

Next, based on these guidelines, our basic research questions, and our readings, we invited a veteran, highly successful teacher to meet with our entire research group for a three-hour, videotaped "practice interview." Esther Dunnington, recently retired from the public schools, candidly explored her processes of renewal, from her early career, when she had "never even heard of a five-paragraph essay," through her moves from rural to urban schools, where she continued to feel isolated. Esther shared the pivotal renewing experiences which "turned her life around." Our work with Esther helped us realize the intricate web of forces within one teacher's renewal, as well as how we might more effectively question teachers about topics they had seldom, if ever, verbalized.

Procedures

Throughout the year, each researcher audiotaped four to six interviews with a teacher in her home, office, and classroom. Each researcher collected approximately six to eight total hours of interviews, then transcribed and analyzed the data. Some investigators conducted additional interviews with the teacher's current and former students, colleagues, or administrators. Researchers also examined other relevant data, including their teacher's (1) published and unpublished writings; (2) classroom assignments; (3) career achievements; (4) letters received from former students, colleagues, and administrators; and (5) actual classroom activities.

During 1996 and 1997, our group met every two weeks. During these three-hour meetings, we analyzed transcripts and critiqued drafts. Each investigator heard several viewpoints to consider for his or her subsequent analysis and interpretation. We asked questions and debated interpretations as we helped each other analyze material. Throughout these meetings, we continued to ask ourselves, "What do all of these case studies have in common?" We avoided stating or implying that any conclusion reached during a meeting was "the final" one. Instead, we offered the researcher a variety of options to take back home and mull over. Once we had explored the transcripts, we distributed drafts of chapters for everyone to read before we met again. During subsequent meetings we responded to the draft, following the same process used with the transcripts, presenting writers with options for revising their next draft. While reviewing drafts, we often returned to the transcripts, working back and forth between them.

Because each researcher focused on a familiar teacher, these meetings helped provide some balance to our analyses. During these discussions, we constantly evaluated the subject's interpretations of her own experiences, matching them against our own perspectives. We did not always agree with the conclusions that the interviewed teachers reached about their own experiences. While this is a typical dilemma of case-study research (Stake 1995), it nonetheless created a richer field of interpretations to negotiate, sending researchers back to their subjects with new questions. Overall, our meetings stimulated deep, collaborative reflection. Throughout the study, we never shared teachers' identities, nor did we use the real names of students, colleagues, or schools in this book.

Only Stories Do That: Narrative as Inquiry

> What matters is that lives do not serve as models: only stories do that. And it is a hard thing to make up stories to live by. We can only retell and live by the stories we have read or heard. We live our lives through texts. . . . Whatever their form or medium, these stories have formed us all . . . .
>
> CAROLYN HEILBRUN, *Writing a Woman's Life*

We selected narrative as our primary mode of inquiry. Here, it serves as the method of, as well as the artifact for, analysis. Carter (1993) argues that stories capture "the complexity, specificity, and interconnectedness of the phenomenon with which we deal" (6) and that this approach avoids the problems of traditional, quantifiable methods which dissect teaching into many isolated parts. Carter concludes that story has now become central to research because of its "richness and nuance [that] cannot be expressed in definitions, statements of fact, or abstract propositions" (5–6). Carter reminds us that this last type of discourse (e.g., law, politics) can be viewed *not* as objective and rational but as rhetorical "posturing." Many teachers also realize that narrative more closely matches what they do every day and how they frame their experience. Stories may be the most efficient and evocative way to learn about teaching because they concretely represent teaching's codes, lessons, practices, attitudes, and values, in much the same way that film and videotape can. Overall, effective teachers are like children deeply absorbed in play. Of course, such immersion can sometimes lead to self-exile, but more often it leads to the best kind of passion. And such passion is best communicated in stories. This research produced many stories, out of which emerged four major themes or processes.

Four Processes of Teacher Renewal

Four overlapping patterns affecting teacher renewal arose during this study: (1) the teacher's social contexts, (2) the teacher's passion and involvement in "flow" experiences, (3) the development of the teacher's voice, and (4) the teacher's relationship with her dual identities: her professional/personal selves and her adult/child selves. The remainder of this introduction provides an overview of these processes. Also, how these processes operate within specific chapters will be noted in the introductions to Part I, Tailwinds; Part II, Crosswinds; and Part III, Whirlwinds. Finally, Chapter 9, "Notes toward a New Model of Teacher Renewal," explores how these processes might function together, before concluding with several recommendations.

Social Contexts

Environment played a significant role in the personal and professional lives of the teachers described in this book. Social contexts—from the family, to the classroom, to the local community and larger culture—affect what we do and how we feel about it. Because the positive influences of social contexts are included throughout this report, here I will focus only on the elements of social context which hampered teachers seeking renewal: (1) teachers' isolation, (2) professional and institutional bureaucracy, and (3) popular culture and media.

ISOLATION

Teaching remains an isolated (and isolating) profession. Throughout these chapters, isolation meanders in and out of teachers' lives like a dark, slow-moving stream. In Lucy Stanovick's "Making Myself Visible: Voice as Renewal," Kate feels extremely isolated from the colleagues in her building: she communicates very little with them about her classroom activities, keeping her classroom door closed. In Marilyn Schultz's "'Miss White Will Not Be Here Today': Feedback as Renewal," novice teacher Julia White had nobody else to turn to when she panicked because she could not adequately teach literature. When Alex, in Susan Baruffi's "The Woman Who Resurrected Words: Writing as Renewal," asked her colleagues for help, they scolded her for being incompetent. Isolation is a fact of life for teachers.

Also, many nonteachers feel somehow intimidated by and resentful of teachers. Maybe it was the bad grade received in ninth-grade math, or maybe it was Mr. Grumby's vaguely snide attitude or offhand remark, but ultimately this view stems from our long habit of distrusting anything intellectual—of anyone "putting on airs" due to educational or economic status. Think of the Marx Brothers and their pretentious counterpart, Margaret Dumont. Think of *The Beverly Hillbillies*, of *Forrest Gump*, of all those "Ernest" movies. Indeed, The Rube is a cultural icon for an upstart democracy which thumbed its nose at King George. Our collective discomfort with teachers runs long and deep. Teachers themselves are aware of these attitudes and even report that their school administrators do not respect them (Frymier 1987, 9).

Sometimes, isolated teachers become cynical and project their problems onto something else, reasoning that "[t]eaching would be great, if only . . . ." Anyone who wants to feel cynical about teaching and learning can find evidence to illustrate the bleakest scenario. The teachers featured in this book also harbored such feelings, but they acted on them. They did not let them fester and mutate into more complicated beasts. When Carole (in Jill Weisner's "Collecting Dreams: Imagination as Renewal") became agitated, she instantly imagined an alternative scenario to play out in her mind. When Pat, described by Marilyn Richardson in "Logic and Sermons Never Convince: Maternal Thinking as Renewal," realized that she did not really believe in "activities," she quickly changed her thinking. Like all of us, these teachers experienced—and still experience—their share of frustration. However, they did not dwell on it long before taking some kind of action.

BUREAUCRACY

Communication experts refer to any element unrelated to a message as "noise." Noise can take the forms of redundancy, irrelevant information, or static on a TV set—all those things that interfere with the message. Teaching is much the same because it involves the constant sending and receiving of messages. We are often interrupted and distracted from our real work of teaching. As T. S. Eliot said, we are "distracted from distraction by distraction."

Typical teaching noises include the following activities: completing attendance slips; attending ever-urgent committee and board meetings (my school has an official Committee on Committees); updating the latest requests from state departments of education; mulling over minigrants; puzzling over purchase orders; calculating and recording grades and written evaluations; completing reports-of-incomplete-grade forms; speaking with textbook committee members and sales reps; submitting substitute teacher requests; writing instructions for subs, absent students, parents, and others; articulating narrative evaluations for student teachers; filling out requisition forms for No. 8 aluminum paper clips and 1.6 centimeter Post-it notes. You know the drill. Frymier defines such bureaucracy as "the purposes, policies, procedures, programs, precedents, and personnel within a building and a school district." He concludes that bureaucracies are "more influential in determining what professionals do than are personal abilities, professional training, or previous experience" (1987, 10). Bureaucratic chores never stop. When one is addressed, five more appear, some of which may even repeat previous tasks. Kim, in Janet Alsup's "Washing Dishes or Doing Schoolwork? Reflective Action as Renewal," must cope with a bureaucracy which even undermines her authority as a teacher.

We have long known that highly motivated people draw energy from within themselves; their inner feelings tell them that they are in charge of their own lives. On the other hand, teachers drowning in piddling tasks can destroy their internalized "locus of control," leading them to believe that teaching is directed by external forces—not by their own skills and instincts. Teachers bombarded with too many distractions become "neutered" and end up lacking motivation, enthusiasm, and energy (Frymier 1987, 9). When this happens, teachers may focus only on protecting themselves—not on changing and growing.

POPULAR CULTURE AND MEDIA

The teachers described in this book were raised with television and other electronic media, and the influence of these media surfaces in their stories, from Carole's visual thinking to Tish's focus on gendered readings of film. These are a few of the positive influences that culture and electronic media had on these teachers. But there are drawbacks, too. Today, our advertising and entertainment industries dominate many other institutions and pathways of life—from religion (thank you, Jim and Tammy), to law (starring O. J.), to politics (vote for Monica), to war making (featuring Desert Storm and its sequel, Desert Shield). The notion that we even *have* a "cultural environment" that needs tending remains a foreign concept to most Americans.

Media and technology do far more than merely communicate information: they also communicate role models, attitudes, values, and ideologies, all of which can influence several types of health. First, electronic media can influence students' *physical health* by communicating about tobacco, drugs, nutrition, and exercise. Second, media influence *emotional health* when they impose definitions of beauty, sexuality, maturity, and problem solving on students, as well as when they glamorize instant gratification. Third, media affect students' *social health* by communicating attitudes, values, and ideologies, including those of consumption, competition, and materialism. Fourth, media affect students' *cultural health* by when, how, and if they "represent" various groupings of people, especially in terms of gender, race, age, and class.

These kinds of health often suffer when media promote image over substance, glitter over authenticity, razzmatazz over rationality, and dollars over everything else. If we can't buy it, it has no value. If it doesn't happen within nanoseconds, it's not worth happening at all. So—how do teachers survive in this pressurized web? First, passion and flow experiences in teaching content areas depend heavily on context. So do the development of voice, identity, and renewal. Unless we know the rich detail surrounding something, it will make little sense. As Fried (1995) reminds us, "A degree of temperature is only a mark on a scale unless it is related to the boiling point of water . . . . Thus a teacher's passion for content serves her best when she draws upon it to help students understand and appreciate what the context is all about" (56).

However, our quicksilver, image-soaked culture forces us away from context. Television news and other programs serve up a series of stories, each unrelated to the next, and these are interspersed with commercials, also unrelated to the program as well as to each other. And now, thanks to TV remote controls, while we're watching this hodgepodge, we can randomly skip around to scores of other channels, further fragmenting our text, as well as our experience with it. To all of this add the fact that technology increasingly shrinks the time in which events are recorded and reported, thereby robbing us of the necessary reflection period we need to draw links between the many disparate bits of information.

Because we have become so conditioned to this lack of context in so many areas of our lives, we seldom question a lack of it in education. We rarely question the notions of variety and speed because they have become sacred. We prefer more to less, and fast to slow. No questions asked. But speed and infinite options tend to militate against context, an essential ingredient in teaching, learning, flow, passion, voice, identity, and renewal. Many teachers enter our profession precisely because of their passion for their discipline—and this includes its complete cultural context. For instance, for Julia it wasn't *only* Faulkner's words that motivated her to learn about him. It was also the details of his life and times in Mississippi and Hollywood and all the forces at play, including Julia's own experience in the South. Teachers who were originally ignited by the rich contexts of their disciplines will be less likely to seek renewal if context—so integral for teaching and learning about a discipline—is chipped away. While we can never return to Mayberry or Pleasantville, we should no longer automatically embrace technology merely because it transmits much information fast.

Passion and Flow

While passion and flow often appear as separate constructs in the professional literature, in teacher renewal they seem interdependent. Here, however, I will first discuss them separately, beginning with passion. While the teachers described in this book are experienced, skilled, and confident, more important is their passion for what they do and how they do it. Kim intensely observed her students and dedicated herself to knowing them as individuals. Passion of some kind is fundamental for these teachers:

> To be avowedly passionate . . . sets one apart from those who approach each day in a fog of fatigue, ritual, routine, or resignation, or who come to work wrapped in a self-protective cocoon. The passion which accompanies our attention to subjects, issues, and children is . . . a gift we grant ourselves: a way of honoring our life's work, our profession. (Fried, 1995, 19)

The teachers described in this book are undoubtedly passionate, as Fried describes:

> When I ask myself what makes the greatest difference in the quality of student learning—it is a teacher's passion that leaps out. More than knowledge of subject matter. More than variety of teaching techniques. More than being well-organized, or friendly, or funny, or fair. *Passion.* . . . By the intensity of their beliefs and actions, they connect us with a sense of value that is within—and beyond—ourselves. (1995, 16–17)

These teachers exceed Fried's (26–29) criteria for being passionate. First, they love to work with students. They like them as *people*—not just as students—which often leads teachers to observe students more closely. Second, these teachers care about their disciplines and are not willing to allow their regard for students to excuse a lack of learning. Third, these teachers demonstrate humor and spontaneity. Tish's dry humor, Carole's playfulness, and Julia's self-deprecation coexist with a deep commitment to their work. Finally, these teachers are not afraid to take risks and make mistakes. For instance, Alex's challenge of her school superintendent's position on hiring was a gutsy thing for any teacher to do. Passion—the intensity of a teacher's beliefs and actions—clearly played an important role in each teacher's renewal. It is crucial that students see, vividly, how their teacher's passion for their discipline connects to the larger world, how it links to current television, film, and music. Students need to see, often and in concrete ways, that it is possible to be passionate about quantum physics or the essays of E. B. White or the paintings of Edward Hopper. If students never experience this, they may well believe that passion is solely the province of rock stars, actors, and professional jocks.

Connected to passion are "flow" experiences. According to Csikszentmihalyi (1991), during flow we become deeply absorbed in challenging yet pleasurable activities. As we interviewed teachers, analyzed transcripts, and drafted chapters, time and again Csikszentmihalyi's concept of "flow experience" helped us understand teacher renewal. Csikszentmihalyi defines flow as

> a sense that one's skills are adequate to cope with the challenges at hand, in a goal-directed, rule-bound action system that provides clear clues as to how well one is performing. Concentration is so intense that there is no attention left over to think about anything irrelevant, or to worry about problems. Self-consciousness disappears, and the sense of time becomes distorted. (71)

Flow experiences are not empty leisure activities or no-brainers. On the contrary, flow experiences depend on our engaging in new challenges with well-defined goals in situations that provide immediate and constant feedback, which clarifies why we are succeeding, and if we are not, why not. During flow we can block out distractions and rely on ritual and habit to free our minds so that we can focus intensely on what we are doing. Such flow experiences result in "refining" the complexity of the self.

Csikszentmihalyi and others define complexity as two broad psychological processes, *differentiation* and *integration*. When we differentiate ourselves, we become more unique and separate ourselves from others. Integration is the opposite—a meshing with other people and ideas beyond our individual selves, creating a more ordered consciousness. Complexity of the self—or growth of the self—occurs when we successfully combine these two "op-posites." In short, flow depends upon increasing complexity, as Donald Murray (1990) illustrates in this description of his own flow experience:

> I come to writing depressed, worried, angry, confused, fearful, unhappy, in pain, and, most of the time, I start a sentence and by the time I get to the end I am lost in the task. I forget the clock, do not realize the CD has played to the end, am not aware of the snow falling outside my window. . . . In the act of writing I experience a serene, quiet joy, a focus of all my energy and knowledge and craft on the task, losing myself in the job that strangely allows me to become myself. (189)

Flow experiences can occur with many activities—biking, as-tronomy, cooking, or surfing the Internet. Like Murray, the teach-ers in this book often depended on flow experiences to energize them, personally and professionally. Some of these activities di-rectly connect to teachers' classrooms (e.g., writing), while oth-ers seem to nurture teaching in more subtle ways. It is extremely important for teachers to engage in impassioned, subjective ex-periences so that they can grow as teachers, as well as help their own students recognize such experiences within the subject at hand.

Csikszentmihalyi (1991) notes that throughout history, flow activity has been viewed as the best way of fulfilling human po-tential. During the Middle Ages, Christians likely believed that peeling potatoes was just as rewarding as sculpting cathedrals, as long as both activities served God. According to Karl Marx, hu-mans create their own selfhood by engaging in productive activi-ties; work transforms the worker. Even two thousand years ago, the Taoist scholar Chuang Tzu described the concept of *yu*, which has been translated as "wandering," "flowing," and "walking without touching the ground" (150). This last translation seems most appropriate, for when we are deeply absorbed in activities such as composing a sonnet or building a fence, we accomplish real tasks by moving from one point to another. But at the same time, our feet do not touch the ground because we are too in-volved to realize we even have feet.

All of these teachers reported having flow experiences—times when they became so immersed in challenging activities, in and out of the classroom, that they lost track of time and awareness of their surroundings. These experiences ranged from Carole's mental scenarios, to Kim's reflections on her students, to Julia's conversations about poetry. The characteristics of passionate teachers summarized earlier—love of content and students, sense of humor—are extremely compatible with flow experiences. When teachers delve into their own curricular and pedagogical preferences and engage in some of their own humor and playfulness, they help ensure that these episodes will more closely approximate flow experiences. These teachers worked hard to replicate such experiences, even if they had to change jobs or grade levels or move to other towns. Once teachers realized the pleasures of passion and flow, they strived to experience them again.

Finally, passion and flow helped teachers through hard times. Kate's pleasurable immersion in reconceptualizing her middle school class helped her cope with the care and eventual death of her brother. A teacher's professional life can affect his or her personal life, and vice versa. Passion and flow also helped wed teachers to their profession, binding their professional and personal identities. Julia's passion for poetry helped motivate and sustain her *while* she coped with self-doubts. Her passion for content thus served as aid or support while she fought battles about teaching it. This resulted in Julia feeling more comfortable in her identity as a teacher.

Voice

Effective teachers employ many voices. A student may need a firm directive one minute but only a raised eyebrow the next, and after that, a patient explanation. Parents or administrators may respond best to a teacher's informed and factual voice, while others will better comprehend a nurturing tone. However, the teacher's most important voice is one which speaks to the teacher and to his or her colleagues about what is most valuable. This voice speaks with fluency, confidence, and independence and relies mainly on "expressive" language, which is crucial for identity formation. Such informal language speculates, doubts, hypothesizes, and wanders—all with little self-censorship.

Like Bakhtin (1981), Elbow (1994), and others, I do not believe that a person's words or other symbols can be divorced from the person who speaks them. Historically, teachers' voices have been silenced or marginalized—by the larger male-dominated culture, as well as by the language of quantitative research designs and its "objective" language of investigation. Even in other forms of academic discourse, "voice" was shunned. It is not surprising, then, that a teacher's personal voice—one which spoke uniquely, directly, and honestly about his or her experiences, questions, and concerns—had little chance of developing.

Teachers' experiences with passion and flow help to develop their voices and identities. That is, intense, pleasurable experiences motivate or elicit a voice in response, constructing a kind of evolving dialogue with self and others. Through language and other symbols, teachers use their voices to record, understand, reflect, communicate, apply, and extend those experiences. Passion and flow can precede the development of voice, but the opposite also seems true—a strong voice can help teachers discover passion and flow experiences.

Teachers depend on voice to mend the contradictions, disillusionments, and other ruptures in a teaching life. National Writing Project sites, for example, have profoundly influenced teachers, enabling them to cultivate their own voices by writing intensively, then giving and receiving feedback on their writing. This simple exercise and acceptance of voice can spur teachers to search harder and longer for passion and flow. Real voices ring with honesty. Like voice, honesty is nearly impossible to define adequately, yet many of us insist that "we know it when we hear it." In these chapters, I hope that you will hear the strong, honest voices which bespeak the heart. This habit seems to help teachers in their quests for renewal.

Of course, the teachers' voices heard here are those that were current during the interview process, since voice constantly evolves. These voices changed pitch, resonance, volume, and melody in their journeys toward expression. As Britzman (1994) reminds us, a teacher's identity (and voice, I might add) is *also* a social fabrication. A teacher's voice and identity evolve from *in-*

side, as well as from the world *outside.* And this glorious, postmodern world outside of us is saturated with information and symbols run amok. The more information we have, the more unstable meanings become, as they slip and slide off their moorings and break free from conventional definitions. The result is confusion.

I agree with Britzman (1994), who concludes that it is difficult for teachers to establish their own identities because, to do so, they must borrow from other discourses, which are "already overburdened with the representations of others" (56). Therefore, at least initially teachers must rely on many sources to develop their own identities, the same way a builder might use cement blocks to construct a temporary frame. Many of these symbols are used goods, with too many fingerprints and smudges on them, and hence too far removed from each teacher's own reality. In sum, voice and identity evolve through a constant struggle or negotiation between ever-shifting internal and external representations. It is not an easy process.

Overall, experiences of passion and flow, coupled with the development of voice, largely shape a teacher's identity. This combination of forces provides teachers with control and autonomy, allowing them to demystify their own careers. And once teachers grow strong enough to be heard and seen—by themselves, as well as by others—they become self-sustaining. Strong voices and identities increase the chances that teachers will thrive—especially those whose identities remain, in part, childlike.

Dual Identities

The teachers described in this book often demonstrated "dual identities": they negotiated between their professional and personal selves, as well as between their adult and childlike selves.

PROFESSIONAL/PERSONAL SELVES

The teachers in this study have struggled to be who they are today. Their success is partly due to the merging of their personal and professional lives, often in unpredictable ways. Most of these strong teachers seemed naturally inclined to ignore certain boundaries between their personal and professional lives, and I believe this accounts for a good measure of their success in the classroom. However, teachers' personal and professional lives were often at odds: their personal beliefs about learning or teaching or relating to other people may not have matched those of their colleagues or the school's official policy. Overall, teachers constantly negotiated perceived discrepancies between what they valued on the inside and what the world valued on the outside.

This negotiation between their personal and professional lives often presents teachers with a conundrum: Do they listen to their intuitive and trusted personal voices? If so, they may risk public censure and possibly their jobs. But if they conform to their school or community's conventions, they risk losing self-respect. Many professionals are embarrassed or reluctant to place anything related to their personal lives on the table for exploration and discussion. Therefore, if a topic or issue is perceived as personal, it is often also considered emotional in nature—something which must remain at arm's length.

Professionalism as a word and concept usually functions productively. But some of its connotations may have outlived their usefulness. "Professionalism" used to mean, "Come into the profession," because novices had no idea of the basics of the professional world, such as calmly reviewing all facts before making decisions, or communicating rationally with colleagues and others. While these things remain an important part of professionalism, I believe that today the term too often means, "Don't dare go *beyond* professionalism, because anything outside it is 'unprofessional.'"

Hence, connecting our professional life with our personal life is still often viewed as, yes, unprofessional. In a classroom, of course, we *should* focus on our students and discipline, not on our own personal lives. However, in regard to several important educational issues, such as curriculum and pedagogical decisions and especially teacher renewal, teachers' personal lives are integral. To deny one at the expense of the other can create dissonance. In some cases (most obvious in Kate's and Tish's narratives), intensely personal elements interfered the most with their professional identities and daily lives. Fortunately, Kate and Tish eventually recognized that the two were not mutually exclusive and reached common ground. When teachers' personal and professional selves are not in sync, they endure various traumas and self-exiles until the two are somehow integrated. This book is about those processes of rebuilding and renewal, those connections between periods of passion and self-exile—those lonely, looping back roads that teachers must travel when their personal and professional lives do not intersect.

ADULT/CHILDLIKE SELVES

As teachers, the individuals profiled in this book *had* to be adults. But most of them also had a strong desire to be childlike—to *play*, to *do* things. Their students sometimes demonstrated a similar dual nature. Possessing a balanced identity translates into equality in the classroom: teachers are free enough to acknowledge the child side of themselves, as well as to respect the adult side of their students. How teachers negotiated the ups and downs of dual identity influenced their renewal processes. These teachers share a desire for respect, though not the kind that comes from being labeled the authoritative adult in charge. They seem to care least about this kind of respect. Instead, they want to be valued for who they are without facing ridicule, prejudice, or alienation. For only in such a safe environment can they and their students take risks, make mistakes, and keep growing as people. Second, these teachers deeply believe in the heart of their subjects—and this is what they want to cultivate and share with others. The childlike part of these teachers values being a participant far more than being an expert source of information and wisdom—a superior automaton who dispenses morsels to its underlings. While these teachers possess abundant knowledge and skill in their respective fields, they prefer to be partners in learning. They relish the excitement which comes from doing things *with* students rather than lecturing to them about done deals. Kate established student committees which determined curriculum, while Julia thought aloud in class about what a poem *might* mean.

Throughout this project, successful teachers spoke mostly about broad or important issues: How can I help my students achieve their own voices and autonomy so that they can become freer than I am? Should I change disciplines or teach a radically different grade level so that I can better help more students? Is teaching what I really want? These teachers focused, explicitly and implicitly, on things that are ultimately spiritual in nature, as art educator Peter London clarifies:

> We are all drawn to the same questions, if not in our work place, in our places of privacy. Where do we come from? Why are we here? What is our place in the scheme of things? How may my life be of service? What the hell is going on here? Is anyone in charge? Whenever this class of questions is raised, the arena of ultimate concerns is being addressed. In this arena, ordinary thinking and feeling and speaking begin to fail us, . . . speech yields to song, walking to dancing, seeing to imagining, reason to intuition, labor to ritual. A deep and satisfying order reveals itself. Music is heard. (qtd. in Dodson 1998, 118)

As an artist and educator, London despairs that these sacred matters are "the one ingredient most drained from our civilization, and from much of our art, and even more so from our teaching" (qtd. in Dodson 1998, 118). These things seem much the same as passion. And when London notes that ordinary communication fails us during passionate times—when "speech yields to song"—he could be describing flow experiences. Like London, the teacher quoted in the following passage also focuses on the arena of ultimate concern:

> Have you ever seen those straight-A students who go directly to college and get straight A's there, yet never experience that *metanoia* that constitutes authentic intellectual awakening? They had high school teachers that "prepared" them for college—that is to say, inoculated them against radical self-examination. I want my students to go to college more passionate than prepared, less defended and more willing to risk failure. (qtd. in Inchausti 1993, 36)

> Students need a perspective that allows them to continue to be transformed, changed, and renewed by their experiences. Ultimately, we want them to surprise us by their futures, not live out some ambitious high school administrator's dream of a successful life. (qtd. in Inchausti 1993, 42)

The teachers in this book sensed the loss of somehow sacred qualities inherent in teaching, so in their own ways they each tried to recapture them, refusing to surrender to isolation, bureaucracy, apathy, or cynicism. Such qualities helped them break out of situations which had confined their spirits and eroded their self-confidence, their identity, their wholeness. These teachers know that real teaching and learning is a spirit. Not a test score printed in a box, not a label such as "Gifted" or "Behaviorally Challenged" or "A.D.D.," but a spirit—an attitude, a stance, a point of view which proclaims with no hesitation: "I am not afraid to change, not afraid to do or become anything that I believe is valuable." It is only natural, then, that, when they find this spirit or inner, higher life, they do not want it to flicker out. These teachers know all too well the cruelest irony of their profession: that meaningful work and a generative inner life—so valuable, liberating, and available to *everyone*—will be found by far too few. This is why we renew ourselves.

So, in essence, what Inchausti, London, and the teachers profiled in this book are all trying to say about teaching and renewal is this: the people who are least afraid of change and experimentation are, well, children. Lindley (1993) explains:

> The source then—the source of the energy that drives good teaching—is the child in the teacher. This idea explains the bond that forms between the good teacher and her students. The students feel they have a kindred child, a colleague, in their teacher. But, *because that inner child is as playful and as irresponsible as they are, they—the students—must gear up an adult part of themselves to take care of (indeed, to teach) the child-in-the-teacher.* Thus, students act more responsibly, stay more alert, and become, in part, not learners but teachers. . . . [T]eachers and students are both split into two parts. Each teacher has a conscious, out-in-the-world teacher self as well as an unconscious inner child. And each student has an unconscious inner adult. (44)

The child within the teacher evokes the adult within the student. And I think that students respond sincerely when they sense something like themselves within adult authority figures because they are too rarely allowed to see it in adults. According to

Guggenbuhl-Craig (1979), an effective teacher "must stimulate the knowing adult in each child. . . . But this can only happen if the teacher does not lose touch with his own childishness. . . . He must not lose spontaneity in his teaching and must let himself be guided somewhat by his own interests" (105–6).

Lindley notes that his own mentors were this way—that they were "encountered fortuitously, like the magical guides in fairy tales" (1993, 15). Similarly, my own mentors represented themselves as *incapable* of lording any kind of power over me—incapable of towering "up there," while I toiled "down here"; incapable of jingling the keys to wisdom in front of my empty hands. The most powerful teacher-student relationships, then, are devoid of fear. Indeed, take this book's researchers as examples. They selected the most successful teachers they knew, and a primary reason for their selections was the equality that warmed the spaces between them.

The teachers in this book have reclaimed their professional (and personal) lives by allowing this childlike part of themselves to regain some of its former power, have reclaimed some playfulness in their teaching, have again immersed themselves in learning. These teachers also reclaim an equality in their relationships with students without forsaking academic rigor. When Carole worked with students who had nothing to say, she encouraged them to "just lie." This and her mental scenarios are childlike in their playfulness and risk taking, placing her alongside students in a shared quest. Kim's intense desire to observe and know her new middle school students demonstrated the equality with which she viewed them. The same is true with Kate, who relinquished control of her lesson-plan book and instead created student committees to make decisions. The same is true with Julia, who elicited questions and answers from students not just so they could think for themselves, but also to reaffirm for both parties that they were partners in unraveling a Gerard Manley Hopkins poem—that they were all in it together.

Of course, our basic systems and ways of thinking about students and teachers do not conceive of them as being at all alike (this would not be "professional"). Instead, we emphasize differences. And of course differences exist—in age, income, and formal education level. However, we can argue that these differences are minor, while the similarities—such as that each of us is comprised of an adult and a child—are major. Because educational systems are based on numerical differences and not on internal, spiritual similarities, teachers face tough (but not impossible) odds in recapturing that spirit of the child that led them into teaching in the first place—those flow experiences during which discovery and learning and immersion made the imposed adult world of time and rules fall away, as they lurched toward just one more peek around that next hill, eager to see what's new.

TAILWINDS

Tailwinds blow in the same direction as our course of travel. The teachers explored in this section sail toward renewal by winds which blow them forward—from talking, to writing, to painting, to making pottery, to visualizing. The teachers in these three chapters illustrate the active forces of teacher renewal. In Chapter 1, "Making Myself Visible: Voice as Renewal," Lucy Stanovick describes Kate, who sometimes stops whatever she is doing to jot down the first draft of the poem that has suddenly surfaced in her mind. Similarly, in Chapter 2, Susan Baruffi's "The Woman Who Resurrected Words: Writing as Renewal," Alex discovers the liberating powers of writing, not just for her classroom, but beyond it. In Chapter 3, Jill Weisner's "Collecting Dreams: Imagination as Renewal," Carole summons her vigorous imagination to launch her into other frames of mind. The following sections summarize how the major processes of renewal—social contexts, passion and flow, voice, and dual identities—influenced the teachers described in Part I, Tailwinds.

Social Contexts

In these chapters, social contexts large and small play important roles in teacher renewal. In Chapter 1, Kate feels isolated from her fellow teachers because she is certain they will scorn her—not just because of her homosexuality but even because of her vegetarianism. Kate, however, bonds with a group of teacher-researchers who mentor her. Also feeling isolated from her fellow teachers, Alex, in Chapter 2, successfully completes a summer writing project, during which she gains the skills and confidence to teach writing effectively. She even changes her career focus to become a media specialist so that she can reach more students by mentoring their teachers. And in Chapter 3, we hear from Carole, who as a young adult felt excluded from her peers because her small, conservative community frowned upon her parents' divorce, as well as the family's poverty. Carole uses mental imagery and drama as escapism and as a means of renewal in her work.

Passion and Flow

These teachers nurture passion for teaching and regularly engage in a variety of flow experiences, which in turn often stimulate their renewal processes. In Chapter 1, Kate becomes deeply engrossed in poetry writing and pottery making. Both function as passions and flow experiences for her, but in different ways. When writing poetry, Kate often invokes painful memories. Using words and images, she imposes meaning and order on the experience. Throwing pots, on the other hand, is a less verbal and less painful form of renewal

In Chapter 2, Alex's passion and flow experiences with her peer writing group, giving and receiving feedback, encourage her to try new approaches in teaching writing. Responding to writing in small groups is such a pleasurable and challenging experience for Alex that she continues this activity for the next ten years. In Chapter 3, Carole's delight in visualizing "alternative scenarios" stimulates her to become a theater teacher so that she can actually stage her own and other people's imaginings, as well as encourage her silenced students to break out of their silence, if only by "just lying."

Voice

Through pleasurable flow experiences, Kate, Alex, and Carole develop their own voices. Each of these teachers' voices had at one time been silenced because other people caused them to feel somehow "less than" the norm. In Chapter 1, Kate explains how she was dismissed as a dumb jock and later rejected for being too different. Through intensive spoken and written language—in college courses, mentoring groups, her own classroom, and therapy sessions—Kate builds her voice. In Chapter 2, Alex's colleagues doubt her teaching ability because she strives to improve it. Through writing, responding to writing, and teaching writing, Alex's voice blooms—to the point that she redefines her job, takes up painting, and even challenges an arbitrary decision by her district's superintendent.

As a child, Carole felt shunned because her parents were divorced and her family was poor. Her passion for visualizing became her expressive "voice," which she acted out in pep rally skits at school. This daydreaming ability led her to become an English teacher and to direct her school's theatrical productions. Carole's visualizing sustains and renews her today, as she describes in Chapter 3. The strengthening of these teachers' voices allows them to question—and eventually dismantle—the realities constructed by others for them. Because these teachers demonstrated to themselves the power of voice, they want their own students to develop strong voices, too. Here again, teachers' personal lives heavily influenced their professional lives.

Dual Identities

The teachers in these chapters negotiate between their professional and personal selves, as well as between their adult and childlike selves. In Chapter 1, Kate's personal and professional selves are tightly interwoven. When she was twelve years old, her mother died. As a young teacher, Kate faced her own brother's death from AIDS—a traumatic experience she knew she could not share with her disapproving family and colleagues. Kate nursed him throughout his illness, holding his hand when he died. She watched her closest ally die in silence, too afraid to speak his own voice because of the social stigma of his disease. Consequently, Kate fiercely prizes not only her own voice but those of her students, as well.

As she describes in Chapter 2, when Alex enrolled in a summer writing project she was "full of self-doubt" about her practices in the classroom. That is, her professional and adult selves were ailing. She completed the project with a revised outlook that stretched far beyond her teaching and continues to influence her now, ten years later. Alex realized that if she could become an effective writer just by writing and receiving feedback—and could enjoy it so intensely—then she could apply this principle to other areas of her life, as well. As Alex states, "I am much more powerful than I ever was before—I can write, I can paint, I can do anything!" The joy Alex takes in these creative activities illustrates a much healthier balance between her professional and personal selves.

Carole, the veteran English teacher in Chapter 3, sustained her professional life through imagination. When life is stressful or boring, she often slips into her imagination: the people around her become actors, as she directs them to move, speak, laugh, dance, sing. Carole employs her visualizing not just to escape boring committee meetings but also to spice up her teaching. She now passes her approach on to her students. Carole encourages young writers who believe they have nothing of value to say to "just lie"—to make things up—so that they can start writing. She tries to help them understand that they too can mentally construct alternative worlds and thereby envision other possibilities. In Carole's teaching life, her adult and childlike selves seem equally at home.

Overall, Kate, Alex, and Carole relish the play that comes from valuing the childlike part of themselves, as well as from valuing the adults residing within their students. Kate allows the child within her to slip out and get her hands dirty in the glorious mud of pottery making. She also encourages her students to make curricular and other teaching decisions—adult decisions—a move that most teachers would never dream of making. Alex expresses the childlike side of herself when she writes whimsical poetry and, in her midforties, takes up painting. Carole releases the kid within her in the same way that James Thurber's Walter Mitty does. Teachers who respect their childlike sides (and the adult sides of their students) will more likely engage in flow experiences and hence further develop their voice—in short, renew themselves.

Making Myself Visible:
Voice as Renewal

LUCY STANOVICK

University of Missouri–Columbia

I have come to believe that we cannot neatly separate our personal and professional lives. I am a woman, mother, wife, teacher, and graduate student, all simultaneously. With skepticism I read the how-to's for success, which make little or no mention of the stumbling blocks or what influences a person's actions. Without these complexities, without the messiness, we have only models of perfection to compare ourselves to. And in the face of that, we inevitably come up short. Especially for teachers, one way to avoid such comparisons is to value the *whole* story. Carter (1993) advocates story as a useful form for teacher research because of its ability to capture the "complexity, specificity, and interconnectedness of the phenomenon" (6). She explains that traditional, quantitative research begets linearity and noncontradiction, while story "accommodates ambiguity and dilemma as central figures" (6). This chapter describes one teacher's complex story, how the stories outside the classroom powerfully influenced the stories inside the classroom.

I chose to study Kate, whose professional and personal worlds constantly fold back into each other. As her story begins, these two worlds are polar opposites, but because of a series of crises in her life, Kate turned to a variety of strategies to help her cope and ultimately succeed. These strategies all seem to have their own language: the language of basketball, the language of writing, the language of talking, and the language of pottery. Their interconnectedness is fascinating: not only can we talk about how Kate employed these strategies, but we can also discuss how three of the four are related to the very content she teaches—language arts—in which writing, talking, and creativity are essential to reconnecting the fragments of her self. In addition, the crises and coping strategies provide the mirrors to reflect on her teaching. At the core of Kate's story is the issue of voice—looking for it, discovering it, and nurturing it.

Kate and I are full-time doctoral students in English education at the same university. Kate had taught middle school language arts for four years. We met in a poetry class. I remember her reading aloud a poem she had written and the paradox of her appearance. On the one hand she was tall, strong, and confident, but on the other, her fine blond hair, gentle brown eyes, and whispering voice made her appear fragile.

Kate's mother died when she was twelve, and her only brother died at the age of twenty-seven from the AIDS virus. How could I talk about such personal events? What right did I have to lay an academic analysis on her very real anguish? I had no idea. But I knew that Kate and I are both teachers, deeply interested in how who we are as persons affects what we do in the classroom. And I knew she was willing to talk. So I decided to be honest, to admit that I was flying by the seat of my pants, and to trust the process. Now, the data gathered, I am surrounded by forty-two pages of transcript, seven full tapes, and countless pages of notes, scraps, and memories. And I wonder how to make this chapter move and laugh and speak like our conversations.

Silence and the Language of Basketball

Kate sits at the corner of my desk in an ancient, high-backed, green vinyl chair that relentlessly tips forward. Periodically, she tries unsuccessfully to push herself back or wrap her long legs under her, or outstretch them, all the while laughing softly that the chair is "just fine, don't worry." Basketball was her youthful passion. Her family—mom, dad, and older brother, Kevin—lived together, but they all moved around separately from each other. She remembers the last few years before her mother died.

> My mom spent lots of time in her office, working. I knew to be quiet and not bug her. So I took care of myself a lot. I know she

loved us, but she had her own stuff going on and I was careful not to get in the way. I was the peacemaker. I knew when things weren't right and made myself scarce.

Kate learned early on to be silent and invisible—the peacemaker—to keep tension from escalating at home. School was barely different. She remembers "sitting in rows, memorizing facts, and having all the spark wiped out very quickly." She told me that she glommed onto basketball and sports by third grade, but that she "never thought that was a very good thing to do because it wasn't violin or orchestra, and my grades weren't that good." It was easy to recognize basketball as the language and voice Kate immersed herself in. After dinner she would go outside and practice "shooting and shooting and shooting." She practiced the one hundred left-handed shots her coach recommended, and in bed she would run plays in her head, even dreaming about basketball. In school she would write notes to teammates, pump them up for the game, or, at the suggestion of her coach, draw up plays during class, putting "people here and here, and I can pass down here or shoot and dribble." She would watch Dr. J. and other professional players on TV all weekend and then lie in bed, basketball cradled under her arm, and envision herself imitating their moves.

Gilligan (1994) states, "To have a voice is to be human. To have something to say is to be a person. But speaking depends on listening and being heard; it is an intensely relational act" (178). Kate wasn't heard in the classroom, but she was noticed on the basketball court. She intuitively knew how to make her identity matter. She wasn't going to blend into the bench, faceless and voiceless. If she was a basketball player, then she would be the best, and as captain of her high school team and a recipient of a Division I basketball scholarship, in her own way she was heard.

The Language of Talk: An Awakening

Kate played basketball at Idaho State University for a year before transferring to a smaller school in Washington state, where she broke her wrist and for the next year wandered in a state of flux. She vaguely felt that there was more to life than basketball, but she just didn't know quite *what*. At age twenty-one she moved east to join her brother at Mentaya College, a small midwestern liberal arts school. She majored in education because of coaching prospects, and she chose English because it seemed the lesser of evils.

> Mentaya's program really changed my life. It was intense. Lots of talking, questions, and you're center stage 95 percent of the time. It helped me realize that I'm somewhat intelligent; it helped me begin to articulate myself verbally. It just shifted me to a whole other person that I didn't know. Before, I was just a jock and quiet, and then all of a sudden, here's Kate who's reading things and interested and talking about ideas.

Kate experienced a major identity transformation. Suddenly, teaching was no longer simply the way to become a basketball coach, and Kate was no longer sleeping or partying when she was supposed to be in class. Instead, she became excited at the prospect of teaching, of emerging into a "new system" for herself—that of talk—which allowed her to see that she was also an intellect.

> I knew I didn't want to give students meaningless pieces of information and perpetuate what happened to me. That's why I'm so particular about how I teach. When you sit in a horseshoe and the teacher sits in the front, and you talk to the teacher and she validates your ideas, that just doesn't work for me. I'd rather be in a circle, with the teacher on the outside and you, the students, are in small groups, exploring ideas, asking each other questions and clarifying, rather than just talking to the teacher and bouncing ideas around like a Ping-Pong ball.

Professional Silencing and Isolation

Kate's first year of teaching was at a middle school in a small, almost all-white, conservative, blue-collar town. Kate always felt like an outsider: "It was all rows and textbooks and corporal punishment."

Lucy: What happened in your classroom?

Kate: I first started with rows and within a month, I moved the seats so that they weren't in rows. I had a teeny library that I kept trying to build up, but what I did was shut my door, every day. I'd just shut my door so nobody would ask what was going on in there, and it wasn't even like I was doing anything radical. Students sat on the floor and read, or they'd talk in groups. So my room had a lot of noise and that was not cool.

Lucy: Did you hear about it?

Kate: No, but you knew whoever had the quietest room had the highest status. The principal was really into control and discipline, and he equated that with silence. I felt isolated at first, until I met Kelly, who taught language arts next door— very bright and creative. She and I just started talking and passing notes, and that was what saved me. It was fun working with her and watching her teaching change.

Kate speaks of silencing images she knows all too well: rows, invisibility, and isolation. But this time it was different; Kate was different. She recognized the oppressive forces and found ways to subvert them—shutting the classroom door to protect her own voice and the voices of her students. By avoiding rows of desks and including a classroom library, she "spoke" against the silencing. And the note passing and talking with Kelly (her fellow teacher) kept her voice heard within a stifling environment.

Kate survived her first year because of her mentor group— three female professors from college. She was in constant contact with them. Once a week, they would meet and talk passionately for hours—over dinner, over coffee, or late into the night—about philosophical and practical teaching issues. These weren't pep talks or gripe sessions; these were meaningful, hard-hitting, collaborative talks. Too often we leave our undergraduate experience ready to go out and change the world, only to find ourselves isolated and perhaps in schools where our ideas may be viewed as radical, unrealistic, or misinformed. Teachers talk to each other about the latest fight in the boys' bathroom or the pathetic new batch of ninth graders. Our visions of how to enrich our classrooms suddenly don't seem so clear. With no one to talk to, no support for our risk taking, we tend not to take those risks.

I taught high school for three years, and I cannot remember one meaningful talk with any of the other English teachers about the teaching in our classrooms. It seemed as though wanting to talk about teaching was interpreted as incompetence—why hadn't I learned that material in college? Since no one talked to me about teaching, I figured I must be the only one who felt like this. Kate was successful at her middle school because of her support system: Kelly and her mentor group provided a community for Kate in which her voice could be heard and nurtured, and where she could be encouraged to forge ahead. This support is essential for teachers to survive and succeed.

With the help of her mentor group, Kate vigorously solicited the voices of her students: "Students made choices about how they wanted to learn certain required material, created types of assessment, defined how much time would be used for writing and reading workshop, decided on the class rules, and generated class activities." Because of a student suggestion made half in jest, Kate and her students collaborated on and designed a highly successful "Talking Workshop" component which allowed "students to generate writing ideas, discuss books they were reading, and analyze conflicts or problems that arose in class." But this took time. Because she had the support of her group, Kate could give the students time to solve their conflicts. This support is essential for teachers to survive and succeed.

Writing to Cope

When Kate first arrived at Mentaya as a college student, the members of her mentor group took her in, gave her a place to live, provided an intellectual community, and attended all her basketball games (the first time, she says, that she felt she had a family, someone other than Kevin, to watch her). This group continued to support Kate while her brother was dying. During Kate's hard first year of teaching, Kevin was living in New York, and for two years he told no one about his AIDS diagnosis. One night he called and told her he "wasn't well" and was coming to stay with her. With no hesitation and no questions asked, Kate agreed—an unconditional understanding between brother and sister to always be there for each other. When he arrived the next day looking frail and weak, she had to ask, "Kevin, what's up?" She immediately got him into the best hospital she could find, which was forty miles away. From then on, her life was filled with teaching all day and driving every night to care for her brother.

Sarah, her best friend and mentor, often stayed with Kate at the hospital, designing her lessons for the next school day. Without Sarah, Kate could not have survived. Routinely, Kate sat in the ICU waiting room late into the night, planning or grading papers in her lap until the nurse let her know it was okay to go in.

KATE: In the hospital, we talked a little. He couldn't really talk, so when he didn't, we'd write. And there'd be hours I'd just talk at him, on and on. At the same time, I was the queen of not feeling anything, not experiencing anything, just keeping busy. Part of that total busyness worked in my favor. I wasn't very verbal. I was very introverted, so I didn't let a lot of things out. People didn't know the extent that I was crashing. I'd hide it.

LUCY: But it has to come out somewhere. . . .

KATE: Mainly in my journal. . . . Saying all this, you know, fuck life. I reread my journal from the month after he died, and the entry was something like, "Well, I guess I need to write, a lot has happened, I need to record it." So it's [journal writing] more of a compulsion to record. Maybe it's a result of having my mother die—just wanting a record of what happened because, until recently, I haven't been able to remember anything about my mother. I know what the grieving process and time can do, so I want whatever I can remember about Kevin to be on paper so I don't forget like I forgot my mom.

LUCY: So your journals are really more record keeping?

KATE: No, it started as record keeping, but then it was big time venting—fuck this, fuck life, I hate this. . . .

LUCY: Was it healing for you?

KATE: I think it was, because I was keeping so much in; it was my one way to let a little bit out before I would explode.

LUCY: Did you discover things while writing? Work things out?

KATE: I *let* things out, let it out, mainly. Just survival, as opposed to therapeutic.

The first poem Kate wrote for Kevin after his death follows.

From a Sister

How can I write a poem
when vivid images of your final days
infect my thoughts
and contaminate visions
of your soft beard laying tightly against your jaw,
that silky hair lapping over your forehead
down to your shoulders
and those brown eyes crying to me for help.

How can I write a poem
when I remember
how holding you caused your tears to run down my face,
stinging my heart and leaving intricate scars.
Feeling the back of your slim, cool fingers
delicately caress my eye lids—cheeks—lips,
seeing your weak diminished
legs lie helplessly against the sheets,
knowing all the time your 27-year-old feet
still longed to jump waves with me at Cannon Beach.

How can I write a poem
when reality reminds me
that I will no longer run my fingers through your hair,
no longer hold your hand
when your fears scream through your eyes,
no longer brush away the tears that tickle your neck
or no longer follow your footsteps in the warm sand.

This poem was lying on my desk among other scattered papers during one of our interviews. After forty-five minutes, she leaned over, turned it face down, and said, "That's all right, it's just depressing me because I know what it's about." I winced at this stark reminder of her pain. We talked about the writing of this poem:

> KATE: I can't remember what impelled me to sit down and write, but I remember being at the keyboard. Okay, you look at the title, it starts, "How do I write a poem?" so something was in my mind that I wanted to write a poem. When I think about that moment, I have another image of when my mom died when I

was twelve. I was always thinking as a joke, "Gee, now I'd have something interesting to write about for my life story." I think I had that same sensation of wanting to get it down in print, or making it last, having something be more permanent for something that disappeared, so I thought I'd write a poem. But at the same time, how can I write a poem?

LUCY: Can you recall how it felt?

KATE: [Long pause] Umm, yeah. Remember earlier, I turned it over? This poem especially is still right there for me. Anyway, I would kind of torture myself with images. I feel like I had a monster of these horrible hospital images that always haunted me: about Kevin and his beard and his hair and wanting to go to the beach, and all these things were haunting me, so that would be one of the feelings—wanting to get those feelings out.

LUCY: Is there some sort of feeling of success when you're writing it?

KATE: Yeah. It's like it's there in me and it's got to get out, and once it's done, I got it out, and then I can leave it. I never have to see the poem again.

Kate's writing, whether poetry or in journals, is clearly a survival mechanism for her. Poetry is for Kate, as it was for bell hooks (1994) in her essay "When I Was a Young Soldier for the Revolution: Coming to Voice," "The place for that secret voice, for all that could not be directly stated or named, for all that would not be denied expression" (52). Writing allows Kate to catch her voice and keep it permanently. Her poetry also moves beyond that. Kate's poetry authenticates her experiences, which in turn allows her the critical distance necessary for personal growth. Even though the emotions it evokes are often painful, the act of writing—the immersion in thought and the creation of the poem—is intensely satisfying. She is, in Csikszentmihalyi's (1990) terms, in "flow," which he defines as an optimal experience, a time when

we feel in control of our actions, masters of our own fate. . . . Contrary to what we usually believe, . . . the best moments in our lives are not the passive, receptive, relaxing times. . . . The best moments usually occur when a person's body or mind is stretched to its limits in a voluntary effort to accomplish something difficult and worthwhile. . . . For or a child, it could be placing with trembling fingers, the last block on a tower, . . . for a violinist, mastering an intricate musical passage. (3)

While in graduate classes or meetings with Kate, I have watched her lower her head, square herself in her chair, take her pen in hand, and attack the page. Her face is taut and her eyes are sharp as she madly writes. She is in flow, and we can *see* it; while it may last only fifteen minutes or even less, she is a different person when she finishes. One day Kate came to my office carrying a piece of notebook paper with black-inked lines stretched diagonally across the page and along the margins, with scratch-outs and rewrites. She told me that while teaching, a memory of her brother came flooding back; she had to catch it. As we talked, it became clear that she was in flow.

> KATE: The other day in class, they were doing the intertexuality thing and throwing the ball of yarn around and everybody was laughing—it reminded me of my brother because he knit sweaters madly two years before he died. So it just gave me this image of him rolling a ball of yarn . . . so I had to write it down. Things'll come to me in poems, not very often, but they do. It's mainly things that trigger stuff about Kevin or my mother.
>
> LUCY: When the memory is triggered, you say, "I have to get this down." Why do you have to get it down?
>
> KATE: Well, one is before I forget it, but the other is that I want to capture that moment. I want to remember it. I want to say whatever it is.
>
> LUCY: So you write by focusing on what you're seeing in your head? Are you trying to describe the image?
>
> KATE: No, it's just something in my head that has to come out. I don't know what it is. It's triggered by an image. I can't do descriptive language, so it's usually an event.
>
> LUCY: Are you recording the image that you see? You said it reminded you of Kevin rolling the ball?
>
> KATE: Well, I think of that as like . . . feeling. I'll think of that image and then it's like there's a feeling there, and then I think, "Okay, what is that feeling?" Then, "What's an event?" Then I think of an event, and then the words that come out describe him sitting with the ball.
>
> LUCY: After you write it, is there a sense of peace?
>
> KATE: Sense of peace like I did it, it's there. I haven't gotten back to it; whether it's too hard or what, it's just like I had to get it out. It was there. I had to get it out.

LUCY: Do you become [so] sensitive to what you're doing that the rest of the class fades out for you? Or is one foot in the class and one in the poem?

KATE: With this poem, I wanted everyone to go away, but I'm the TA, and I don't want it to look like I'm not paying attention. Also, a student was next to me, and I didn't want her reading my poem, but I had to write it. With poetry it might be a five-minute flow, but I don't totally lose a sense of what's going on. I'm very aware of what's going on around me. Being in the moment as well as in the poem go hand in hand: fade back in to the class and they're throwing the ball, and I look at the faces and watch somebody, how they turn the ball, and then I think, "Okay, how will that go?" Then I go back and watch someone else catching it and tossing it and think, "Oh, the word *toss*." So I fade in and out of the experience. . . .

LUCY: So is that a flow experience?

KATE: Yeah. Sounds like the whole experience.

LUCY: Right, because when you're watching them throw, you're watching them for very different reasons, concentrating on what they're doing for the poem.

KATE: Yes. Concentrating for the purpose of writing the poem as opposed to learning about the activity's concept.

Growth and the Personal-Professional Cycle

How does this connect to Kate's teaching? Kate is an English teacher, a writing teacher, and as National Writing Project teachers have been saying for over twenty years, the best teachers of writing are writers, and Kate is a writer. In the previous transcript, Kate analyzes the specifics of her writing process: she distinguishes between descriptive writing and writing about an event. She explains that while she narrates what she is seeing in the classroom, she attends to specific word choices which she can then use in her poem (e.g., the word *toss*).

I observed Kate teaching her own class, Middle School Methods: The Teaching of Writing. She requires her preservice teachers to write constantly and then write and talk about their writing. One student asked if she could turn in a poem she had written during another class. This student explained that, despite the fact that she knew she was no longer paying attention to the teacher, she simply had "felt compelled to write." Soon, all the students were sharing their own experiences of feeling compelled to write. In full understanding, Kate confidently allowed her students to explore the relevance and usefulness of writing. Because Kate understood the intellectual implications of these experiences, she helped students connect their personal gains to educational goals: her students were talking about and using the terms *reflection, the writing process, metacognition, purpose, audience, form,* and *context.* In Kate's classroom, the personal and professional double helix flourished. bell hooks (*Teaching,* 1994) argues adamantly against the mind/body split so popular in academia—the notion that the personal and professional sides of ourselves bring nothing to bear on each other and are thus best left separate. hooks points to the "self-actualized" teacher as one who seeks the union of "mind/body/spirit" (18) and argues that personal growth is not only important, but also directly related to the success of a "liberatory classroom"—one where teachers and students are engaged and "in the present" (158). And just as it is important for students to connect the content of a course to their own lives, it is just as important for teachers. Teachers should not forget themselves but, rather, continually self-evaluate the personal and professional selves to see where and how they intersect. Kate's poetry does this. In the midst of teaching writing (her professional self), she writes about her brother (her personal self). On a more elemental level, Kevin—who he was and how he died—profoundly affected Kate's teaching. Like hooks's self-actualized teacher, Kate is ever cognizant of this connection:

> KATE: I think one of the most significant changes was finding my voice and being more comfortable with myself. One of the most valuable things I ever heard and learned about teaching was at a conference about drugs and alcohol. The man said if you don't have your shit together, you're not going to be an effective teacher. If you're dealing with all sorts of emotional stuff, you're not gonna be effective with kids. You know, after Kevin died, for the next year and a half I went way down, and when I heard him say that, it hit home because I knew I had to get myself together because I was, if not at least committed to myself, committed to the children whose lives I touched. That's when I started getting into therapy, and through the process of

therapy and learning to talk about things and be more present with myself, I was much more present with the students. I think the other piece of that question is about voice and how I keep saying "voice." It became important through my education program, and then the issue around my brother's death and having a lot of gay men die in silence. For my brother not to be able to tell anybody—for two years he was diagnosed and didn't tell a soul—and just all the political and social and personal silence around that issue, suddenly reiterated the importance of voice and silencing. I realized how important it is to give kids opportunities and ways and invitations to talk. Not psychotherapy talk, just voice.

LUCY: What was school like while you were taking care of Kevin?

KATE: It was hard because it was my first year and I didn't know anybody. I knew Kelly, but they didn't know me, and I was working for tenure, so I was afraid to miss days. I only missed three days during Kevin's time. But actually, I needed the relief. It was nice to get to work and have a routine and be away from all the hellacious stuff, but it was also hard because I was teaching and creating and not using the textbooks—I was different and I knew it. Plus, I didn't tell anyone about Kevin but Kelly, because the school is so conservative. If I said AIDS, they're gonna think I'm sick, and gay bash, and be homophobic. The year after Kevin died, there was an article in *Newsweek* about gays in the military; it was laid out in the teachers' workroom with a note: "If we can't bash homosexuals, who *can* we bash?"

As we talk, she speaks in her signature whisper while huddling under her coat, pumping her legs. I comment on her posture because I'm confused—my office isn't cold. She hesitates, then leans over and turns off the tape. For Kate to be true to herself and honor her voice, she has to tell me she is a lesbian. As a teacher, she was committed to nurturing and validating her students' voices, while at the same time her own was silenced by the bigotry of her fellow teachers. And she has been graciously letting me into every crevice of her life, talking the last month about the importance of voice, and yet she has felt compelled to silence a part of herself. The irony of it. But at the same time, I could sense an obstacle removed and see the road in front of us smooth out. She had trusted me enough to peel back another layer. In that moment, my role in this study changed. Some distance between us had been erased. I no longer felt like an awkward "interviewer" collecting information *from* her. I understood that getting to something meaningful meant working *together*, figuring it out together.

Another piece fell into place for me: bell hooks defines "liberatory teaching" as that which "does not reinforce the existing systems of domination" (*Teaching*, 1994, 18). The dominant ideologies of our culture include those of being white, male, and heterosexual. Thus Kate, as a female and as a lesbian, is a minority, and as such, stands in opposition by not remaining silent. And the lesson is not lost on her teaching: she is committed to student voice in a system which still values student silence. Michelle Fine, who has extensively researched student silence in public schools, concurs that "silencing constitutes the process by which contradictory evidence, ideologies, and experiences find themselves buried, camouflaged, and discredited" (1987, 243). Fine concludes that "the typical classroom still values silence, control, and quiet" (249).

Renewal and the Flow of Talk

One day when we were winding down from an interview and we were feeling talked out, my office mate, Cathy, joined us. The three of us intersect in many ways: we are all the same age, all in the same doctoral program; Cathy co-teaches with me and with Kate. With amazing ease and fluidity, we started talking about our morning classes. The conversation moved to our own teaching philosophies and ways of de-centering ourselves as teachers. In what seemed like minutes, an hour passed. When I reminded Kate of a computer seminar she was late for, she decided not to go, saying this was much more fun. We were in flow.

Was our discussion renewing and transforming? Yes. From that one conversation, I revamped the rest of my syllabus for my new class. Whereas I had felt anxious, I now felt confident about my teaching decisions. In that class, I slowed down, listened more, negotiated rather than dictated, and let students make decisions rather than deciding for them. Kate said she had longed for but rarely encountered this kind of talk in graduate school. We are fully committed to our conversations—we meet over lunch, at the bar, across e-mail, even interrupt each other when we need to talk. Whether we are talking about how to teach something or about our own writing, it is the flow of our talk, the shared discovery, the *process* that holds the renewing, transforming power.

Talk has been central to Kate's growth, both personally and professionally. After Kevin died, Kate floundered for a year; she describes herself as "going way down." Initially, I was uncomfortable asking about her therapy; it felt like prying. But she kept mentioning therapy every time we talked about flow. Somewhat timidly, I asked if we could talk about her therapy and whether it was a flow experience. Kate leaned forward and planted both feet firmly on the ground, her brown eyes fixed into space so she could keep up with the words that tumbled out:

KATE: Oh, yeah, that's the key ingredient. That's what made things open up, made me see the world differently and be in the world differently, to make time for pottery, to be able to write, walk in the woods. That has all come from the work I've done in therapy. And the connection to therapy is voice. Up until that time, I silenced myself, hid myself, my writing, my speaking, my feelings. But there, I have this safe space for fifty minutes where we get to focus on me.

LUCY: Did therapy affect your teaching?

KATE: Yeah. I can remember I was teaching seventh grade. It just gave me more of a sense of presence of myself. I was able to not be so scared of feelings and just talking to people. I had this student, Troy, who was one of the Outsiders [referring to Hinton's novel *The Outsiders*]. Troy's brother was in jail and his dad had also been in jail. He was a Lorton and everyone told terrible stories of the Lortons. He was tough, but just sweet to the core on the inside, and I got him in my language arts class. He was flunking, but I took him on as a project and got him into wrestling. He was the best wrestler. He became student of the week and passed all his classes. Then, just as all that was happening, his dad died suddenly. I remember we had been reading *Bridge to Terabithia* and I had a really neat activity to talk about Leslie [the main character], death, and life. The very next day his dad died, and the kids came in the room, and they knew I'd talk about it. It was very meaningful, connecting talk that dealt with the literature and their feelings and real life. When I think back, I could never have done that before therapy.

The Language of Pottery

It was the beginning of winter break and I hadn't talked to Kate for a couple of weeks. I work like that: go great guns and then cool off, put it on the back burner, and then without warning, the impulse comes back with great urgency. Standing in the mall trying to do all of my Christmas shopping in one day, I got that sense of urgency. Draped with shopping bags, I called Kate from a pay phone and asked if it would be too big of an imposition to stop by to talk. She said no problem. A string of Christmas lights hung from her front window, and the house emanated warmth— soft lamp lighting, wonderfully soothing holiday music (a mix of melodic female chants), and a festive, full Christmas tree.

In the past, Kate had mentioned pottery more than once as a flow experience, and every time, her face would light up, but we had not pursued the subject. After every interview, I would write myself a big note to start with pottery next time, but it never happened. I was curious to find out if pottery connected to her voice and renewal, and if so, how. Tonight I was determined to find out.

Kate said she had immersed herself in writing poetry and found it rewarding. During the same semester, she and her partner, Terese, by chance walked through a pottery shop, and Kate suddenly remembered how in grade school she used to love painting and drawing. At Terese's suggestion, Kate signed up for a pottery class.

> KATE: Right. And I started pottery, so I remember just thinking a lot about different words or different language. I'd leave pottery and everything would be pottery to me; I'd see things in a pottery shape as well as think about words and language and try to think about how I could write about pottery in my poetry and how my pottery could be poetic. They're both creative processes that I never took time to do and it was fun, satisfying.
>
> LUCY: What does that mean, you'd be doing pottery and thinking about language and certain words?
>
> KATE: It was more of a feeling. With poetry, you have an idea or an image or a feeling in your mind and then if you stick with it, out come some words in language which could be turned into a poem. So, from thought comes this thing. That's the same

with pottery. You have a thought and then all of a sudden it becomes this thing. . . . My pottery just felt like it came from somewhere down inside me that wanted to come out.

LUCY: Different from poetry?

KATE: It's the same. It was like a gift that I was giving to myself by taking the time to do pottery and poetry. I never really thought of myself as creative before and then all of a sudden these creative things were coming out. Suddenly a door had opened to allow myself to have these things emerge from my thoughts or from my self or my being. I felt like the pottery was from so deep inside me.

LUCY: So does pottery have a language to you? When you're working on the pottery, do words come to you, random words?

KATE: No. More just an idea, like the idea of the pot. With poetry there is something in my mind that has to come out. My pottery is more relaxing, opening up and letting something come out, something that is deeper and in a different place. But it's not words; it's more the image and the shape and the feeling of the pot going around.

That "different place" is probably her calm, creative, happy state, whereas her poetry seems to cope with anger and hurt. Yet, as I closely examine the preceding passage, I hear Kate connecting writing to pottery—she talks about the "thing," whether it is a poem or a pot, coming from the "thought." To her, the process is the "same thing." Talking about the poetry and pottery in tandem signifies growth, and while her poetry may still be the way she deals with her tragedies, she is now also talking about it in the context of something that is fun and creative. The pottery and the poetry and the talk—the symbol systems—are not isolated parts of her whole; they are interwoven. I doubt that Kate could have reconnected those memories and that creative part of herself had she not done all that writing and talking. The talk and the poetry freed her voice.

LUCY: Voice and pottery—do you think that in some way your pottery allows you to find your voice?

KATE: Well, that's the thing that's deep down in there. I have this urge to give my therapist a pot because it's a way to say, "Thank you, you've helped me get here." And when I say it's deep down inside, the voice is my creative self, my kid self—it's playing in the mud. Pottery is great, very tactile. You just get muddy, dirty, clay all over your hands; it's just like playing in the mud. That is a voice, so that is a way to speak; it's a way to have me. You know, voice is more than words, it's expressing myself in some way.

The beauty of this is that, given what Kate has gone through, she could reconnect with this creative, childlike voice. She had, unbeknownst to herself, protected the most precious parts of herself. She hadn't let them die, but they had lain dormant until she was ready to reconnect with them. Pottery is the conduit for reconnection. It may be the symbolic representation of hooks's union of mind/body/spirit.

I think the most important thing in terms of renewing or sustaining is just having perspective, making that time to do pottery or write in the journal or take a walk instead of getting lost in my work—taking time for other things that I never did before. You know, because when you're so busy and so stressed, you're not as effective.

To do our best work, we have to have time away from it—this is what Kate is saying. I have learned the truth of this statement in a new way since beginning this project. Whereas I used to see exercising or leisure reading or watching a film as precious time away from my work, I now see the interconnectedness of these activities. As Kate has experienced (and as Csikszentmihalyi observes), I have discovered the flow involved in these experiences. Instead of feeling guilty, I now know that I am better for the time away. It isn't easy, especially for teachers, who are notorious for putting themselves last. But these other parts of our lives open up a gap that makes room for some new connection or insight. Then we return to our work, clearer, calmer, and sharper.

Conclusion: "Making Myself Visible"

Through Kate's story, we have come to know each other. While I admire how she has survived, what strikes me is how she has not allowed these events to be the sum total of her identity. They are integral parts that shape who she is, but she is also more than that. Drake, Eliot, and Castle (1993) examined how the process of telling one's story can actually empower the teller. Unbeknownst to the others, each person studied had been plagued in his or her professional career by feelings of "inadequacy and low self-esteem" (297). It wasn't until they began sharing their stories that they realized what had been holding them back. By sharing their stories, their feelings were made explicit, and then they could move beyond the confines of past experiences and grow. Kate's very act of telling her story further develops selfhood, her identity. As Drake, Eliot, and Castle (1993) discovered, the telling of the story becomes another step in a person's "journey out of silence" (298).

> Yeah, I think it's the impulse not to be invisible or not to lose my story. I told you when my mom died, I realized I suddenly had something to write a story about. So my process from then until now, especially the last five years, is retelling my story. That's more voice, giving life to myself by telling my story. So when my brother died, telling his story and at the same time telling my story is [a way of] recapturing me. It's a way of making myself visible.

CHAPTER TWO

The Woman Who Resurrected Words: Writing as Renewal

SUSAN BARUFFI
Sackman High School, St. Louis, Missouri

After all, I've known Alex for five years now, and I've spent two hours every working day carpooling with the woman. I should know all about her by now, right? Maybe two hours a day gives one a little insight into a person, but I'm finding that describing this sometimes wild, sometimes pensive, larger-than-life enigma of a woman is a hefty task. I sit here now and write, and the same things that always swirl in my head are back again, bewildering me. How do I write about someone I admire and, to be fair, someone I am still a little intimidated by? How do I stay true to who she is? How do I make sure that I don't just start writing and, pleased by the way I phrase something or by a colorful word, let the writing take over and dwarf her story? At some point, Alex is going to have to see this—what will she think? Will she say it's a fine piece of writing, but it's not about her—it's not honest? Her words chime in my head: "When you write, you don't have to be faithful to the facts. But you *must* be faithful to the truth."

Will Alex, a veteran writer, whip up a new draft and say something like, "I thought this might be closer to the real story?" Will she take a look at my draft and begin to "workshop" it? I have been in at least two writing groups with her and have more than once heard something along the lines of, "This part . . . hmm . . . I'm not sure this works here. . . . " While these self-doubts assault me, I try to fight back by repeating chunks of this mantra:

Relax. Who could write her story better than you? You know her. You've argued with her about movies, you've squashed her (and been squashed by her) on the racquetball court. Long before you knew you would ever write about her, you studied her as she puffed on candy cigarettes and cruised down Highway 36. You've compared family histories and you've road-tripped with her—six hundred windy, nausea-filled miles. You've shared your writing with her, reviewed hers. Remember, Alex is the one who pushed you to start writing. She is the poster child for a study on how teachers reinvigorate and reinvent themselves—and you are a decent enough writer to capture her essence on paper, even if you don't know everything.

And then, after a few minutes of pumping up my writer's ego, I am ready to sit down and start writing. For at least a half hour. Until I have to take a deep breath and repeat my mantra. Now, though, I have to tell you about our first meeting. We were at Mountjoy High School, where Alex taught Spanish and English. It was early August. She was cleaning her classroom, packing up piñatas and posters. I was standing there feeling awkward, trying to figure out how I could possibly decorate the bulletin boards of my first classroom.

The Alex I met that day was the post–Missouri Writing Project version, and to hear her tell it, the previous version was quite a bit different. Really, to tell her story right, I have to go back about ten years before I met her, when she was a new teacher at Mountjoy High School. The following excerpt of a poem she penned during her early years there might give you a glimpse into her state of mind back then:

The Contract

Over there on my desk it silently sits;
It's driving me crazy, it's giving me fits.
Now it starts talking, it's calling my name,
"Next year will be different, it won't be the same.
Come here and sign me, you know it's your fate,
I'm due the fifteenth, you don't want to be late!
With me signed and delivered your job is secure,
Don't think of the year you will have to endure."

The fact is, Alex walked into her first Mountjoy classroom ready to teach Spanish. She had studied the language extensively in the United States and in Costa Rica and had helped develop the Spanish curriculum for the district where she began teaching. A great start, since her six-hour teaching day would include Spanish I and II. But what about the four different English courses she was expected to teach? Because Alex had only completed six hours of English in college, she crammed as many college English classes as she could into her after-school and summer schedules. She also attended as many English conferences as possible. Despite her efforts, she remained unsatisfied with her teaching.

> I always knew that I was supposed to teach writing, but all I could teach them to do was to capitalize, indent, and maybe organize a little--all surface stuff. It was like I had to teach them to build a building without ever talking about what we were building and why.

It's not too often I hear Alex reminisce about those years, but she got a little agitated remembering The Teachers' Lounge Incident.

> I told you about the time when I talked to Marie and Joan in the lounge and said something about "How do you know what to do in the English classroom, how much time to spend on what things, what to concentrate on?" Then one of them looked at me and said, "If you don't know, Alex, then you shouldn't be teaching." They were acting like God was speaking to them, telling them what to teach. Well, it wasn't the first year I'd been teaching; I'd been at Mountjoy for a number of years. But it made it obvious to me that they didn't have the self-doubt that I had about teaching, and I had a lot of very strong self-doubt. I felt like what I was doing was junk.

I'd heard about The Teachers' Lounge Incident before, but this time Alex clarified her frustration. She had taken a shot at collaboration, trying to get practical feedback from her colleagues, but all they offered was sophomoric condescension. This agitated Alex because it emphasized not only her floundering but also her isolation; these co-workers weren't anywhere near throwing Alex a lifeline, let alone encouragement. Even as she sought their advice, Alex realized that these two women "didn't have the answer, but they did a good job of making me feel stupid anyway." The irony was that they were doing just as much "junk" as Alex, but they were both comfortable with their mediocrity. The combination of Alex's self-doubt and professional alienation motivated her to continue looking for answers—in arenas outside of the teachers' lounge.

The Writing Project: Getting Rid of the Junk

Nine years after Alex walked through Mountjoy's front doors, she felt dangerously close to "becoming one of those teachers who don't know what to do, so they give their students a lot to do." She was fed up with wasting her students' time. She had heard about the Missouri Writing Project and hoped it would provide some answers. She was on the verge of committing a large chunk of her summer to this seminar—at least seven hours a day for four weeks to writing, talking about writing, thinking about writing, researching writing, and sharing writing.

She even had a problem just writing the application (she had done little more than compose anniversary ditties in the past). Simple questions like, "Describe yourself as a writer" intimidated her. Application in hand, she called the institute director and bargained to forgo the $500 stipend and pay the course fee—in lieu of submitting the application. According to Alex, "I very honestly went into the Writing Project without wanting to write!"

Finally, she got her ink flowing, finished the application, and was accepted. Surrounded by twenty other teachers, she found herself in a small writing group with three other people. There it was, her tiny captive audience, and she immediately felt a responsibility—not to her writing, but to the group. Alex explains, "Here are these three other teachers who are going to sit here and listen to what I've written. There's no reason to skimp or waste their time."

Every day without fail Alex and her writing group met for at least an hour. (Writing group time is "sacred," exempt from any scheduling changes.) By the end of the project, the four named themselves The Fireside Chat Group. The group's bond has held them together for the last seven years, and they meet regularly to share their most recent writing. This solidarity was not forged over time but was soldered at The Fireside Chat Group's very first meeting.

Megan, one of the group members, passed out a piece on her father's recent retirement. As she read, Alex scrambled to correct all the grammar errors and all the run-on sentences, but as Megan reached the halfway point, Alex remembers,

> She got really choked up and started crying as she read. Carla finally hugged her, and John and I joined in. But it was a real revelation for me. Something I was treating as an inert thing, waiting for me to fix up, was obviously much more to the person who wrote it. It taught me about ownership and also, what a piece of writing says is much more important than how it says it.

And that is how her stifling assumptions about writing—which Alex had never been able to shake—were jolted free on the first day of the Writing Project. Finally, after years of seeking answers, Alex discovered how to radically rethink, resee, and revise her attitude toward teaching, learning, and writing.

Building a New Classroom

According to Alex, teachers unknowingly but *constantly* waste their students' time.

> Writing for punishment is still going on. There are teachers out there who think it's perfectly okay to have kids copy five-hundred-word reports verbatim out of *The World Book Encyclopedia*, even taking points off if they don't stop at exactly five hundred words! They consider this a writing assignment! We have all these English teachers who are teaching their students to write who don't believe that they, or their students, *can* write. So we set up false parameters; we stick to things that are "safe," like the five-paragraph essay and the term paper. We have had it drummed into our heads that we are successful if students can pump out a decent term paper. But what does the term paper have to do with life? Name one great five-paragraph essayist in the world! We will force-feed our students with bibliographic form and grammar terminology because we don't know any better, because that's all that we—without being writers ourselves—

can grasp. We teach them not to be readers, not to be writers—because, basically, *we're* not readers, *we're* not writers.

Of course, this is Alex's thinking after spending three weeks in a National Writing Project Summer Institute. Alex isn't shy about admitting her faults as a writing teacher before this transforming summer:

> When my students did write, most of it was in response to other people's writing. It was like telling them, "All the good stuff's already been written. Don't you try and write anything; just write about this really great writing by someone else."

A fledgling graduate of the Writing Project, Alex was ready to overhaul tradition. She was ready to model her English classroom on Writing Project philosophy, ready to put into practice some of the strategies she had tried during the institute. The next year, her English classes devoted three periods a week to writing workshop, and students chose the type of writing and their own topic. At the end of each quarter, students were evaluated on a certain number of polished pieces. Alex diligently protected these blocks of writing time. She set up two desks off to one side of the classroom for kids to talk about their progressing works with someone *other than the teacher*. While theoretically a great idea, Alex had reservations: "I was just sure that it was going to be a mess—that I was going to have kids fighting to get over there to sit and gossip." She kept vigilant, ready to break up any chatter about the homecoming dance or football rivalries. Instead, she found that the students

> genuinely got up to go over there to talk about their writing to other kids. I mean, they saw each other as valuable resources. Plus, they wanted to conference with me all the time about their work, even before or after school. I cannot tell you the number of rewrites they did on their work.

There were other obvious successes. One of her students published a writing workshop creation in a book about rodeos; another won a contest for her composition on wildlife. But the less apparent successes—such as kids giving up those few minutes of pre–first bell socializing so that they would have a little one-on-one time to ask for Alex's writing feedback—are the ones that convinced Alex that she and her curriculum mutiny were on the right track.

Resurrection: Life after the Writing Project

Participating in a writing group was the catalyst for Alex's first revelation about writing and teaching. I've never known her to turn down an invitation from a writing group, even when her daily planner was crammed. She has juggled commitments to three or more writing groups simultaneously. She dragged *me* to my first writing group. Therefore, I would have bet that the most valuable part of the Missouri Writing Project for Alex was her writing group. I was wrong. According to Alex, the value was a lot more abstract. First of all, the Writing Project demystified writing for Alex:

> Most people will tell you that writers and artists are born. Gauguin was born Gauguin, Hemingway was born Hemingway. Now I realize that isn't necessarily true. Maybe I can't write Hemingway's stuff, but I can write good stuff—and I never did that until I was forty years old. There was never anything in my life before the Writing Project that taught me to do that, or that it was a worthwhile endeavor—writing just to write. And if I could, anybody could.

Second, the Writing Project led Alex to see the power inherent in writing:

> If you need something—bookshelves, a telephone, whatever—and you can put down cogent reasons why you want it and put it in the right style, you can get it. You gain credibility. If you write something creative that's decent, the whole world thinks, "Wow, only really intelligent people can do this." All of the sudden you have this new persona as a really bright, talented person.

Third, the Writing Project introduced Alex to her potential:

> There was something about somebody saying you have to sit down and write for an hour every day. You owe yourself that

hour every day, and it doesn't matter how it turns out. This gave me the discipline to sit down and do it. But then the possibilities opened up. What could I do with my writing? I learned how to invest myself in something, and I got to build whatever I wanted.

And this is why the woman who decided to give the Writing Project a chance, to try one more thing to transform her classroom into a valuable learning environment, ended up with a whole lot more than she bargained for. Although she could not have anticipated it, Alex ended up on a pilgrimage toward resurrecting words.

Writing and Truth

Alex might have started out her writing career producing "little more than cute little ditties for people's birthdays"—in fact, she still might whip out a few limericks for fun—but that's certainly not the extent of her work these days. I have sat with her in many writing groups and been blown away by the way she can turn a phrase, click out a rhythm, or build a piece to its climax.

At one writing-group session, I listened to her read her satire about Washington politics. I loved listening to the way the words flowed from Alex's mouth. I loved that the piece was full of her spunk and attitude, her humor. But I also felt miffed. The poem was a workshop piece, and we were supposed to give her suggestions to improve the poem; but what could I say? We all agreed that it was a finished, polished piece. Alex became sort of agitated, stuffing the paper back in her bag, and I knew what was bothering her: that sort of feedback, the fatal, "It's-perfect-the-way-it-is" kind, seemed to lack sincerity. Alex thought the readers or listeners owed her piece more thoughtful, probing counsel than that. For Alex, writing is never a detached exercise. That is, no matter what form her writing takes, it always remains a part of her, an extension of her worries, attitudes, regrets, philosophies, outlook.

I have pieces of myself that I didn't have before, and I have outlined pieces of myself. It worries me a bit, but everything I write turns out to be, in some way, about me. But there are truths and revelations in writing. You have to face things you never faced before.

Her analysis here definitely applies to her piece "The Perfect Picture," which explores one of the less picturesque realities of life. "It doesn't particularly work as a story. It's not one of my best pieces of writing," admits Alex. "But in another way, it *is* one of my best because it puts things in perspective." In this excerpt, Alex remembers an uncomfortable childhood scene: eavesdropping on her parents as they circuitously refused to let an African American couple tour the house they were selling (the same parents who banished a child from their home for using the word *nigger*).

The Perfect Picture

. . . . I didn't confront my parents then. I was too embarrassed and ashamed. But a month later, after the house really had sold, to a white family with four children, I was alone with my mother in the attic packing, and I confessed I had been home when the Andersons came. I asked her why she and Dad had lied. She at least had the grace to blush before she answered. "We would be happy to have the Andersons in the neighborhood. But you have to remember, we won't be living here. Some of our friends don't feel the way we do, and we can't impose our beliefs on them, especially when we won't be here. Besides, there is the ugly but very real fact that if we sold to the Andersons, property values would go down. We don't have the right to do that to our neighbors." She held my eyes then, and I was the first to look down.

Nothing more was ever said either by my parents or me. It was one of those painful moments of doubt in a basically secure life that children are afraid to examine too closely for fear they will lose something important. I dealt with it in my dreams, where I haughtily presented them with a set of crisp white sheets and invited them to try them on for size. In real life, there were no more confrontations. But I remembered and from then on, I think I felt tainted and burdened with the guilt of racism.

When we moved to Missouri and actually saw Klansmen handing out leaflets in a mall, I cringed and looked away, but it was no longer terror that made me do it. I had lost my mantle of righteousness, and I was afraid, if I looked, I would see something familiar in their eyes. Or worse yet, they would find kinship in mine.

According to Alex, all of the story's details aren't necessarily true, but that's not the important part:

There is this real dichotomous thing going on: when you write, on the one hand you don't necessarily have to be faithful to the facts, but you must be faithful to the truth as far as who you are.

In real life, Alex never dreamt about the gift of sheets. Plus, she never made the connection between her parents' actions and the rally of Klansmen until many years later. For Alex, committing this memory to paper was essential:

"The Perfect Picture" gets to the truth of how I felt, and of course it helped me get to the truth of how you can't say things. If I didn't commit it to writing, it would have always been kind of amorphous, kind of uncomfortable. If I were not writing, but only telling the story, I would have made excuses for [my parents]. . . . You commit to writing some of those things you could never say, things that would be familial treason or something. A lot of my writing is an attempt to resolve or explain something I see. I avoid talking because that's sometimes seen as a betrayal, but in writing you get resolutions you don't get in real life.

Lamott (1994) would likely agree:

You need to put yourself at the center [of your writing], you and what you believe to be true or right. The core, ethical concepts in which you most passionately believe are the language in which you are writing. . . . But needless to say, you can't tell them in a sentence or a paragraph; the truth doesn't come out in bumper stickers. . . . Your whole piece is the truth, not just one shining epigrammatic moment in it. There will have to be some kind of unfolding to contain it, and there will be layers. (103–4)

Maybe this is what we rookie writers find so intimidating. We know we are good with words, that we are adept at phrasing and playing with language until we mold what others call "good writing." But it's not so simple once we realize that writing demands more than the skillful arrangement of words, once we accept that real writing exists in multiple layers.

Writing, Alex-Style

I have spent many carpool hours listening to Alex rave about the transformational powers of the Writing Project. As a walking sandwich board for the project, Alex has goaded, cajoled, and prodded several struggling teachers into participating. This includes me, but we'll get to that later. Somehow, I always pictured her fresh out of the project, religiously carrying around a little notebook to record insights that popped into her head and writing impromptu vignettes. She would lay that little journal on her nightstand so that whenever she awoke with the inspiration for a poem, editorial, or novel, it would be within arm's reach. The random hours she devoted to writing would flower into lengthy spans, until she would be completely consumed by each piece, oblivious to the ringing of the telephone, the growling in her stomach, the twitching of her tired eyes.

Well, this certainly wasn't and isn't Alex's experience—and my scenario definitely would be too Harlequin romance for her anyway. Alex would never claim that the act of writing is her passion, her obsession. She's frank about it: "I don't stay awake at night and say, 'I've got to write!' It's not this, 'There's a song in my soul, and I've got to let it out.'" Many contemporary writing gurus agree with Alex that not all writers live with pen in hand, writing constantly. Goldberg (1986) attempts to dispel writing myths like these by claiming that writers, like runners, need to practice. "You don't wait around for inspiration and a deep desire to run. It'll never happen, especially if you are out of shape and have been avoiding it. But if you run regularly, you train your mind to cut through or ignore your resistance" (11).

Alex no longer heeds anyone's writing prescriptions. She writes prior to each writing group meeting. That means that even during periods when she belongs to three groups simultaneously she averages only three hours of uninterrupted writing a month. That's okay, though. For Alex, the magic in writing has nothing to do with romantic inspiration or even tenacious, scheduled, methodic commitment to practicing. The beauty of writing for Alex lies in one simple truth, which she often states: "Before the Writing Project, before I really tried it, I never knew I could do it."

Overcoming Limitations

During our carpooling, Alex muckered about how she was surrounded by artistic people and how she was the least creative person in the world. Then one day she jumped into my Honda and announced that she had enrolled in a drawing class. Later, as we sat in her living room to talk about her writing, we digressed: we giggled about her thirty minutes of fame as a contestant on the TV game show *Jeopardy;* we discussed the pros and cons of sponge painting her bathroom; we argued about the worth of Quentin Tarantino as a director; she even tried to pawn her cat off on me. But when we touched on the work she had produced in her art class, she lit up and started talking rapid-fire. I didn't interrupt.

Pulling out a how-to-draw book and watercolor pencils, she showed me her terriers and Scotties. She talked about the shingles on the house she was sketching, how the instructor would point her in the right direction, and how she was able to go with it, experimenting with brush strokes and shading, so that the result was distinctly hers. She bent close and lowered her voice:

> I'm never going to be a great painter, but, um, I'm working on this piece for Frank [her husband] for Christmas. He doesn't know about it, but I've got to finish it up this week. You know, she [the instructor] has to show me how to do it, like I was doing the shingles, and she has to show me how to put down the paint. It's a watercolor and you go like this [she demonstrates]. To see that physically happening on paper and to know that I did it, and that I could do it, was just amazing.

After Christmas, I was back at Alex's house, and there it was, hanging next to the entranceway and matted in a light blue: the watercolor winter landscape of Alex and Frank's house. That day, she talked more about the painting and its importance to her:

> This became the most intense project perhaps of my life and largely because I didn't believe I could do it. I honestly believed I could not do this. It was like starting with nothing. I had no talent. But you can sit down and just do art. There ain't no way in the world that anybody would hang my painting in a museum, but it's a picture of my house, and there's lines on the eaves, and I did it. And I learned things I didn't know anything about. I would never have done this before the Writing Project.

According to Alex, art, like writing, is mythologized into a herculean task. So when the Writing Project redefined writing for her, showed her that the average person could create some extraordinary prose and poetry, it gave her a glimpse into other areas of life that might be conquerable. Now, with a pinch of anger, Alex talks about our tendency to view creative endeavors as "off limits to the regular Joe. You would never say, 'You can't drive; Mario Andretti can drive.' But we do this with writing, and we do this with art!" Those people who never graduate past paint-by-numbers are missing out. They never get to experience the high that comes with wading into untested waters, and according to Alex, they are denying themselves something essential to personal growth: "Something comes out of a new and different experience, some self-knowledge. You are a different person when a piece of art is done." So, will Alex limit herself to writing and art as her paths to personal enrichment? I doubt it.

> After the Writing Project, I found out that I really can accomplish things, that I can figure out how to do it. I am much more powerful than I ever was before—I can write, I can paint, I can do anything!

The Tough Part

It is easy to see that the Writing Project was a necessary force behind Alex's personal and professional rejuvenation: it gave her the practical insight into how to revamp her English curriculum to make writing relevant for her students; to expand her writing repertoire to uncover personal truths; to unlock potential and reveal new possibilities. It is easy for me to enumerate Alex's successes. Yet it is not so easy to explain how the Writing Project contributed to Alex's decision to leave the classroom, or how this exodus is also testament to Alex's personal and professional renewal.

At first, this was the part of Alex's story that was difficult to explain. I couldn't quite grasp why, just one year after her Writing Project experience, just when her classroom practices had finally started to gel, Alex decided to leave her position as Mountjoy High School's English/Spanish teacher and become the middle school's media specialist. I have long wrestled with this thought: here I am, writing one story about what keeps teachers vibrant in their professional world, and somehow I need to justify Alex's decision to leave her classroom.

At first, it seemed like the end of a teacher's story, because Alex offered no enlightenment. She hedged, gave evasive or labyrinthine answers to my questions. I pushed a little more: "You taught English and Spanish at Mountjoy and then you did the Writing Project, and after that you became a librarian? You figured all this out [how to make writing meaningful for her students] and then you left the classroom?" She picked up some watercolors.

> Think of all the people who, if you asked them to pick up a pencil and draw, would say, "No, I can only do stick figures." I guess I'll go back to what the guy says, that the best English teachers are those who do it for themselves. And being a really good English teacher, given the structure of the school system, may be impossible. It's really such a hard thing to do, so time-consuming, so outward-focused. For me, being an English teacher is the guiltiest job in the world because there's always a billion things being written that you should read and there's your kids' writing. No matter how much you have them read, no matter how much you have them write, it's never enough. You never really feel like you're doing a good job. . . . I feel like the year we did writing workshop [the year after the Writing Project] was my most successful year of teaching, and I got their writing back to them in two

days, tops. But we did workshop three days a week and I had seventy-five students in English classes alone.

It is problematic to consider that teacher renewal has been successful when the teacher opts to leave the classroom. We at first assume that a white flag was raised, that the teacher left an impossible situation because he or she didn't have the chutzpah to stick it out and triumph. A primary aim of the National Writing Project is to help teachers become writers themselves, so that they in turn become better teachers of writing. But what happens when the teacher abandons the teaching of writing? Has the project failed? Knowing Alex, my answer is, "Positively, absolutely not." It's almost tragic to lose any teacher who values student writing. It's tough to lose a colleague who is committed to becoming a better teacher, willing to go back to school, give up a summer, tap dance—or whatever it takes—to make his or her classroom a potent learning environment. Unfortunately, not all teachers share Alex's zeal. I agree with her estimation that

> most people out there who teach don't really know what they're doing. Most of the better ones will tell you they don't know what they're doing, but they are trying to figure it out. The poorer ones will tell you they know exactly what they're doing, and their curriculum is written in concrete.

Now, as a media specialist, Alex sees part of her job as helping those teachers who are fighting to make their curriculum meaningful.

> I guess I like this job so much because I get to work with both the teachers and the students, and I feel more effective than I did as a classroom teacher. . . . I am able to stay current with the technology and the literature, and a major focus of my job is to help the other teachers on the staff stay current. I try to funnel information and programs and curriculum ideas to them. I get to collaborate with them in lesson planning. This keeps me in direct contact with the kids. It also helps me influence the way things are taught.

Of course, Alex did not make the change to middle school media specialist easily. In an extended confrontation with

Mountjoy's superintendent, Alex explained why she should be considered for the newly available position. The superintendent did not agree, so Alex asked to address the school board personally. The superintendent refused. But Alex ignored his mandate and contacted board members individually to plead her case.

> I would never have done this before the Writing Project. But now I knew that I knew more about what was supposed to happen in the classroom than the superintendent did. He had no power over me. He had made up his mind that he did not have to give me this job, and I didn't feel he had the right to do this. I knew I was justified. I valued myself. And I prevailed.

Alex alludes to the fact that her success was due in part to the Writing Project, though she has never fully explained why. I think the answer lies in a *cycle* of renewal: once Alex revitalized her own voice as a writer through the Writing Project, she created a domino effect. Her revived words led to the "resurrection of [her] students' writing souls," which in turn led to her increased confidence as a professional. Each step of this process of empowerment and self-validation naturally guided her to resurrect her words in an unexpected venue: a confrontation with Mountjoy's superintendent. And consider the result of Alex's efforts: After nine years of struggling at Mountjoy High School (and one year of triumph), she is now in a position to collaborate with every teacher and connect with every student. As a media specialist, she finally feels potent, powerful, and influential. How's that for renewal?

Alex and Me

I have come full circle: I met Alex as she was packing up her classroom, the one I was inheriting from her. She seemed—even in the act of cleaning—a seasoned, confident pro. Tossing a Julio Iglesias cassette in my direction, she simultaneously rifled through the file cabinet and kicked crumpled papers toward the trash. In those first few minutes, my arrogant, first-year-teacher attitude shriveled, and I had the uncomfortable realization that I was a bland and awkward successor to this woman.

Quixotic and paranoid, I spent my first days at Mountjoy trying to ferret out information about Alex. I uncovered a few facts: she was leaving the classroom to become the media specialist; she was about forty; she had a dog named Lulu; she had lived in Central America for a year; she owned a boat and was an avid sailor. Not exactly what I was looking for. At the end of the day, I summoned the courage to look the counselor straight in the eye and frankly probe: "So, what kind of teacher was Mrs. Columbo?" He raised his eyebrows, screwed his mouth into a sarcastic scowl, and I was sure I had hit the mother lode. Images swarmed in my head: students tied to their desks, mechanically filling in worksheets; Mrs. Columbo at her desk, slumped over the latest *Soap Opera Digest*. I waited. Finally, he responded slowly and deliberately: "She was one of those feminist types who kept her name when she got married."

I wasn't exactly sure how the decision to keep the name Columbo had any relation to her classroom persona or ability to teach. But I didn't like what I thought I was hearing either: Alex Columbo sounded a bit more progressive than I wanted her to be. I smiled politely at the counselor, grabbed my book bag, and figured I'd just have to continue the investigation on my own.

Before the first full day of school, I heard about some out-of-district teachers who carpooled to Mountjoy's schools. Great, I thought, that will save me some cash. But included in the package was Alex. I began to imagine a nightmarish ride with the ex-Spanish/English teacher. I could see her climbing into the car and shooting questions my way—in Spanish, of course—and I would haltingly mumble answers in my unpracticed tongue. Then she would give me unsolicited tips on how to arrange desks, how to teach *Romeo and Juliet*, how to introduce the argumentative essay.

And so I silently and consistently worked on excuses to escape the carpool (and Alex specifically): I was going to have to stay after school for this or that; I was claustrophobic and allergic to perfume. Then, about one week into school, the thermostat of my 1987 Caprice up and quit. I was stuck. The first half of the drive was usually okay; I asked the other three teachers questions about how to fill out and submit requisitions, how to get the janitor to empty my trash. We chatted aimlessly about the weather, the school calendar, the school board president.

Then we picked up Alex. Surrounded by two or three tote bags of books, computer disks, and random papers, she shoved herself into the back seat. Then everything changed. The three other women, who for the last twenty miles had been rather reserved, were transformed. In lightning succession, the four exchanged stories about their families, latest love interests, dogs, realtors. They laughed about principals' antics, argued about the origin of one urban legend or another, discussed how best to deal with prickly classroom situations, and even belted out show tunes. Silent and distant, I daydreamed of lower gas prices and a new, dependable car.

Five years later, I honestly can't pinpoint the moment that my opinion of Alex changed. At some point, I stopped worrying about her judging my faulty Spanish or my ability to teach writing. (In fact, about the only time she brought up my classroom was to ask if everything was going okay or to give me something to use in it, like her authentic Mexican sombreros.) I started to realize what most of the people around me already knew: Alex was an amazing woman.

When she convinced me to visit her writing group, I had a somewhat mixed reaction. With a master's degree in English literature under my belt (which meant I had written a smattering of papers about Milton, Hopkins, and other authors I cared nothing about), I felt overqualified to join this writing soiree. At the same time, underneath my cockiness, I was scared to share my writing with anyone. At our first meeting, I read my own piece of writing, which was extremely stilted, wordy, and artificial.

Thankfully, the group, with Alex at the helm, was kind, restricting its feedback to questions and gentle suggestions. I exited my first writing group feeling exhilarated, validated, and ready to start writing. Before long, Alex raved about how the Writing Project had changed her life. She soon convinced me that I could have a similar experience if I committed a chunk of my summer to learning about myself as a writer. To top it off, Alex offered to write a recommendation for me. The deal was sealed. Along with twenty other participants ranging from elementary teachers to college instructors, I spent four packed weeks exploring writing. I left the project motivated, rejuvenated, and powerful. I was ready to write my young adult novel and anxious to jump back into the classroom.

That post–Writing Project feeling is one that does not dissipate, and as I watch my students give each other thoughtful writing-group feedback, I realize that the project saved me from becoming one of those lecturing, podium-glued teachers who, in the words of Alex, "constantly and consistently waste their students' time." I am also relatively sure that without that "Writing Project feeling" working in me, I would never have had the moxie to attempt to write this chapter. That's why I stay connected. This will be my fourth summer working in some capacity with the project. Without a smidgen of doubt, I thank Alex for all of this. Without her support (and, let's face it, her relentless nagging), I never would have attempted the Writing Project.

Right from the start, Alex took special care to mold me into an assured, risk-taking educator. But now I understand her concern for me as more than mothering or mentoring: it was an outgrowth of the Writing Project philosophy. As Alex once wrote, once you are "Redeemed by the cleansing waters/ Of the Missouri Writing Project," you cannot help but shepherd others into the flock. And that is how two past graduates, two women who *could* be joined by nothing more than a couple of sticky, cramped hours carpooling each day, ended up on a similar mission.

Alex speaks for both of us.

> Most people spend their lives bitching about how everything in the world has kept them from accomplishing what they should have. What a terrible way to see things. But all life is really about thinking like this: "This is not the way I want this to be; what do I have to do to get where I need to be?" After the Writing Project, I figured out I really can accomplish things, that I can figure out how to do it.

Collecting Dreams: Imagination as Renewal

JILL WEISNER
Maryville University of St. Louis

W hen I first learned about this project to explore teachers' experiences of renewal, I was eager to participate. Interviewing teachers who love teaching and have found ways to stay renewed was right up my alley. I thought it might even offer some inspiration for my own teaching. For too long, I was frustrated by the lack of enthusiasm I saw in my colleagues. The negative talk in the teachers' lounge, apathy toward trying new things in the classroom, and impatient attitudes toward the students often made me feel a little hopeless about the future of teaching. I learned to stay out of conversations about students and to avoid the smoky lounge when certain teachers were there. I did not want to isolate myself from other teachers, but I was not about to get sucked into the black hole from which so many of my colleagues seemed to function like automatons.

After our first meeting as a research group, I realized it would be my responsibility to find someone to study. My excitement dissipated. Who would I interview? What veteran did I know who still loved teaching and was great with students? I knew a few inexperienced teachers who maintained high expectations for themselves and their students, but I could not think of any "renewed" veteran teachers. After a few weeks, I received a phone call that turned my perspective around.

The phone call was from a former student, Samantha Jordan. She called to wish me happy birthday, but she also nonchalantly mentioned that the utilities had been turned off in the trailer where she, her baby, and her boyfriend lived. To make matters worse, they were being evicted from the trailer court. I could only imagine what life was like for them. Samantha, who has surprising passion for life, also told me about the volleyball team she was joining with her mom and the deer she and her boyfriend had killed (out of season). When we hung up, I knew I could not help her do more with her life. Too proud to accept money and too unaware to seek social services, she appeared to be stuck. I remembered the first time Samantha and I met. Ten years ago, I walked through the student cafeteria during lunch at Cleveland High School when Samantha, tall and sturdy, ran up to me. I was student teaching and coaching first-year basketball for the first time, yet she had somehow figured out who I was, what I looked like, and how to find me. She asked, "Hey, can I still come out for the team?"

"Why didn't you come last week?"

"I got in a fight with my older brother. I've been out of school all week with this broken nose." She pointed to her bruised and swollen nose. Her words sent a chill through me. I was expecting her to say she had been out of town or something. Not knowing what to say, I told her to be at practice at three P.M. She bounded off toward her friends and huddled by the soda machine, pretending not to watch me. Later, I quickly gathered information on Samantha. A school counselor directed me to her team of four teachers—one of whom was Carole—who team-taught one hundred first-year students labeled "at risk." When I first talked with Carole, she told me about Samantha's extremely abusive family background and her lack of academic ability (she was assigned to special education services). But she said Samantha was an excellent athlete who would benefit from being on my basketball team. I was immediately struck by how much Carole knew about Samantha and by the amount of interest she appeared to take in her. Samantha was a student whom most teachers tried to ignore or sent to the office to get out of their hair. Samantha was self-righteous, protective, and temperamental—she took no orders or disrespect from anyone.

During that first conversation with Carole, I realized how different she was from the other English teachers at that school, especially from my cooperating teacher, Dorothy Wilcox. In contrast to Mrs. Wilcox, Carole offered me a safe place to vent my student-teaching frustrations. Mrs. Wilcox and I had little in common. I was twenty-three and sported an Izod shirt and penny loafer shoes and could not relate to the veteran English teacher's heavy eye makeup and frosted beehive hairdo. I was an idealistic young teacher who wanted to have fun with the students and engage them in writing and reading. Mrs. Wilcox had received her educational training years ago and developed her classroom around diagramming sentences, memorizing vocabulary words, and implementing assertive discipline techniques. This approach was not me. After spending a month with Mrs. Wilcox and hanging out in the English teachers' workroom, I harbored little hope for my future as an English teacher. I thought that if I could not get interested in gerunds, appositives, and five-paragraph essays, I would not fit in anywhere. Because of my own desperation about teaching, I was relieved to meet Carole, who was interested in and positive about students. Of course, there were other good teachers at Cleveland High. I just had not met them yet.

After my first encounter with Carole, she agreed to let me observe her in the classroom. I noticed immediately that her classroom looked and sounded different from all the others: it was cluttered with piles of books and magazines, the desks were crammed into a circle, the students were focused on projects, and they were buzzing with talk about their work. Most of the other teachers in that school had bare walls, neatly aligned desks, and consistent silence. Throughout the year, I continued to spend time with Carole and her team members. They helped me through my difficult student-teaching situation. During my lunch period, I often wandered to Carole's building and sat in on her team's meal. In the other lunchroom, teachers' talk consisted of racist, pessimistic, almost hateful gossip about students. Carole's team members complained, but they planned strategies for dealing with their students rather than resigning to a sense of despair. This proactive approach is what drew me to Carole's classroom and taught me the importance of seeking out colleagues with positive attitudes. Ten years later, the phone call from Samantha reminded me of Carole and how much she helped and inspired me during that difficult time. Over the years, I have revisited those memories of Carole and her kindness and compassion toward the students. I knew she still taught at Cleveland High School and decided I would call her to see if she would be willing to talk with me.

But I was nervous about calling her. I wondered if she was still committed to teaching. Had she continued to be empathetic toward the students? Was she burnt out? Would she have time to participate in this study? I put off the call for a week before finally picking up the phone.

Fortunately, Carole remembered me, and we agreed to meet during her preparation hour. I arrived at her room just as the bell rang. I stood quietly at the doorway as thirty-one first-year students filtered out of the room. Once the crowd cleared, I saw Carole and a student standing near her desk. Unaware that I was there, she handed him a hardback book and said, "This isn't about the mob, but it is about gangsters, and I thought you would like it. You don't have to give this book back; it's yours to keep." Holding back a smile, he thanked her and ran out the door. Later, I asked Carole why she gave him the book:

> He has an absolute admiration for Al Capone. When we were doing something earlier in the year, he wanted to do it on Al Capone. Then I realized he was infatuated with him. I was at a bookstore and I saw this book on the mob and it was relatively cheap, so I just bought it for him. It's something I can do. I love books. I think it is a real gift when somebody gives me a book.

During that first visit, I was relieved to discover that Carole had not lost her enthusiasm for teaching, nor did she lack interest in the students. I saw how important it was for her to offer them moments of happiness by capitalizing on small opportunities to let them know she is interested in and cares for them. This first visit convinced me that Carole was the right person for my study.

Seeing Scenarios

For the second interview, we met at Carole's house, which is situated in a well-maintained suburban cul-de-sac in a large midwestern city. During that session in Carole's sunroom, I accidentally stumbled on her love for fantasy, imagination, and creative thinking. Her sunroom, located at the back of the house, affords an easy view of the neighborhood from several different perspectives. As an aside, I told her how much I enjoyed watching my neighbors and creating stories about their lives and families. It was then she revealed her creative interests: "I see moving pictures always. When I'm bored or when I'm sitting at these meetings, I'm seeing these people as stars in a full-blown motion picture. They may be tap dancing; they may be running down hills. I see things in movies all the time."

Carole calls it "seeing scenarios." Her imagination often takes over during boring meetings or in situations she wishes she could change. Using the people who are present, she will "fantasize what a movie would be like if that person [anyone from the meeting] was in the starring role." What can get Carole into trouble is that she enjoys her scenarios so much that she likes to share them with her friends. Telling the story is just as much fun for her as imagining it.

> I tend to get so delighted with my creativity that I want to tell everybody. I have to share it, and I get people off track and in trouble. For me, it is so much fun. I just think it allows me to change the circumstances of a boring meeting a little. I do like telling the story. If I can't embellish it, if I can't make it better, if I can't add to it, then it's no fun.

Sitting on the couch with the tape recorder between us, Carole suddenly came to life. Describing these stories brought on animated gestures, fast talking, and a smile, which lit her otherwise subdued face. Up to this point, we had discussed her teaching and involvement in the school plays, but she had not shown this kind of energy about those topics. I suddenly found myself amused by the stories and fascinated by her ability to turn dull, real-life experiences into fun adventures. I figured we were on to something. Then she told me of an adventure that filled her fifth-through eighth-grade years.

> For several years, my two best friends and I pretended that we were married to the three stars of the TV detective series, *77 Sunset Strip*. We always did the [scenarios] in my garage. We did our whole life. We would just reenact whatever we wanted to. I remember when my mom came home and opened the refrigerator and there was no food in there. I had taken everything out, and we filled it with lilacs for the [made-up] wedding. We

also buried every dead animal that we found. We made an or-
gan on the back of the garage. We just drew it on with magic
markers and pencil and we would pretend to play hymns for
them.

Every day at school she and her friends planned the scenes
they wanted to act out that day after school. She loved it and
they loved it. It became an obsession for them. Carole said that
once they began acting out their detective-series scenarios, dialogue popped into her mind. Ideas, events, and images appeared
without effort. Her imagination simply took over.

Carole did not let me in on her ability to "see scenarios"
right away. She revealed this gift only after a great deal of talking. Slightly embarrassed, she made several comments like, "Now,
don't think I do this twenty-four hours a day or anything" and
"I'm not seeing you in some movie where you are dribbling bas-
ketballs and acting like Whoopie Goldberg or something." She
wanted to make sure I knew she didn't do this all the time. Possibly unsure of how I might respond to her ability to create stories
and imagine different worlds, she was at first hesitant to speak of
her interest in seeing scenarios. Gradually, though, she became
more comfortable talking about the subject.

> When I was in high school, I struggled a lot with where was I
> going to fit in, because my high school was very cliquey. Very
> small. Everybody knew everybody all along, but everybody had
> labels. My little group was called the "Golden Girls" because we
> had real good values and real good grades, but we weren't real
> popular. We were kind of klutzy with boys and kind of indepen-
> dent and goofy. We had to kind of carve out something that we
> could do. And so we went to the principal and said, "Our pep
> assemblies are just horrible. We need to have better pep assem-
> blies. We have some ideas." We told him that we were going to
> do these skits. We just kind of took over. And the man just kind of
> lost control and didn't know how to get it back. We organized
> these humongous pep rally skits that would be done in the gym
> right before school was let out on Friday afternoon. We got real
> dramatic and really into this stuff. We would write them and
> produce them and carry them out every week of football season.

Early in her life, Carole developed an active imagination and
visual way of thinking, using this imagination to play with her

friends as well as to fit in with her peers. What is remarkable about her experience is that she not only possessed the imagination, but she acted it out as well. She turned the stories generated in her mind into adventures that she and her friends participated in. As the ringleader, Carole transformed what could have been an ordinary life into one filled with excitement and experiences that many children never have.

Shifting Priorities

Carole describes herself as an optimistic person. I asked her several times how she sustains her positive outlook, and she always replied, "I guess I was just born that way. . . . I basically like everything I have ever done. I feel very lucky and have tremendous support from the people around me." I have wondered if there is a cause-effect relationship between the way she creates stories in her mind and her outlook on life. Even though she clearly let me know that she is simply an optimistic person, I could not help but wonder how her active imagery and seeing scenarios kept her positive in difficult situations and sustained her genuine interest in students and teaching. Csikszentmihalyi (1991) offers an answer to this question:

> One of the simplest ways to use the mind is daydreaming: playing out some sequence of events as mental images. . . . [D]aydreaming not only helps create emotional order by compensating in imagination for unpleasant reality . . . but it also allows children (and adults) to rehearse imaginary situations so that the best strategy for confronting them may be adopted, alternative options considered, unanticipated consequences discovered. . . . And, of course, when used with skill, daydreaming can be very enjoyable. (120)

Csikszentmihalyi might label Carole's talent as daydreaming. As a child, when Carole created mental images that did not match her real life, she created a world that was fun and sometimes outrageous. As an adult, her daydreams are not as elaborate, nor does she act them out, but they still provide opportunities for her to momentarily escape unpleasant situations. Additionally, as an adult this daydreaming talent has translated into an ability to manipulate her mental focus (such as imagining her principal tap dancing on the table during a boring faculty meeting). But at other times, she can turn what disturbs her into something more positive.

While Carole may not describe her daydreaming and job satisfaction as a cause-effect relationship, there is a natural connection between the two. At one point, she said of her imagination: "That's how I change unhappy things into happy things." When she experiences challenges with her teaching, and because she is a "real big believer in being optimistic," she often turns things around in her mind by taking control of her internal world— reshifting her focus.

> CAROLE: When I am depressed and things aren't going right, it's not comfortable for me to just sit around and feel sorry for myself, to be discouraged or unhappy. It's not something that brings me pleasure, so days that are bad or if things didn't go right or whatever, I don't spend a lot of time agonizing over them. I try not to spend a lot of time in depression if I can help it. So, one of the ways out for me is to just consciously say that I'm not going to be depressed and I'll try something different tomorrow.
>
> JILL: So you can almost will yourself out of it?
>
> CAROLE: I think so. It's just sort of a matter of shifting priorities. Well, that didn't work, that's not going to work, you're stuck with that person, so could [I] be happy if I changed something else? So then I just kind of change how I view things. That's one of the reasons why I can have good days: I just change my requirements for myself. I find so many things interesting and fascinating to pay attention to.

Carol readily shifts her focus. Csikszentmihalyi (1991) explains how our mental abilities help us control our internal world: "The better route for avoiding chaos in consciousness, of course, is through habits that give control over mental processes to the individual, rather than to some external source of stimulation. . . . To acquire such habits requires practice" (120).

In addition to internal stimulation, Carol also experiences external stimulation in the form of the annual school drama production, which she directs. Working with large numbers of students over a short period of time is extremely demanding. The schedule is often grueling.

> I would stay after school to try to do my schoolwork, so I would get home around 4:00 P.M. I would start a little dinner, then I would change my clothes, get a couple of jugs of water ready, and return to school at 5:15. Then I'd open the gym up, rehearse from 6:00 to 10:00, then usually stay until about 11:00 P.M.

Like all after-school activities, directing the school play takes its toll on teachers. Juggling an English teacher's workload is difficult enough, but add to that hours of play rehearsals, and there are few hours left for eating or sleeping. Carole describes the complexities that arise when directing the annual school play or musical. She obviously enjoys drama a great deal, yet it requires enormous amounts of time and energy. But once she arrives at the rehearsals, she loses herself in the play and the students, an intensity of concentration that Csikszentmihalyi (1991) defines as a "flow" experience.

> I wake up when I get to rehearsal. On the way here, I sort of physically feel myself changing gears. It's like I am totally unaware of the time when I'm here. I don't even look at my watch. I will look up and it will be four hours later and I had no idea. But equally, it's just like anything else. Anytime you have highs, it takes a large toll on your energy. I don't sleep well when I do shows because I'm charged up. When I go home, I don't want to go to bed. I am on a high! But it's already 11:00 P.M. and I'm up at 5:00 A.M. Then, the next morning I think, "Why do I do this? This is not worth it. This is horrible." And then I get into my teaching. I get very engaged and don't pay much attention to lots of other things. And then there's this period of shifting.

Her flow during a recent production was interrupted by a personality conflict with another faculty member involved in the production. Many times Carole was left alone with all one hundred students and had to be both music and drama director. The stress was unbearable. She described how she shifted her focus onto other things and survived the production. Her daughter, Holly, gave her the most helpful advice. Holly suggested, "I'll tell you what you do. You do a really good play next year that you really want to do and make it be your swan song, and do it really well, and then say good-bye. That's it and it's over; let somebody else move on." This comment encouraged Carole to set her eyes on next year. Her daughter's reminder was "a sanity moment for me. . . . It was like, yeah, that's what I'll do. And so that got me through it."

Rather than become frustrated by situations she did not have control over, Carole focused on spring vacation and her yearly trip with good friends (the Golden Girls). "I kept looking at my calendar thinking, when I'm on vacation this will all be over. This will be over!" Refusing to crumble under the pressure, she found a positive focus. Her process of sustaining herself as drama director, teacher, and mother depends on the gift she has turned to for years—her ability to create a world with fewer worries. Carole also focused on her students in the production. "Honestly, the kids were absolutely wonderful. . . . The moments with the kids were an absolute joy." Her time with the students was certainly not free of problems, but overall they helped remind her why she was involved in the production in the first place.

By focusing her mental energies, Carole is not simply overlooking the negative parts of her life. She capitalizes on the moment and does not waste time worrying. "I'm one of those people who is not going to walk around and go, 'Man, I was waiting my whole life. I was just getting ready to start enjoying it.' I try to enjoy the moment a lot. I really try to live by the seize-the-day philosophy." Her strong desire not to let life pass her by helps her create the life she wants.

From Imagination to Drama

Carole's interest in seeing scenarios manifested itself in a love for drama. Throughout her schooling, she became involved with school plays, ran a video camera, and hosted her own radio show.

> My whole growing-up period in Iowa was sort of filled with these little adventures. I could tell you all kinds of capers. Early on I was cast as the lead in a play. That was a big deal. That was usually a senior/junior thing. They rarely used freshmen in the

plays. And so I did that and I also took part in speech contests, which they don't have nowadays. My dream was to be a television anchor. I was going to go away to college to be on television or maybe radio. I know I had no encouragement from anybody there that I can remember. And my mom didn't have any knowledge base to help me in that type of thing. And when I got to college, they didn't offer broadcasting there, so I had to figure out what to do. I got a job at the television station where I ran a video camera. They also had a student-owned radio station, so I went over there and did my own little radio show.

Once she became a high school English teacher in 1969, she got involved in directing school plays.

I really like to make people do things that they don't want to do. I like to get kids acting silly. Drama allows you to do that. And then I have this remarkable chance each year to do those plays, which is probably the way that all education should be. It's supposed to be guided. I don't lecture them about it. We do have a little period where we study the script together, and I give them some reference points. You could call those minilectures, but they are very small. It is totally student-as-worker. They get to try out their own work. They get to demonstrate it.

The student-centered, student-as-worker, and teacher-as-facilitator methods Carole uses when directing plays also operate in her teaching.

Any time I ever read anything on education and how it's supposed to work, I think, "There it is—it is a play." I keep thinking that drama is the model for all education. I try to use the drama model as much as I can, so it is definitely important for me to get the kids out of their seats. But I also know that every single time I've gone to a meeting and I've thought it was boring, it's because I didn't participate. I was just sitting in the back, thinking, "When is this going to be over?" Every conversation that you were ever actually engaged in—even if you didn't come out the winner but you were actively talking—I think you come away with some ownership. And so that's what I try to take from drama and put into my teaching.

Carole's enjoyment of play and making the ordinary extraordinary translates into an active classroom. Her students shed their self-images as noncreative thinkers, poor readers and writers, and/

or bad students. She said, "It's just amazing to me how sterile some of these kids are!" She described one way that she encourages her students to visualize scenarios and shift their self-images.

> I change unhappy things into happy things. I'm convinced that everybody can do it. And so I try to get my kids to do it. I always try to tell kids that are so turned off and so negative about school. I just say, [whispering] "Lie. Just make it up. Do you know how much more chance you are going to have to get a few points? Just lie!" So I won't let them write "I don't know" or "Nothing." I tell them, "Just lie about it." And then they say, "You're telling me to lie?" And I say, "Don't tell your mom—we'll both get in trouble. Just try it."

Using dramatic techniques—dialogue, charismatic voices, and gestures to retell events—Carole's love for telling a good story is evident. From a young child to a college student, she created narratives when she and her neighborhood friends spied on neighbors or produced skits for her high school pep assemblies. As an English teacher, she continued to do the same thing.

> CAROLE: I'm trying to get them to understand that you've got to first of all observe. So many of these kids are just sleepwalking through everything. They're just not even picking up anything because they're not opening up any of their senses. They could learn so much if they would just observe. Their own lives do have stories to be told. They need to be the collector of dreams. They need to be the collector of that story. And then I think that if you can get them to start collecting and listening to their own stories and their own hearts and own dreams, that you then need to teach them to listen to others.
>
> JILL: Can you think of an example of how you get kids to be collectors of stories?
>
> CAROLE: Well, just like this story that we're doing right now in class. They're writing their own stories, and it's nothing new and I'm not the only person that ever does it, but they are being allowed to publish. It becomes a very individual thing. A lot of kids write stories that are sort of just their lives. We talk a long time about the fact that where you live is where you should start from. And that's where a lot of story ideas come from. I just try to do it in everything. I try to allow them to use what they have and go from there.

She pushes her students to think creatively and play with language and ideas. In telling students to lie, Carole encourages them to do as she did when she was a child and continues to do as an adult. She says, "If I can see the pictures, then maybe I can get the kids to see the pictures." Getting students to "see the pictures" or imagine scenarios is the first step. The second step is to help them elaborate their stories. As she sees it, "A story is just so plain unless you embellish it." Developing stories and transforming everyday occurrences into exciting adventures is how Carole renews herself. It is also how she wants her students to renew or awaken themselves.

Carole also uses her imagination to brighten her students' days. Sometimes scenarios that involve her students come to mind. When one does, she shares it with them, trying to make them smile or give them hope they otherwise might not have.

> I [shift my thinking] for myself sometimes. I know I do it in my teaching 'cause I just did it on Friday. I thought, "God, I'm going to be in a kick-back mood. I'm going to tell all the kids I'm going on vacation and I am going to buy them all Nautica jackets." I just looked at them and thought, "I am so excited about going on spring break that I wanted to tap dance the whole day." It was the anticipation of the moment for me. I'm going to be leaving the students and was thinking they all deserved to have this experience [going to a resort]. I said to them, "I'm going to go shopping and I'm going into the Nautica store to buy you each Nautica jackets."

Carole's desire to help students have the privileges and pleasures she has encourages her to share made-up stories with them. She really would like to buy them all Nautica jackets, and likes to imagine that she will someday.

> I did really visualize myself coming back from the resort with a huge carton of Nautica jackets and being able to say, "Here's one for you and here's one for you." Thinking, "Wow, when I win that lottery maybe that's what I'd do—something extravagantly stupid for each of them instead of something practical."

Winning the lottery and buying all of her students jackets is a near-impossible proposition, yet sharing her story with her students added a little extra fun to an otherwise typical day, transforming it into a more enjoyable one. She says, "For a brief moment, maybe in a way, it's [the Nautica jacket fantasy] my wish of giving these kids the knowledge that everything is possible. I'm trying to give them some hope." Carole "sees pictures," plays with the scenarios, and enjoys the process. Passing the powers and pleasures of her imagination on to her students is an important part of Carole's curriculum.

Divorces, Dramas, Dreams

Perhaps Carole became so good at embellishing her stories and shifting her priorities because of her own difficult childhood.

> I lived in this tiny town that was very isolated in the middle of Iowa cornfields. We didn't have a car until I was sixteen. We didn't have hot water until I was in sixth grade. So I was really stuck in that town and its belief system and its way of doing things. Until I went to college, I had no idea that I was as poor as I was. I realize now that we were on welfare. I didn't know that that's what it meant when my mother said to take the pink slip and they will give you some groceries. I was also a member of the only family in that town that was divorced. There was no other kid in the entire town that was from a divorced family.
>
> I can remember having to pay all the bills from about age nine up. Writing the checks. Deciding to pay this and that. Doing all this walking up to town. My mom didn't handle that kind of stuff very well at all. Bills that she didn't have money for she just didn't open. They just got thrown into her purse, and we wouldn't worry about them until they [bill collectors] came to the door. When I got old enough to understand you are not supposed to do things this way, I took over the job.

Carole did not have the money or the kind of family her friends had, but she could create the ideal family in her mind. It seems feasible to make the leap to say that when she sees students who are equally deprived of family, money, or stimuli, she wants to help them transcend their situations—using humor or fantasy to change their attitudes, perceptions, or responses to life. I asked Carole what role her childhood played in the formation of her vivid imagination. She remembers fantasizing a room in her house that was well stocked with paper, gift wrapping paper, pencils, and other niceties. This room obviously did not exist, but her imagery helped her cope with poverty.

> One of the reoccurring things that I'm sure happened because I was so poor was that I pretended that I rode in Roy Rogers's saddlebags. So wherever he went, I went. In retrospect, I think it was probably part of missing my dad, and here was this big protector that was going to take care of me. And wherever he would go, I would go.

Carole's mother played an extremely influential role in developing Carole's imagination. She gave Carole the inspiration and motivation to create for herself any life she wanted.

> Mom was probably the perfect example of motherhood in that she just believed that it would just all work! She was one of those mothers that would think that whatever I would decide to do, she would celebrate just for the very fact that I'd decided it. If one day I would come home and say, "I'm going to be a brain surgeon," she would say, "Oh, that would be wonderful. You would do so good in brain surgery. We'll get you one of the Dr. Casey shirts." She just gave me this power to believe.

Whether Carole wanted to be a brain surgeon, television newscaster, or tap dancer, Carole's mother was the first to praise her and even help her elaborate the scenarios. In her mother's mind, Carole could do anything, and her mother shared this sense of empowerment with her daughter. The fact that Carole's mother was able to share this uninhibited outlook on life is remarkable, given her own background. Orphaned as a child and divorced as an adult, her mother had more than her share of challenges to deal with. "My father just dumped her in this town and left her there. She was an orphan by the time she was eleven. So she had no family of her own to turn to. She didn't have that support system at all. She couldn't turn to his family either. But she was an amazing person." Amazing because she managed to help both her children believe that the world was theirs to conquer. She had little money, no spouse, and two children, and she lacked some parenting skills, yet she motivated her daughter to strive for a life better than that which society expected of her.

> To my mom, every play I have done was the best she'd ever seen. I wondered how it could always be the best. I learned after I started doubting it that it didn't matter. That it still felt really good to have somebody say to you it was the best they had ever seen and say it with enthusiasm. But it never ceased to make me feel good, as opposed to someone saying to you that it was really stupid. It's harder to pull the head up when someone is slapping it down. I learned a lot more from my mom than what I ever thought. You don't spend time ever thinking about those things too much—at least I didn't, until my mom died. Then I realized she really taught me a lot about being a good teacher, good parent, good person.

Carole obviously absorbed her mother's belief about having the power to create an ideal world for herself. The Nautica jacket scenario is just one example. Like her mother, Carole wants to give her students the "power to believe" that the impossible just might happen someday. Evidence of this attitude and lifestyle is also clear in her sustained enjoyment of her career, her long-term success with the school plays and musicals, and the impact she has had on her students. Toward the end of our last interview, Carole recounted a common conversation she has with her ninth graders. As I heard her speak, I could imagine her mother's voice echoing in the background: "I think that the neatest part about teaching ninth grade is that there is some hope. I sometimes say to them, 'You have got a bad deal of cards. I just don't think things sound very fair at your house. But you have a choice. You can control your destiny.'"

Carole's optimism and control over her life, I believe, come partly from her challenging childhood and a mother who supported her active imagination. Her love of play and stories makes dealing with the day-to-day struggles of teaching possible. As she says, "I'm a big believer in being in touch with dreams and believing in dreams." Whether she puts herself mentally into another world, shifts her focus to more pleasant experiences, or shares her scenarios and beliefs in self-actualization with her students, she effectively uses her talents to renew herself and others.

When I started writing this chapter, I wasn't sure how believable Carole's story would be to readers. After all, I had not believed that anyone could maintain the positive, optimistic attitude Carole possesses. Then I remembered Samantha Jordan and why, as a student teacher, I had been drawn to Carole. Samantha's dire emotional and intellectual circumstances made most teachers give up on her. But Carole didn't. She wasn't sure if Samantha would graduate. In fact, she probably could have guessed that Samantha's life would turn out much the way it has. But during the year that Samantha was her student, Carole encouraged her not only to dream but also to believe that her dreams could become reality. Samantha managed to graduate, and while in high school, she kept in touch with me even though I was no longer teaching at Cleveland. She told me how she turned to Carole for frequent advice and support. I am not saying that Samantha graduated because of Carole, but it is obvious that Samantha was influenced by Carole's interest and concern.

Carole's story is about taking control of her experiences. Carole's mother was irresponsible, poor, and undependable, but she was also unique. She too had an active imagination and wanted her daughter to "will" herself out of their situation. After her mother died a few years ago, Carole realized how much about life and teaching she had learned from her: "I learned a lot by my mom dying. It was a real hard moment, and I learned that she will always be alive as long as I model the good things that she taught me. My passing on gifts that she gave me is keeping her alive. I think that's a little bit of what I'm doing here—passing a little bit on to kids."

I am touched by Carole's story. She does not ignore the hardships of life, but she believes there is a way out and wants to find it.

> I think I own my own happiness! I don't think you own it; I don't think he owns it; I think I own it. I think that's one of the ways that a lot of people let themselves get disappointed, depressed, or unhappy—they allow too many other people to own their happiness. I see that with kids a lot. They set out in an okay mood, but they let other people tell them how they are going to be. They give it away. I don't believe in that.

II

CROSSWINDS

Crosswinds blow across our line of travel. They do not parallel our path but come from perpendicular directions. In the following three chapters, you will meet teachers who were influenced by breezes from unexpected directions—from Kim's dishwashing, to Julia's absenteeism, to Pat's love of spontaneity and surprise.

In Chapter 4, "Washing Dishes or Doing Schoolwork? Reflective Action as Renewal," Janet Alsup describes how Kim Stover stayed alive in her classroom by engaging in informal, reflective action research. Kim typically lost herself in deep reflection about her teaching day when she washed the dishes after dinner. Kim, however, never thought of these periods as constituting "schoolwork." Nonetheless, her cycle of closely observing students, responding to their needs with modified practice, and then reflecting upon these changes enabled her to continually improve her teaching.

In Marilyn Schultz's Chapter 5, "'Miss White Will Not Be Here Today': Feedback as Renewal," Julia White realized that, even with a master's degree in English, she could not fathom the literature she was to teach without consulting notes from her professors or published critics. One early morning, she slipped into the classroom to write on the blackboard, "Miss White will not be here today." She then returned home to wrestle with how to teach literature. Despite this fizzling start, Julia went on to earn many teaching awards during her long career.

In Chapter 6, "Logic and Sermons Never Convince: Maternal Thinking as Renewal," Marilyn Richardson describes how Pat Pollack returned to graduate school in search of ways to transform traditional and dull learning activities into learning that was fun for and accessible to students. Instead, she discovered whole language and other theories which resonated with her own beliefs. The following sections summarize how the major processes of renewal—social contexts, passion and flow, voice, and dual identities—affected the teachers described in Part II, Crosswinds.

Social Contexts

In these chapters, various social contexts both help and hinder teachers seeking renewal. In Chapter 4, Kim's administration, without consulting her, reassigned her from high school to middle school. This decision favored bureaucratic expediency far more than student learning or teacher renewal. Kim later disparages the excessive bureaucratic tasks which distracted her from teaching.

In Chapter 5, Julia learned from her own experience early in her career that teachers need to support each other through mentoring, in-depth conversations, and friendship. Thirty-five years later she is sustained by links with professional organizations, as well as by informal gatherings for food, song, and, yes, talk about literature. Finally, in Chapter 6, Pat is convinced that students need to define and investigate their own interests. Student collaboration and inquiry often create flow experiences for students as well as for Pat. These shared experiences not only improve students' learning, but they also help them bond more with each other, thereby encouraging Pat's development as a teacher.

Passion and Flow

In Chapter 4, Kim's passion was to get to know her students. Her flow experiences occurred when teaching and especially when reflecting on each day, puzzling over her students' actions and responses, hypothesizing which approaches might work more effectively. In Chapter 5, Julia realized that if her students were to truly understand and appreciate Shakespeare and Hopkins, they must engage in many dialogues—with themselves, with their peers, and with their teacher. Through questioning and conversing, Julia's students stimulate her to work even harder. The interactions between teacher, students, and texts create flow experiences for Julia, which continue to renew her even after thirty-five years of teaching.

In Chapter 6, Pat was an unusual physical education teacher and coach: she happened *not* to believe in competition. She returned to school to study literacy and found, to her surprise, that her real passion resided in "big ideas" that helped her make sense out of the teaching strategies she embraced—those emphasizing cooperation instead of competition. Her immersion in big ideas also enabled Pat, a mother of four, to understand how "maternal thinking" operates effectively in the classroom.

Voice

In Chapter 4, Kim was "robbed" of her voice fairly early in her career when her administration made some drastic changes without consulting her. The administration's failure to treat Kim as an equal motivated her to respect and treat her own students as equals. Kim observed her students closely, and by evaluating, reflecting, and modifying her approaches, she worked at meeting their needs. Her cultivation of students as individuals greatly strengthened their voices.

Julia, in Chapter 5, seems to clarify and enrich her own voice every time she converses with her students. She patiently waits for students to respond to literature. When they do, she often encourages them. For example, she might write a note in her own book so she "won't forget" the student's insight, or she might say, "I wish I had thought of that." Students respond positively, creating a cycle of dialogue which reinforces the voices of teacher and students.

As we discover in Chapter 6, the more Pat learned about philosophical and educational ideas, the more she applied them in her classroom. To comprehend, implement, and evaluate such ideas, Pat needed to talk with colleagues, mentors, and students. Such cycles created an "intrinsic desire" within Pat to learn all she could. These flow episodes simultaneously strengthen Pat's voice and allow her, through differentiation and integration, to become more complex—to grow.

Dual Identities

The notion of dual identities functions effectively in these teachers' lives. In Chapter 4, Kim acknowledged her childlike side by enjoying humor in the classroom: she was not afraid to joke freely with her students and even taught units on humor. When teachers share humor with students, they demonstrate that students are equals (in fact, there is no other way to share humor). Such sharing means that Kim acknowledged the adult side of her students—that they could laugh together but still work seriously and respect each other.

By the same token, Julia, in Chapter 5, discovered that functioning purely as the adult in the classroom—as the expert who dispenses knowledge to students—rubbed against the grain. Eventually, she allowed more of her childlike self to operate when she engaged students in conversations—authentic discussions which demand that all parties be equal. When Julia asks her students questions to which she herself does not know the answer, her childlike self comes into fuller play.

In Chapter 6, Pat regarded the competition inherent in her physical education classes to be wrong. She did not care whether her students won or lost games. In a sense, she viewed students as too individualistic or too adultlike to focus on competition. When she returned to college, she affirmed her deep belief that students should be masters of their own destinies—that they are their own best teachers. In short, she continues to value the adult selves of her students. To accomplish this in a classroom requires that teachers relinquish much of their own power as adult authority figures—they must become more equal with students. In other words, their childlike selves must operate in greater balance with their adultlike selves.

Washing Dishes or Doing Schoolwork? Reflective Action as Renewal

JANET ALSUP
University of Missouri–Columbia

The room was silent, and it was my turn to read. I felt vulnerable, like I always did in high school. Like something was out of place. Was my shoe untied? My belt missing a loop? The assignment was to write a personal narrative. But how could I share a personal memory with my fellow ninth graders who might not understand? So instead I had written a story with personal narrative trappings. I had used the first person, and I *said* it really happened. It was about using my mother's credit card in a fashionable and expensive store. Which, of course, never happened. My mother never had a credit card. My mother didn't even have a checkbook. In fact, I had never seen a credit card. And I certainly didn't know how to describe using one.

But it was time. I stood and began to read. Soon my worst fears came true—my classmates had questions: "Did you actually forge your mother's name on the receipt—or did you sign your own name?"

"Didn't the clerk realize the name didn't match that on the card?"

I now know why I couldn't do the assignment like everyone else. It was because I knew the other kids were writing about things I couldn't—trips to Disney World, family reunions, car wrecks, broken bones, none of which I had had. Nothing "exciting" had ever happened to me. In fact, I remember one day at my rural elementary school standing next to a girl who was writing on the board the names of all the states she had visited. She kept listing and reading them out loud as she went along. I listed only Illinois and sat down. I couldn't write about me: the family farm, fantasy games of intrigue with the neighbor kids, my mom's greenhouse, or my isolated parents. If I had written a personal narrative, it would have had to be truly personal. I had no Disney World vacation to fall back on. I would have been forced to write about things I really didn't want anyone else to know: painting my room green because I wanted it to look like a forest, or filling up the back of our pickup with water and using it as a pool. What fifteen-year-old thinks those things are important enough to write about?

I was about to weave another web of fiction when Mrs. Stover stepped in. "Janet," she asked calmly, "is this fiction?"

"Yes," I quietly answered.

"Well, that's fine. It's a good story."

I sat down. She had saved my writer's ego. She had saved me. She never mentioned that I didn't "fulfill the assignment," never used a judgmental or teacherly tone.

Sixteen years ago as a ninth grader in Mrs. Stover's English class I was validated as a writer. I remember long, detailed responses (yes, responses—not comments or corrections) on journals she asked us to write. I remember being trusted as a writer. She allowed me, although only a first-year student, to write articles for the school yearbook, and I remember the two of us finishing the yearbook together in the summer. Most of all, I remember being liked. I couldn't remember ever before having a teacher who seemed so responsive to me as a person, not just as the girl in the second row, third seat.

This is the story of Kim Stover and her experiences as a teacher. As Carter (1993) reminds us, story has in recent years become a way for teachers to talk and learn about teaching. Educators have moved away from purely quantitative data to describe their experiences. She writes, "The core knowledge teachers have of teaching comes from their practice, i.e., from taking action as teachers in classrooms. Teachers' knowledge is, in other words, event structured, and stories, therefore, would seem to provide special access to that knowledge" (7). This is Kim's story as seen through Kim's eyes, and through mine, since my own story has intersected with Kim's for years. After being Kim's student, I also became a teacher and eventually taught English for seven years in the same district. So when I learned of this project to explore teacher renewal, I knew I wanted to tell Kim's story.

To learn more about Kim, I listened to her complex story with its cycles of discouragement and disillusionment, satisfaction and accomplishment. I not only want to tell about her practice, but, more important, I want to describe how she emotionally and psychologically sustained herself and her teaching through the years, how she reinvested her teaching with real meaning after difficult times when it seemed meaningless. In even the best of circumstances, teaching is a profession which has cycles of highs and lows, sequences of successes and failures, as we change and adapt. In Kim's case, she had to confront more than the normal challenges and still sustain her enthusiasm. Her times of difficulty, questioning, and then reconnecting occurred in waves throughout her career.

Learning to Teach

I interviewed Kim at her home in the small town where she also taught English. She is a smallish, attractive woman in her late forties with an easy laugh and a strong, confident air. We met three times for a total of seven hours, which generated more than thirty transcribed pages. Her home is an old, white, colonial-style house set on a narrow, small-town street, with a large backyard and a red porch swing. Her husband, a carpenter and contractor, had remodeled the house, combining old-style charm with modern convenience. A piano greets me as I enter, sheet music waiting to be played. A compact disc from the play *Rent* lies on the kitchen counter. Kim's bookshelf dominates the living area. Books range from Louisa May Alcott and Shel Silverstein, to Shakespeare, to what Kim calls "smutty" romance novels. We sat at an antique table in the dining room and talked about her teaching, my teaching, our students, our futures.

Kim spent her teenage years in a neighboring, somewhat larger, town, where she also attended high school and college. She had always loved literature and language but pursued a degree in education at the urging of a favorite college professor.

Teaching was something she chose to do because she loved English, not because she felt any overwhelming desire to work with adolescents. Despite this uncertainty, when Kim graduated from college she found her first teaching job in the small town where she still lives. Living and working in this rural area was at first difficult—in a town with a population of only three hundred people, Kim experienced culture shock. She was surprised at how different the students were from her own high school peers, even though she was only eight years older than her students when she began teaching and her alma mater was only twenty-five miles away. She was sometimes frustrated by her students' lack of motivation.

> I was naive my first few years. I had kids in junior and sophomore English, transient, because of the nuclear power plant. I thought that by the time they were sixteen they had decided whether they were going to graduate from high school or not . . . they were going to do it or they weren't, and I didn't go out of my way for kids who didn't come to school or who didn't do their work.

She often taught traditional grammar in these early years (e.g., the parts of speech) and thought of education as transmitting knowledge from teacher to student, because that is how she was taught.

> I know that I came in with a strong background in grammar and believed that students in this district really needed correct speech habits. So I thought that going over drills in subject-verb agreement would improve their speech, but I found that it didn't. You had to weigh in your mind in the scope of the normal school year what was important, so what eventually became less important were parts of the grammar book that I had seen fail time and time again. You know, what point is there in pursuing strict traditional grammar instruction if students couldn't even analyze their papers? I didn't see the subject-verb agreement thing having any impact on their lives.

Even near the beginning of her career, Kim observed students closely, seeing that they differed from how the college psychology textbooks painted them and from how their academic records defined them. Kim found ways to connect with the so-called difficult students and developed a rapport with them, to the extent that sometimes students and even teachers accused her of having favorites. Even in these early years, Kim began to see that she was viewed as an advocate by those kids other teachers often did their best to ignore. "We talk about dealing with very rural children and at the same time, after two or three years, you're getting to know them and understand them better, which allows you to rethink what you're doing in the classroom. First you show an interest in them. You show them that you care, that you're not an ogre."

After five years of teaching high school, Kim's administration abruptly reassigned her to the middle school. Several events led to this change. Her district expanded and separated the high school from the middle school. More important, her curriculum came under scrutiny. While teaching at the high school, Kim devoted nine weeks to teaching the research paper to all students who took her junior English class. When she was first hired, Kim said she was specifically asked to include the research paper in her curriculum. The project came to symbolize what Kim wanted her students to achieve.

> It may have represented a skill, a life skill, that I saw beyond the actual act of reading, into investigating a problem and knowing where to go to get the answer and then fitting your thoughts into a pretty strict format. As for those kids going on to be farmers or going to trade school, I was confident they would face situations in their life completely unrelated to the research paper. But there were skills they would learn from completing the paper that would help them through [those situations].

The administrative opinion on the paper changed when some kids failed Kim's class because they didn't complete the paper. If students failed her class as juniors, they could have difficulty graduating the following year. This possibility caused an outcry from the parents of one student who had not completed his research project. Because this student happened to be the child of a board member, Kim was pressured to stop teaching the research paper. Her principal questioned her closely about her reasons for requiring the paper and how important it was in her curriculum.

Despite the administrator's position that her expectations were unreasonable, Kim strongly defended the inclusion of research in her curriculum. And so she found herself in the midst of a power struggle early in her career, a struggle over curriculum and educational purpose. As a result, Kim suddenly found herself teaching middle school rather than high school English.

Learning to Reflect

The abrupt transfer from high school to middle school was Kim's first experience with school bureaucracy and the politics of a small community. "I was bitter because I felt I did a good job in the high school, and I had a lot of support from the students. My first year in middle school was very unhappy. The difference in children was something I was not prepared for. They perhaps were petty. They perhaps were tattlers. They whined a lot."

The sudden switch upset Kim and caused her to lose faith in the wisdom of her district administrators. Her frustration also made her first couple of years in the middle school even more difficult.

> It killed something in me as far as enthusiasm for the whole big picture, the district, and it made me aware of the politics and the inner workings of the school board and the administration. I became suspicious of almost everything. I know I took it out on the students and expected too much. And my lack of experience with kids that age was part of it, but I was really unfair to them. It took three years in that system to understand the mentality of seventh and eighth graders. So the thing that changed was me: I discovered that those kids have personality and they have needs. You have to give them the opportunity—give yourself the opportunity—to know them better. I learned their special characteristics. I learned what failed in the classroom and what succeeded, and that was an impetus to change my methodology and rely less on textbook-driven lectures. I tried new things with the same goal in mind and found what worked and fine-tuned them.

How did Kim once again transform her attitude and find her connection—this time to middle schoolers? The answer seems to be sensitivity, perception, and acting on her instincts, as well as her habitual reflective thinking. She began to look closely at her teaching and modify it to suit her new, younger students. She saw that middle school kids were different from high school students—yes, they were perhaps needy and clingy, but they were also bright and energetic. As she had with her high school teaching, Kim was searching for—and finding—a sense of renewal through positive interactions with students. The disequilibrium caused by the change in teaching environment, which she was powerless to prevent, was balanced by her inquiring mind-set and her tendency to look and listen to her students, as she had listened to me in high school. She allowed herself to get to know and like them. This change in attitude began to influence her practices.

> I put more emphasis on experiences in the classroom that I thought would carry over into the high school curriculum and into life in general. I stopped relying on a textbook and started developing units of my own that would complement academic needs. I began relying on my understanding of what was needed.

Kim was learning to trust her instincts and use a process of observation, evaluation, and modification that she modestly calls the "trial and error" approach. Zeichner and Liston (1996) define reflective teaching as "a recognition, examination, and rumination over the implications of one's beliefs, experiences, attitudes, knowledge, and values" (33). Kim was beginning to recognize and ruminate; she stopped being primarily a problem solver, or a "technician" in Zeichner and Liston's terms, and she began to be a reflective teacher, constantly examining her own presence and power in the classroom. Kim admits that these changes were a natural progression and would probably have occurred no matter what grade she was teaching. As her thinking about students changed, her philosophy evolved and she continually modified her pedagogy.

Also instrumental in Kim's success with middle school teaching was her participation in the Missouri Writing Project, a four-week summer institute. There she learned strategies to use with her seventh and eighth graders, strategies that moved beyond traditional textbook-based instruction to more teacher-developed units that suited students' needs and interests. Kim's students began writing children's books and then sharing them with elementary students, creating authentic writing assignments, and publishing their work. They completed individualized reading units and wrote stories, journals, poems, and letters to foreign tourist offices to plan dream voyages. Kim sometimes used television commercials or current news issues to help her students invest in literature.

> I would take a novel as timeless as *To Kill a Mockingbird* and present it in a way that connects to students' relationships, family. Almost inevitably something would happen in the news that I could tie it to: what is justice? The Mike Tyson decision, O. J., other things. The man who killed his pregnant wife and stabbed himself and then he said a black man did it. You talk popular culture, news, and relate it to the timelessness of a novel and try to get kids to understand that not everything changes. I think that timeless literature allows you to do this—like Mark Twain. You can talk about childhood experiences. "Have you ever fought with your brother? Have you ever gotten into trouble for something you shouldn't have said at school?" So even though this book took place in the 1850s, the heart of the matter still takes place today.

Kim connected her students' experiences in English class to their lives, enriching both. She had the same students for two years in a row, and she continually evaluated and reacted to their needs. Her view of students and their learning went beyond the single school year to the whole middle school experience.

> The majority of the writing that was done in the seventh grade year was personal narrative. I felt that the best way to get kids to write was for them to write about themselves. I felt that was what they were most interested in. Let them tell a story, and by the time they were in the eighth grade, funnel some of that into responding to literature. I don't have the documentation to support what I did, other than [that] I had a large amount of cooperation from the kids. If my judgment means anything, I saw growth.

Kim was viewing herself as both a teacher and a researcher. She was clearly making changes based on her own analysis of her classroom. So I wondered how could she doubt that her experiences in the classroom were documentation enough? How could she doubt that her judgment was valuable to the practices in her own classroom? Perhaps this doubt in her own abilities to evaluate her students' needs and make changes comes in part from her experiences with the academic community. As a high school student, Kim found her classes primarily lecture and teacher driven. She also does not credit her graduate school experience with helping to transform or inspire her teaching, even though she says being a student again and dealing with "motivated colleagues" was important to her self-esteem and often enjoyable. Many times during our interviews she pointed out that her views diverged from those of mainstream academia: "Sometimes you have to lead [students] through the paper. Again, academia would say you shouldn't do that—you shouldn't give them ideas. But I'm here to tell you that a seventh grader who refuses might produce if you plant the seeds."

In defending her opinions (e.g., she does not favor block scheduling), Kim told me, "Yes, that is my gut reaction. But I don't have stats to back that up. Except my experience in the classroom." More than once she mentions that she cannot justify her curricular choices quantitatively. While it is true that Kim could have taken her researcher stance a step further and gathered hard evidence in the form of audio and video recordings or more detailed notes, it is clear that she often used a reflective thinking process that enabled her to make necessary and effective classroom changes when she thought they would help students.

North (1987) contrasts teacher "inquiry" with teacher "lore" and states that much of what classroom teachers do is simply lore or the passing down of strategies that work, rather than actually asking questions and then searching for answers in their own classrooms and basing practice on close observation and reflection. Perhaps the tendency to label much of teacher knowledge building as simply "lore" (which suggests fluff or even gossip) has led teachers like Kim to doubt their own abilities to participate in actual inquiry and to make informed decisions about their own field. Teachers like Kim, however, make it clear that teacher thinking and problem solving should be highly valued, especially when it leads to positive change.

Kim described many other examples of modifying her pedagogy in response to students. Take, for instance, her changes to what started out as the "hero paper," which was assigned in the seventh grade during a thematic unit based on the concept of courage. Kim asked students to choose someone they admired, someone they wanted to emulate, and then write about that person. Kids wanted to write about Michael Jordan or Madonna. Although these people may be worthy heroes, as Kim said, writing about them was "empty" because her students didn't have real knowledge of them: "I wanted [students] to get away from celebrity worship. You are dealing with seventh- and eighth-grade minds and students going from being self-absorbed to taking others' needs into consideration." So, by understanding her students' stage of development, Kim modified the assignment to, "Tell me about a positive experience that you've had." The lesson broadened but encouraged students to write more about what was real and true for them.

Kim's observe-and-evaluate approach to teaching often was most obvious at the end of the year or even at the end of the day: "At the end of the year, you sit back and think, 'That just didn't work!' I'm not willing to say that it's always the kids' fault. At the end of the year, I would spend time thinking, 'Why didn't I get across to Jason?' 'How could I have been more effective with Emily?' Or, 'Why [did I allow] Chris to needle me?'" At the end of school days, washing dishes at her kitchen sink, Kim would continue her "thinking like a researcher"—thinking which often sustained her in the classroom.

> Before I got a dishwasher, I would stand right there washing dishes, and I would reflect on my day and what my units were and how I could get done what I needed to get done. That's something the Writing Project made clear to me—that composing didn't actually mean sitting down with a pen and paper. I was washing dishes, but I was really doing schoolwork.

Csikszentmihalyi (1991) might call this flow, the flow of thought, which he defines as "joy, creativity, the process of total involvement with life" (xi), a mental approach through which people can make many everyday experiences more meaningful.

Here, Kim is involved in thinking about her work, using the act of washing dishes as the time and place to plan and set goals for future lessons. She has turned a mundane, daily activity into an often productive, pleasurable time for reflection.

After several years of teaching middle school by the traditional schedule of fifty-minute class periods, another challenge arose that created disequilibrium in Kim's teacher identity: the institution of block scheduling. Block scheduling required Kim and her colleagues to teach in blocks of ninety minutes every other day instead of fifty minutes every day. Once again, Kim received no time to plan for this change. And again, she observed and evaluated the situation and changed her practices accordingly. She added art to her curriculum: students created newspapers based on a theme, complete with cutting, pasting, and drawing, in addition to reading and writing. Although these kinds of activities seemed tailor-made for block schedules, Kim continued to have doubts about the new schedule—what about day-to-day consistency?

Kim's story about Chad best exemplifies her reflective-action approach to teaching. Kim saw Chad as an extraordinary student. In fact, she observed that his entire eighth-grade class had unusual talent and energy. Therefore, Kim modified her curriculum to accommodate their enthusiasm. The students encouraged her to teach more poetry, so she taught more poetry. She chose poetry she liked and thought they would like too, not relying on the standard textbook. The kids wrote imitations of poetic styles, including that of e. e. cummings. She remembers Chad's response:

> He was very reluctant because that wasn't the type of poetry he was used to. He was heavily into narrative poetry. So I took him aside. He was having some frustration, and he came up to me at one point and asked, "What do you want me to do?" I said, "Whoa, whoa, whoa. It's not about what I want you to do. I want you to be you. I want you to find your voice. I want you to experiment and challenge yourself a little bit." So he did some imitative poetry, and he created some original poetry that was completely different from the narrative, which was so startling and shocking, yet so brilliant, in my opinion. Our relationship evolved to the point that he felt that he could take chances with me and he wouldn't offend me. And that doesn't happen all the time.

One poem Kim remembered was titled "Kids" and appeared in Chad's class project. She remembered it because it was such a change, such a risk for Chad. He stepped into another persona, one completely different from his true personality, which is shy and unassuming. Kim was shocked by the poem's violence: "Oh my God, you would not have believed his poetry. This is a kid who was a model student!" But instead of remaining shocked, she decided to appreciate Chad's risk taking and praise his creativity. In "Kids," Chad pretends to be, as Kim defined it, a sociopath, as he experimented with the power of language:

Kids

Yes, I recall Mary Jane,
Quaint, little Mary Jane.
With a face like a flower,
And a scream like a train.
Her blood was sweeter than acid rain,
Quaint, little Mary Jane. . .

Oh, I remember Elizabeth,
Quaint, quiet Elizabeth.
She wasn't loud like the other kids,
She even let me slit her wrists.
Those dogs had fun with her head in that ditch. . .
Quaint, quiet Elizabeth.

How can I forget about Jill?
Bad, mean, naughty Jill?
She wasn't nice like Jane or Beth.
She sprayed mace, I can feel it still,
She pulled out a gun to kill, kill, kill. . .
Are all kids turning into Jill?

I visited Chad, now a first-year student in high school, and we talked about this poem and his experiences in Kim Stover's class. He explained that the poem was an experiment for him, an opportunity to step out of himself and write fiction as poetry. He also shared some of the other poetry he had written. He described Mrs. Stover as encouraging: "She didn't want to stifle our creativity or anything. She didn't have limits on any of these poems." Because of this freedom, Chad was able to dive head first into poetry and a year later continues to write volumes of it. Over three hundred poems are available on his own Web site. He talked with me about using color words, adjectives, and analogies in poems. "I don't think I'd be writing as much if I hadn't had Mrs. Stover as a teacher. She started all this." In the eighth grade, one of Chad's poems won a National Council of Teachers of English Promising Young Writers Award. Kim had seen Chad's class as different, as special, and had given her students the opportunity to take flight. She had told Chad, "I will accept whatever you do because I know you are a poet." Chad had flown.

Collaboration, Connection, and Humor

Kim also kept her teaching rewarding by collaborating with other teachers. "I found that my associations with people at school have helped me inordinately," she said. "I have very good, supportive friends." This collaboration included some projects with Lisa, a middle school science teacher.

> I remember being in the library and kids were giving speeches and acting like political candidates and Lisa had such a lively face. Her blue eyes would just dance, and I remember her bending over, laughing at some of the stuff, because she has a wonderful sense of humor. Lisa saw kids for what they are and allowed them to be kids.

Lisa loved kids like Kim loved kids, so they worked on a project together in which students wrote essays to become astronauts and "fly" in a space shuttle they had built in the school gym. Since students spent the night pretending to be on a mission, as chaperones Lisa and Kim took turns sleeping on the gym floor. Such collaborative efforts and friendships clearly played a role in sustaining Kim as a teacher. Collaboration was also the highlight of her graduate school experience: "As much as whatever content they presented you with, just sharing things with people who were in the trenches with you was great."

For a long time, these positive experiences also helped Kim counter another aspect of teaching that eventually drained her enthusiasm and confidence: the tendency of the school bureaucracy to rob her of her voice, her teacher voice as well as her personal, human voice. As Kim explained, "When administrators questioned my judgment as a teacher and what was best for the class or the individual—you know, that's my integrity." As in the struggle over research papers, Kim felt powerless when confronted by an administrator who left her out of major decisions that affected her job, curriculum, discipline, and scheduling. Kim thought that she and her students should make such decisions. Her administrators seldom agreed. As Dana (1995) notes, however, the role of the administrator should be one of "facilitating and celebrating teacher self-direction, and the development of teacher voice" (59). Because Kim's teaching, though often successful, was not valued by school administration, she had to locate her own sources of renewal and professional motivation.

Despite these disabling factors, Kim's connections with students continued to give her much satisfaction, which prolonged her career. Csikszentmihalyi's flow was alive and well for Kim as a teacher.

> We discussed race relations in the U.S. at length, and it was like a twenty-minute discussion when kids stopped trying to call attention to themselves with some off-color remark and actually began discussing adult moral issues with intelligence, acknowledging a point here and admitting they were looking a little bit wrongly—some admission of being enlightened. It was just amazing for me.

Kim was in flow. She was totally immersed, connecting with students and becoming part of the learning community in her classroom. She had set a goal and was reaching it. Just as she experienced flow while washing dishes in her kitchen, here Kim turned a "normal" class meeting into a rewarding teachable moment. At the kitchen sink, her flow consisted of mentally rehearsing lessons and reflecting on her students. In this classroom flow, Kim—and her students—experienced the results of that thinking.

Action Research

The more I read and talked about action research or teacher research, the more I understood Kim. The following definition of action research especially applies to Kim.

> Teacher research means seeing what has been in front of us all the time. It means seeing something we didn't expect to see, a sure sign of learning since what we expect is what we already know. Teacher research is not about what we can prove but about what we can learn—about what we can see in our classrooms that we have not seen before, that instructs and empowers us. (Bissex 1994, 90)

Kim observed and evaluated her own classroom and made appropriate changes. She was not a cookie-cutter teacher, stamping out the same shapes year after year.

> When you spend four weeks on a grammar unit on the parts of speech and a kid didn't understand what a verb was coming in and didn't know what a verb was when he left the unit, then you have to sit back and say, "This isn't right, this isn't working. What are you seeking here?" You want them to have experience with writing. You want them to have experience with oral expression. You want them to read, read, read, read. You want to read to them. After my third year in the middle school, I decided that the traditional text is not the way to go, so I developed units that suited me. I never did use the teacher's edition. Never used it. Even the questions at the end of a story might not necessarily suit me. I'd look them over and use what I wanted.
>
> It was basically a sensitivity to, "Are they responding?" So, they weren't responding to traditional instruction, even though it's the easiest to teach. Get a book. Get a worksheet. I would have left the field if I had hidden behind an instruction booklet. So if you care about kids at all, if you like people, you listen to what they say. And you can get honest responses from children that may be critical of what you're doing, but not critical of you. And that's the beauty of middle school kids. They sometimes tell you how they feel, and you have to rise above your personal feelings and sometimes say, "I know you don't like it, but believe

me, you need it." You have to have some sense of evaluation, not just whether they did well on the test, but it's a day-to-day thing. Responses, looks on their faces, how many of them are trying to snore. And think about what you would have liked. My guiding principle for curriculum development has been, would I have enjoyed it? Would that have been fun?

Kim believes this reflective nature and willingness to make changes helped her to enjoy a successful teaching career. I linked Kim's method of seeing, thinking, and teaching with the methods of other action researchers I had read. Atwell (1987), for instance, also evaluated her middle school teaching and middle school kids and found that what she was doing was not working—for them or for her. So she changed.

> What I do in my classroom next year will not look exactly like the classroom I described here. New observations and insights will amend theory; the process by which I translate theory into action will change. The agents for change are my students. The classroom itself becomes an evolving text—a communal scribble we revise together. (254)

I certainly see Kim in this passage, but perhaps Kim's story is more about a teacher learning to research and thus learning to be a better teacher. This process is recursive—the researcher looks and learns, and the teacher uses this knowledge to teach. But don't think of the teacher-researcher as a schizophrenic phenomenon. Kim is a perfect example that the two roles can work very well in tandem, one invigorating the other.

When one looks at Kim's development over time and how her view of students changed, a pattern emerges. Kim's teaching changed, yes, but primarily her thinking changed. She developed as a thinker and a learner, as well as a teacher. Kim came to like students, first in the high school and then the middle school, and because she liked them, she began to care if they learned, what they learned, and how they learned. Empathy led to observation and searching for the right teaching approaches. The most important result of teacher research is not necessarily immediate changes in pedagogy, but the changes in how teachers think and evaluate their own teaching and classrooms. Suddenly, nothing seems simple or static. With the classroom in a constant state of flux, reflective teachers forever think differently about their own teaching. Likewise, Kim's thinking changed as she developed as a reflective teacher, becoming more aware of her students. Her best memories are those of times she and the kids "got along," when they connected as people, not just as teacher and learners.

> Following that third year, I found myself gravitating to being more student centered than teacher centered. Eventually, my personality is such that I am going to know these kids. And I can't say that I knew all of them. And then with the proximity of other classrooms to yours, you saw them in the hall, you saw them in the cafeteria, you saw them a lot more. You saw them so much that it was just very, very close. It really was like a big family.

It became important to Kim to learn what students liked and if they had fun.

> If you don't maintain a sense of humor, if you can't laugh at yourself and get a laugh out of it—that has been another saving grace. And the kids can make me laugh. One time my principal came into the room, and I don't know what we were doing, but I'm pretty informal. But I said something like, Here's Mr. S., and I want you all to show him how much control I have over the class, so get on the floor and say, "Hail, Mrs. Stover!" Every one of them did it!

Kim also put herself in her students' shoes, identifying with their confusion in the face of learning new material. She spoke fluently about her own learning process, which she described as wading through the "fuzziness" and letting information "filter, boil, and simmer" until it made sense. In analyzing her own thinking, Kim became more aware of her students' cognitive processes. She not only became more aware that there *is* a process, but that there are *many* processes—a fact many teachers seem to deny.

Belenky et al. (1986) define a connected knower as one who builds on personal experience and also "gains access to other people's knowledge" through empathy and seeing through another's eyes (113). Kim started at the opposite end of the spectrum, thinking of herself as a "banking teacher," described by

Freire (1996) as the giver of knowledge to students' minds, as one deposits money to be withdrawn later. When Kim came to like kids, her thinking changed. She can almost pinpoint the moment this change crystallized for her.

> It was probably my third year in high school when I started loosening up and we could actually have some fun with some of the things we were reading. And I'll never forget when reading *Romeo and Juliet* out loud, and Dave and Kevin—Dave played the part of Juliet—and we just laughed a lot, and, of course, when it was all over we had to look at it a little more seriously, and it showed me that there was a place for laughter in the classroom.

Eventually, Kim based her teaching decisions on individual student and class needs and interests. Teaching became more difficult but more satisfying and more successful. Teacher and students were learning together. Kim didn't want her class to be one in which students couldn't "second-guess the teacher, where [students] couldn't propose a dissenting view." Her class was quite the opposite. As Chad said to me, "I was pretty sure she'd understand my poetry. She seemed like the teacher who would." As Kim grew as a thinker, she grew as a teacher.

The Difficult Decision

Kim outgrew her administration. In Csikszentmihalyi's terms, her self became more complex. Her intuitive knowledge and concern for kids did not merge with administrative procedures, which were often arbitrary and dictatorial. So, after nineteen years, she quit teaching. "Everything that comes through the administration is not consciously trying to tie teachers' hands, but it does. When you spend your whole preparation period documenting an incident in the classroom instead of reading papers or developing plans for a unit, then I think that's robbing you and your students." Feeling alone, without either administrative support or respect, she left the district where she had spent so many years. She told me that she does not miss "the bureaucracy and the lack of the true regard for students." But she does miss the people and the profession that often brought her great joy.

As I sat down at the computer to tell Kim's story, I struggled with her decision to quit teaching after so many years. She had dropped this bombshell when I asked her if I could write about her methods of staying successful in the classroom, and she told me she had quit her district the previous spring. I had also left my job to pursue my doctorate, so I had not been aware of her decision. Upon hearing her news, I wondered if I could include her story in a book about teacher renewal. How could I say Kim renewed herself in the classroom when she had just quit? How could quitting be reconciled with her years of effectiveness?

When I began talking to Kim, however, I realized that her quitting did not undermine her effectiveness as a teacher or her ways of finding success. Nor did it undercut the power of her story. In fact, in many ways her leaving teaching invests her story with more power. Unfortunately, good, strong teachers like Kim can sometimes be labeled "rebels" and seen as troublemakers by those at the top of their school's power hierarchy. Such teachers are not valued, their knowledge is discounted, and they often find themselves frustrated and without support. The lesson of Kim's story is not that all effective, outspoken teachers must eventually leave teaching. Rather, the lesson is that teachers like Kim are essential: their skill and experience must be recognized.

Not only did my current status as a student and graduate instructor help me understand Kim, but interviewing and writing about her also helped me as a teacher. Coming to know Kim again has given me a connection in the real world with the names and terms of my research. Instead of a reflective teacher being a hypothetical abstraction, I now can think of Kim, and the term means something. And, since I have a real-world example, I can more easily work to apply the idea to myself and my own teaching. I now try to be a reflective teacher and an informal action researcher. I now pay more attention to my students than to myself as a teacher. I am not a performer; I am a coach, an interested mentor. I try to observe and reflect on my teaching and reevaluate what I do regularly, always asking, Am I teaching in a way consistent with my beliefs?

Kim's story contains much good advice: listen to students and respond to their needs, develop strong relationships with colleagues, have high expectations of students but also realistic demands, and, most of all, allow yourself to truly like and enjoy young people. Kim's story also teaches us that critical reflection and flexibility are key to teaching success. Understanding how Kim succeeded with so many students has motivated me to try to do likewise. And sometimes when I wash dishes I stare out the kitchen window and wonder about tomorrow's class.

CHAPTER FIVE

"Miss White Will Not Be Here Today": Feedback as Renewal

MARILYN SCHULTZ
Lincoln University

Julia White personifies the student-centered teacher. A master of her subject, Julia's teaching style is deceptively simple: she asks questions, questions that she has prepared as thoughtfully and arduously as the most polished lecture.

JULIA WHITE's department chair

Teaching awards and student testimonials illuminate Julia's success at asking questions. In fact, the statement by Julia's department chair in the chapter-opening epigraph was one of many provided in support of Julia's nomination for the award for excellence in teaching in the College of Arts and Sciences at the university. In presenting the award plaque, the dean observed that Julia is no newcomer to awards. She was previously selected by the Council for Advancement and Support of Education (CASE) as her state's Professor of the Year, and she recently received the Governor's Award for Excellence in Teaching. Her students are regularly selected to present papers at the National Undergraduate Literature Conference. Her English education portfolios have been evaluated as excellent by the State Department of Education, the National Council of Teachers of English (NCTE), and the National Council for the Accreditation of Teacher Education (NCATE). In presenting the award, the dean concluded, "Julia's teaching *is* informed every day with her determination to reach the minds of her students, to focus on *their* learning."

This determination has shaped Julia's teaching. She expects her students to understand what they read. In turn, she nods her head and smiles after responses that reflect insightful and thoughtful reading. She has developed tolerance for silence, so she can refrain from answering her own questions. Most teachers answer their own questions within seconds. Thus her patience forces her students to find something to say.

Texts from Julia's Life

At age sixty and after thirty-five years of teaching, Julia still enters the classroom with energy and the desire "to model for students the kinds of questions that they need to learn to ask to be independent thinkers." She was interested in her subject matter long before she became a teacher: "I first loved words—their power to move, to enlarge life, to clarify it. I was fascinated, and sometimes awed, by the literary works of art and by the aesthetic experiences they could give me." Her interest in what she does is not overlooked by her students, one of whom writes, "There is no doubt that Dr. White loves to teach and loves what she teaches, but what is amazing is that she manages to transfer that love to her students." Another student, who is also presently teaching, agrees: "Through her passion for the subject, I saw what great literature was capable of emotionally provoking in a person." Julia permits her students to move from the classroom to her office to continue class discussions. Her office is an unofficial refuge and support center for students, who know they will always find, if not Julia herself, an open door, a comfortable chair, books to peruse or borrow, and perhaps a fellow student. Another former student concludes that "Professor White was a mentor before it ever became fashionable."

In Julia's office, students drift to the sitting area furnished with a desk and two chairs for quiet study. They use the shelved books, not only for exploring questions raised in class but also for pursuing extended reading on assigned writing problems. Julia's personal relationships with her students and colleagues are reflected in the framed pictures perched on top of a bookcase—photos of Julia and her students and friends, including some from her undergraduate and graduate days, taken during casual dinner trips to surrounding small towns or summer excursions to London or Ireland. When given a new picture, she softly smiles, "This is a wonderful picture. I am so glad you gave it to me." Soon the picture is framed and added to the office collection.

Julia's southern graciousness is not limited to her office. It is not unusual for her honors English students to gather at her apartment for informal meetings. She may invite students and colleagues to her modern apartment, decorated with prints and framed literary quotes, for a simple lunch. A bowl filled with rocks from Wordsworth's Lake District sits on her coffee table and generates conversation and questions. Compact discs play on the portable stereo sitting amid the shelves of books. After she has welcomed her guests with coffee, tea, cola, or wine, Julia "volunteers" someone, usually a student, to play the piano, and invites her guests to join her in singing. After laughing and singing, everyone sits around her table. The guests persuade her to sit still, although she insists that she is fine and moves from the kitchen to the table, filling glasses and offering more food, still attuned enough to the table conversation to share her views.

Julia's southern roots resonate in her voice, despite the years of midwestern influence. When she sits around the classroom table with her students and smiles or nods in agreement, it is like a subtle gift, a sign of her approval. By ceasing to smile, she appears to anchor herself in silence while awaiting an appropriate response, sending students to their books to read more carefully, to find a response that will raise her bowed, white head and brighten her face. After asking a question, she has the patience to sit, perhaps giving some additional direction, but without answering her own question, even when the passing of time creates an uneasiness among the students browsing through their open books. One of our colleagues who joined Julia's poetry class summarizes Julia's Socratic questioning: "Early on, Julia taught us that every word counts in a poem. She taught us by asking questions about the word and lines that we thought we understood. As we answered her question, new meanings emerged. A special kind of energy is generated in a classroom when words on a page change their meanings."

All text pages are turned to John Keats's "To Autumn" when Julia asks a general question: "Do you see more than *autumn* in this poem?" Students, peering directly at the poem lines, immediately respond that they do. One answers, "Warm days make me think of summer." Julia, dressed in a solid-blue linen jacket coordinated with a long print skirt, has her head resting in the palm of her left hand and a pen in her right hand as she guides the pen to the line containing the phrase "warm days." Soon other students are chiming in: "I think of winter with the line, 'Thou watchest the last oozings hours by hours.'" The same student adds, "It makes me think of death, too."

"There's summer 'with the fume of poppies' and with 'twined flowers,'" another inserts at a moment of silence. Pointing to the open book, a student adds, "'the songs of Spring,' and, of course, there are lots of references to autumn." Soon the students are excitedly talking about the poem and asking their own questions. Occasionally after a comment Julia makes a note in her text, saying, "I wish I had said that. I don't want to forget it." Thus she is modeling how texts are open to more than one reading. Her text is penned with notes, creating a record of students' comments for future discussion or reference. Eventually her students are recording comments of others in their books. Expressing satisfaction with a student's response, Julia sometimes vocalizes an "Ahh" or gives a fast affirmative nod.

Referring to Keats's poem, one student asks, "What's 'the winnowing wind'?" Another interrupts arrogantly, "Didn't you look that up? I don't know if we will tell you." The fifteen students are soon giggling. A playful interaction develops among the students while Julia sits in the background, shaking her head and widening her blue eyes. She drawls approvingly while giving emphasis to the name, "Mary, I knew you would remember." Everyone giggles some more, for Mary had previously come to class without looking up word meanings unknown to her. Another reminds the class, "How could you read the poem without knowing what the words mean?" The student, realizing his transgression, momentarily slumps into his chair. Their talk soon returns to the poem, and someone says something about the wind separating the chaff from the grain, so the question has been answered while the teacher's expectation that each reader look up any unknown words has been reinforced. The remainder of the class is devoted to discussing lines and words in the poem. Julia ends class by passing out an assignment. Before leaving, the students turn in their responses to reading the poem and pick up the previous day's ungraded writing. Most students leave the room reading Julia's comments, while three gather around her.

Not only do students, especially English majors, express satisfaction with her classes, but Julia also enjoys her profession: "I feel blessed that I am in a line of work which I will never quite learn 'how to do' and which keeps being interesting to try." How does Julia develop a sense of renewal despite doing the same work for so many years? Has she experienced this high level of enjoyment from the beginning of her career, or has her job satisfaction fluctuated? What does she do, in or out of the classroom, that makes her stand out as a teacher? These questions frame this chapter.

Already we have a partial explanation for the first question. Csikszentmihalyi (1991) points out that studies on optimal experience "have demonstrated repeatedly that more than anything else, the quality of life depends on two factors: how we experience work, and our relations with other people" (164). By her own admission, Julia feels fortunate to be teaching. She finds pleasure in her work. She also strives to develop personal relationships with her colleagues and her students. Several colleagues have taken her poetry classes, and her students are invited to her home to join in various activities, extending the relationship beyond that of teacher and mentor to one of friendship. Her relationships with her students are also enhanced through her inquiry teaching method. Through her questions, Julia focuses students' attention, provides order for their thoughts, and diverts their attention from "whatever is most problematic at the moment" (Csikszentmihalyi 1991, 119). Preoccupations and other distractions retreat as the questions engage students in learning. Any aberrant disposition affects the mood of the class, and withdrawal, anger, frustration, fatigue, or exhilaration will be noticed around the civilized discussion table. The silence must be filled to reduce a mounting tension, and the students must do the talking.

Since I have worked for fourteen years in the same department with Julia, I was also able to talk to her students and colleagues. Together we attended meetings and shared lunches at her apartment. Thus any weakness in this study may be related to what may also be its strength—my familiarity with the subject. Like other colleagues, I have also been a student in Julia's poetry classes, where I always wondered if she had struggled with teaching during her beginning years, or if she was a natural teacher, never sweating about what to do on Monday.

"They Said I Was Fine, but I Wasn't"

Julia began her teaching career in 1959 at Western Kentucky University, where she "survived on personality during the first couple of years." She then echoed my question, "When did I know that I didn't know? As soon as I tried to teach literature." She explained her early paucity of knowledge about her discipline, with its unclear and sometimes uncomfortable boundaries:

> JULIA: You know how subtle short stories are. Highly literary short stories are subtle as all get out. And here were all these short stories in this book, and I was supposed to be teaching Introduction to Literature. Eventually I was assigning three or four for one night, just hoping I could say something about one of them. I was given the book only two or three days before classes started. I realized that I couldn't teach these stories. I was not a skilled, independent reader. If I did not have notes on what some professor or critic said about a work, I usually could not read it with understanding. One day my inadequacies caused me to creep into the classroom early and write on the board: "Miss White will not be here today."
>
> MARILYN: You actually did that?
>
> JULIA: I did that at least two times, maybe three. I went into the classroom just after 6:00 A.M., after a security officer had opened the building and before my department head and the students arrived. After leaving my message, I went home and stayed all day in the house, trying to figure out what to do when I faced students the next day.

To illustrate her ignorance, Julia recalled her discussions with a teacher at Western Georgia and how she discovered vicariously what a teacher should be:

She and I talked about teaching a lot, and she was the first person that I could talk with about teaching. Many of her ideas were the kind that, when I heard them, I thought, yeah, that's what I think, too. I had never heard teaching concepts articulated. Even the word *pedagogy*, the first time I heard it, sounded like a word being mispronounced. I had never heard *pedagogy*, much less talked about it with anyone. I learned some approaches to teaching, and she talked about an influential teacher at Peabody College. What she said about this teacher shaped my decision to enroll at Peabody College for my Ph.D., where I found my own influential teacher and learned worlds about teaching from her. Her techniques were what I was trying to do, raised to the ninth power. When I first started teaching literature, I asked [the students] questions sort of sheepishly, because I thought that I should be lecturing, telling them stuff, if I were teaching well.

I inquired whether methods other than lecturing were modeled, observed, or even noticed during her school years.

That's all I had seen through the completion of my master's. I said, wait a minute, wait a minute. Look at what those lectures produced. They produced me, who had a master's degree at age twenty-three from a reputable state university. The professors said I was fine, but I wasn't. I could produce more people like me. After I started using this inquiry approach to teaching, I thought, I don't know the name of this, and I don't see anyone else asking questions, but this must be legitimate. I decided asking questions was okay, but experience gave me the confidence in what I was doing.

Her students' responses inspired Julia's confidence in teaching by the inquiry method. She also credited them with willingness to learn: "I had students who were pretty excited about learning themselves. I thought, I'm just dragging them through the same process that I went through to find out what's happening in this story or poem. They're excited about the language and the insights gained." A colleague describes Julia's lessons:

Julia planned her lessons in a careful sequence. Indeed, the artful sequence of her teaching was almost as beautiful to read as the poems. She began with simple questions, brief assignments requiring that we tell only who we were and what we thought. She read and listened well to our responses. Each lesson challenged us more. Each person was pressed to think and to explain his thoughts. As the lessons progressed, Julia would remind us of things we said earlier that we might use as we responded now. There were times when we failed to respond to her promptings and urges, so she stepped in to lead us. We loved to listen to her, but she never said a word if she could coax that word from us.

A former student writes that, after fifteen years, Julia's questions "still sound in my head as I attempt to guide students today. She taught me that students value learning when they are active participants in the process, rather than passive receivers of knowledge, disseminated by an all-knowing professor." These questions direct students to take responsibility for their own knowledge. Julia purposefully chooses books without specific commentary and footnotes because less dependence on what others say leads to confidence in their own voice and opinions. Such discussion and interaction consumes time, so Julia focuses on a few poems or literary genres. Reading one genre or format, such as sonnets, prepares students to read another. Recognizing structures helps shape readers' expectations for content. Julia's students learn to interpret messages contained in the form and to anticipate the structures (ballads, sonnets, couplets, blank verse, limericks, hymns, odes, lyrics) that guide the content. Along with the structures and their concepts, students identify specific writers' themes, sentences, views, images, metaphors, words, or anything else that makes each writing unique. Reading and discussing a few pieces of literature carefully builds internalized touchstones for reading many more independently. Teaching depth, as opposed to breadth, is what Julia does well.

Years of Experience

In teaching writing, Julia focused on essays because she could get students to read well. She talked about how the writers constructed their essays, but she didn't make many connections between the readings and the students' writing. She explains that she never anticipated that reading George Orwell would make students' essays sound like his writing. She also recalls that some writing practices, scrupulously avoided now, were quite legitimate until 1969.

> Writing impromptu papers was something to do if you were not quite prepared for class. And the teacher would say, This is the subject. Now write. If the writing assignment were more structured, I would tell the students to get the subject and to produce the outline by a certain day before writing and handing in the paper.

Julia taught writing by instinct. She maintains that she never really learned anything formally about teaching writing until 1979, during a series of faculty workshops. For twenty years, she taught without understanding how to do it. Referring to the workshop presenter, Julia reports:

> She helped us by asking questions and introducing ideas that gave us insight into how we taught writing. I had been so busy trying to teach literature, and I didn't really work at teaching writing. I didn't have any idea how to. Before 1969, nobody was talking about the teaching of writing. My strength in teaching writing was my ability to write good comments on students' papers and to talk well with students who came in to see me, but I really didn't know what to do in composition classes. To be a good citizen, I thought I had to correct every error they made. And now I don't correct any errors. Virtually none. I make some kind of mark, but I don't tell them what the error is. I believe they have to find the problem to learn something. If I mark the paper, what is left for them to do? I was really interested in teaching, and I recognized Diane was bringing to life the ideas I had begun to see in journals. I was forty years old before I learned about teaching writing.

Discovering a way to teach writing that was similar to her current method for teaching writing through literature was uplifting for Julia. She shook her head.

> It's pretty humiliating to think that I'd been teaching almost twenty years before I did see these methods work for composition. What could I have done to make these connections earlier? I don't know. But it's nice Diane and I ran into each other. She also asked me how to teach students to read poetry. Our working together has been beneficial to both our professional lives.

I wouldn't say that I was completely worthless as a teacher of writing all that time. I do think that I was able to help fairly capable students get more reflective about their writing and improve. I was asking the questions I ask now—"What are you doing here?" and so on. I think they profited. But I spent a lot of time like other teachers saying, "This is bad." So I corrected the heck out of those students' papers. As a result, the first twenty years of students who took English composition with me learned about next to nothing. That's what I would say. They may have learned something because I could make pretty good comments. Of course, I made those comments and just returned the papers. They were supposed to get better writing the next paper.

That "next paper" is one Julia now reads, comments on, and grades. Students turn in their first drafts. She doesn't grade this draft, whether written for composition or literature; she only responds to it. She returns the papers and allows students several days to revise. Her comments on the first drafts are suggestions or questions that lead to improving the draft: "Are you satisfied with this phrase?" "You're onto something in this paragraph, but one can scarcely even suspect what it is without reading the paragraph that follows." Her suggestions are in the interest of precision. Students turn in their revised drafts with their first drafts. Within a couple of days, Julia returns the revised drafts—retaining her reputation for speed—and comments on the writer's revision success: "Yes, this is a better word choice." "This is even better the second time I read it." "You'd have to feel good about writing a paper such as this." "Inspired." "You demonstrated the point instructively for me—I never appreciated this point so much." Students are anxious to have their papers returned, especially with feedback that assures them they have helped their teacher, a literary expert, see something new in a text. These personal responses strengthen the feedback loop between teacher and students.

Why did Julia discover an approach for teaching literature fairly early in her career but not an approach for teaching writing? Personal interest in reading poetry may partially explain her tunnel vision. Even today, the overwhelming praise for Julia's teaching comes from English majors, especially those who take her poetry and Shakespeare courses. Another factor dampening her enthusiasm for teaching writing may be related to the academic perception of these skills. During this period, professionals tended to approach writing and reading as separate subjects, requiring unrelated skills. Many looked at reading as decoding language and writing as encoding language. Although a relationship was acknowledged between reading and writing, teachers often focused on one or the other, without much regard for their connections.

I can see another source for the difference between Julia's early views of teaching literature and teaching composition: the traditional rift within English departments between those who teach literature and those who teach writing. This division was often perceived with smugness and arrogance on one side and abasement and inferiority on the other. Literature teachers held more power and prestige than writing teachers. Writing teachers felt they were treated as "less serious, intellectual, and scholarly— indeed, less a member of the profession" (Elbow 1990, 127). Signs that this hierarchy still exists in many institutions include an inordinate adulation for literature teachers, whereas writing teachers are often hired as part-time or adjunct faculty who are not provided offices or entitled to health benefits. They are often paid less and hired last and teach the larger classes. Julia's speciality was literature, so it was natural to invest her energy where interest, prestige, and rewards were greatest.

The faculty workshops inspired Julia to examine the imbalance between literature and writing. The collapse of the distinctions between reading and writing—eventually referred to as a paradigm shift—stimulated questions about whether meaning is located in the text or in the reader. Eventually many scholars answered "Neither," preferring instead to view meaning as emerging through interaction between reader and text or as being socially negotiated. Within these amorphous but more flexible reading/writing boundaries, Julia realized that students in writing classes could make order out of chaos through many of the same methods she used to teach reading. Struggles are inherent in both reading and writing. Calloused fingers or strained neck and eyes, crumpled paper around the writing area, and teeth marks on pencils nag the writer and make the discomfort visible. Nevertheless, Elbow (1990) asserts:

Because the reading process is more hidden—and also quicker—it seems less fraught with struggle for someone who is good at it. Therefore literature teachers often fail to experience themselves in the same boat or engaged in the same process as their weak students. When it comes to writing, however, almost all teachers experience the common bond of struggle or even anxiety, no matter how good they are. Writing is a leveler. (131)

Students often feel they are struggling alone, reading closely for the "correct" interpretation of a text, whereas their teachers did not have to work at acquiring literary knowledge. Julia, sharing in the struggle, teaches students to explore literary texts. She invites students to negotiate meaning with each other—and with herself, the teacher, a teacher without all the answers, who finds new evidence for altering her interpretations. This approach enchants students with the power of language and imagination. Authoritative voices emerge and reading independence develops. Coming to an awareness of this literary self-sufficiency, they send Julia, one way or another, a message of gratitude.

"If There Is Energy . . . I Feel It"

Julia maintains that "for more than thirty years, what has interested me the most about teaching is the minds of my students. As a consequence, the focus of teaching is not on my learning but on theirs." She suddenly stopped and said, "I come out of class some days just as high as I can get in my life." Pressed to recall one of those days, she smiled, "We had one day like that recently. . . . I can't think of what we were doing. But I thought, 'Yes, this is it. This is the way it should be.' And I wanted class to go on and on."

Noting similarities between this day and others, she asserted, "Well, I was doing the same kind of thing I do any other day; it's just that I did it better, and they did it better. I know that I feed off their responses. The better they are, the better I am." During these times, she can forget other worries, and she feels stronger. I asked how she handled student responses that were dull or lifeless. She explained, "If their responses are just negative but passionate, I can work with that. It's just that if their responses are real flat, it's hard to get anywhere. If there is energy in what they say, I feel it, and I know that I am better and better. I know I am."

A former student credits Julia with the ability to bring Shakespeare's characters to life: "We don't just talk about them in class. She has us read what others say about Cleopatra, Hamlet, or Othello. Eventually we feel like we're talking about living, complex people, not just characters in a play." I asked Julia if she thinks exhilarating days just happen or if she does something to create them. "Well, you can't just order it to happen. I believe the students have to allow themselves to be engaged for that feeling to happen. That's why this feeling develops so many more times in literature classes than it does in freshman composition."

Julia believes that meaning is socially constructed, so she and her students explore literature together, dipping into bits, hearing the words, rolling the words over their tongues, and following voices toward familiarity and insights. If reader-response theory is used properly, Elbow (1990) maintains, it "promotes professionalism in the good sense (nondefensive thinking together) and undermines professionalism in the bad sense (trying to hide your struggles and to erase bonds within the unwashed)" (132). Julia and her students keep the struggle visible and create bonds themselves. Since she engages in the struggle too, students feel more open to speak.

When we talked about teaching first-year students, Julia concluded, "I don't think I'm particularly good with freshmen. It's not that I don't like freshmen. I think one-on-one I do all right with them. I don't think my freshman classes are wonderful." I asked if she thought students' lack of willingness to engage themselves was especially noticeable in writing classes.

> There's hardly anything they want to know. When I ask them what they're hoping to learn, what they want to know in this class or any other, they are usually at a loss for words. Now they want to complete certain steps to get certified to enter professions. As far as what they are hoping to learn, or what they hope to change about them at the end, they look around and ask, "Different about us? We don't want to become different. We're checking out of here. We want to stay like we are."

On the other hand, she observed, "Students identifying themselves as English majors want to know about certain pieces of literature or writers. I'd say that's what distinguishes the better students from the lesser ones: some really want to know." She thought this difference distinguished her first-year composition classes from her literature classes:

JULIA: Many freshmen want to make good grades. Many are conscientious, but very few want to become good writers. Do you see what I am saying?

MARILYN: Yes, they just want the credit.

JULIA: They want to be approved of and thought well of, and they want to make good grades. To say that they had some sense of how becoming a better writer or becoming more aware of language is going to improve the quality of their lives or change the way they live, I don't think most freshmen think about these possibilities.

MARILYN: Do you get bored with freshmen?

JULIA: I don't know. I wouldn't say that I get bored with them. I probably am, too. . . . I don't know. Maybe that is bored?

MARILYN: Does this mean that you don't try to capture their interest as you might in an English major's class?

JULIA: Just rarely do I see a freshman become excited about learning. It's so labor intensive working with freshmen. I know it's a weakness in me as a teacher. Maybe other teachers have wonderful classes about learning to write. I don't think I do . . . very often. Anytime I do have a good response to teaching writing, it involves a one-on-one situation or a personal dealing with their writing.

MARILYN: Do these freshmen give you much feedback about your teaching compared to your English majors?

JULIA: [without hesitation] No.

MARILYN: The students' responses seem to be an important connection to your [ability to relate] to the class. The more they're engaged, the more you're engaged.

JULIA: The English majors don't have to come tell me that they think I'm a great teacher. That's not necessary. I know when they think I'm a great teacher. Usually their responses make their feeling about the class clear. I think they're great too. They want to know something. And so I can ask questions that lead them somewhere, and they have such satisfaction from learning. . . .[As for the most meaningful feedback] Just seeing what happens in their heads is really the most meaningful to me, or seeing them understand something well in class. We shout and holler as we see growth in reading and writing: "Yes, *this* is what we were talking about!" Sometimes they don't know [but] they understood the concept in class.

MARILYN: So it doesn't have to be something that *they* articulate? It could be changes that you see in their behaviors?

JULIA: Oh, yes, and then they are so pleased. Discoveries happen with freshmen too. But it's just harder, much harder for me to teach freshmen.

I asked Julia if she felt more confident going into a class for English majors, Shakespeare, for instance, compared to a first-year writing class. "Well, whatever the class, I have butterflies the first day. I always do."

"Even after all these years?"

"Even after all these years," she repeated. "I still do. I don't think having butterflies the first day is bad. I realize that students usually have them too, so I work from that point."

I pursued, "Then do you still feel more confident about going into a majors' class than a freshman writing class?"

Oh, probably, yes. I am too accepting, just getting by, in a freshman class. It is so hard to have a wonderful and productive and exhilarating fifty minutes with a freshman class. It just takes so much energy. You can do everything in trying to engage them but not get a response because they really don't want to know. They want to succeed, but they don't want to know. Most don't want to be good writers.

Encouraging more definition of her view of first-year college students, I speculated, "They don't recognize the importance of writing?"

"No, they don't. They feel no satisfaction from writing, so I think it's hard to teach them."

Julia's engagement with English majors and her contrasting view of teaching first-year composition as "labor intensive" (even though it comprises half her teaching load) seems to be a conundrum. She has won awards for teaching. The students most vocal about her teaching expertise felt they had made some transformation in reading, writing, and talking about Romantic or modern poetry, Shakespeare, or introductory literature. The vocal ones are generally English majors, but I can verify that some first-year students, generally those who work toward improvement and/or are mature, older, nontraditional students, appreciate her instruction and style. A number of first-generation students from impoverished academic backgrounds, however, deal ineffectively with disagreements and problems. Naturally, these students do not praise teachers such as Julia, who don't allow them to turn in late papers or come to class late.

Julia feels that she gets little feedback that can inform her teaching of first-year composition classes. She knows that she does better when she has feedback, whether students show passion for or against a subject. Csikszentmihalyi (1991) would agree with her approach: "Almost any kind of feedback can be enjoyable, provided it is logically related to a goal in which one has invested psychic energy" (57). Some students, of course, do not invest themselves in composition or generate energy in class. Julia is aware of the students' nonchalant responses. Student resistance to talking, writing, or reading in class allows problems to filter through to her consciousness. Her first-year students' lack of willingness to explore questions and language issues drains Julia's psychic energy and detracts from her enjoyment of teaching. We are left then with the question of what criteria she uses to assess her success with first-year students. Although Julia interprets the placid atmosphere as unwillingness to engage in the course, she has succeeded in doing something right, since many of these first-year students, at the end of the course, express satisfaction with discovering how to improve their writing. Then there is the issue of literature. Julia respects good writing, but her love is literature, and so students don't expect her to emphasize writing. Hence, during the course, the feedback is minimal.

The Organizational Woman

Julia has been involved in professional organizations such as the state association for English teachers, the T. S. Elliot Society, the Modern Language Association (MLA), and the National Council of Teachers of English (NCTE). She has been discreet about her contributions, both voluntary and solicited, to these organizations; her colleagues frequently were unaware of the responsibilities she assumed within these organizations. She reflected, "I was on the board in various capacities of the state association for a dozen years. And finally, you're president. Also, I was the editor for eight years of three publications, and I liked editing. I wouldn't take anything for my experience with this group of English teachers."

> MARILYN: Do you think that your work with professional organizations has contributed to the enjoyment that you derive from teaching?
>
> JULIA: It was wonderful for me to discover through those professional contacts and writing projects and the state organization that the teaching of writing uses similar good practices at any grade level. It's energizing to know that there are other people working at many different levels and using the same techniques I use because they work. I also liked drawing from them to shape my own teaching.

Julia also edits the T. S. Eliot Society's newsletter and reviews manuscripts submitted for publication.

> I read one this year, not knowing who wrote the article; it's all blind. The writer does not know the reader's name. Sometimes I think that whoever is sending an article to PMLA would probably freak out if he or she knew that somebody unknown from an institution unknown to many was judging the article. But it's always engaging because I get to think again what they are saying about Eliot and how they're writing their articles. This editing adds variety to my work. The few times I've been sent a manuscript of a book, a textbook, I enjoy the editing. When MLA first did the handbook, I read and commented on the entire manuscript, a line at a time, and that's exciting and engaging. I thought through the whole manuscript.

I asked whether Julia's professional activities increased her teaching confidence. "They do. Because if I never talked to another professional, I think my confidence would be lower. I would have a weaker sense of what is appropriate or what expectation to have at a given level. We establish this sense through working with each other." Julia also worked as the poetry classroom edi-tor for the *English Journal,* an NCTE publication aimed at sec-ondary school teachers, for a couple of years:

> JULIA: This was interesting because I had manuscripts coming to me. I edited them and responded to them. I suggested changes and returned them. Sometimes I talked with people on the phone.
>
> MARILYN: Did this editing increase your credibility with students and colleagues?
>
> JULIA: It would if anybody knew about it. Most of the time people didn't even know I was editing manuscripts. I think confidence comes from this work for organizations, the sense of knowing something beyond ourselves and in connecting with others who also teach. This participation leaves me with a sense of the profession as a whole. I think that is important.

These professional activities tighten and broaden Julia's rela-tionships with others who teach English, giving her a sense of what to expect from her students and boosting her professional credibility. Naturally, all of this activity seeps into her classes, creating connections to current professional thought. Julia's pro-fessional activities are another source of feedback and renewal.

New Challenges

> Since we last talked, I got an invitation to give a paper on Gerard Manley Hopkins in Ireland. The day I got the invitation, I was already thinking about the paper I was going to give. It's about teaching Hopkins, and I started thinking about [a] new book [I got] on Hopkins. I know it is a good book, a new critical biogra-phy of him. There's not that many biographies about him, and this new book is well reviewed. I've had it several months, and I hadn't started reading it before that night. I was thinking about our conversations and the important reasons to give a paper. It is what the giving does for you in the process of getting the paper ready. The paper helps you focus your thinking, gives you a question to concentrate on for a while and causes you to go through the same process that students go through to write pa-pers. It's important for me to write something that somebody else will read or hear. To have this Hopkins paper just hanging out there does something to my head in all that intervening time.

And I'm excited about it now and have been before. . . .[In preparation for this presentation, Julia wanted to read all of Hopkins's poetry.] Even though some of the poems won't have anything to do with my paper, I just feel energized in this way. Any presentation that I've made anywhere gave me more energy. It's like exercising does for some people. These presentations do the same for me.

Although Julia would not be teaching Hopkins between now and the presentation, she wished she were. She predicted that there would be an interaction between writing the paper and teaching Hopkins. Since she won't be teaching, she will be contacting some former students who found Hopkins's poetry difficult in the beginning but who liked it eventually. She commented, "I would like to see what they can remember and the difficulties they recall."

MARILYN: Do you have some way to determine whether the paper is successful for your purpose?

JULIA: Well, that's interesting. If it's a critical paper or if it's what might be called a speech somewhere, as opposed to a workshop or some interactive presentation, if it's a canned deal, something all prepared, I think I have a good sense of whether I've written well or not.

MARILYN: Before you present it?

JULIA: Yes, I think I am a pretty good judge of my own work as far as critical writing or composing. I also think I'm a pretty good judge of whether my speaking works for the audience. I had some validation when I wrote my dissertation, not one page of which was returned for more revision.

MARILYN: Wow!

JULIA: Not one page all the way through. I do so much revising as I go along. When I finally had it together, I had it together. The way I can tell whether a speech works is that the room gets completely quiet, and I figure it must be all right with them too.

MARILYN: Can you articulate how you feel when these are successful?

JULIA: [Smiling]: Well, how I feel, the biggest charge comes when I'm getting the thing together and doing it. I really get exhilarated when I know I've written something that is right, feels right. I hoot and holler and fly around the house a little bit.

These outside professional demands give Julia a goal, something to organize her thoughts around, a barrier against distractions or problems, and an opportunity to enhance her reputation and résumé. Good work brings compliments, attention, and respect, providing the feedback that keeps her engaged in her work.

"It's the freshness of them," she said, explaining what keeps teaching interesting:

> JULIA: Through the years, I also get a new course to prepare. For instance, I thought it was lovely to celebrate the start of my thirtieth year of teaching by getting Shakespeare for the first time. I put a lot into that course, just thinking about how to teach the course and trying to learn more about Shakespeare. I'm not the greatest expert on Shakespeare. I've put lots of thought into how to help my students become independent readers of Shakespeare.

> MARILYN: And making them independent readers keeps your work from becoming routine?

> JULIA: That's absolutely right. The focus is on their minds, and that's not just a slogan. That's something I have realized.

One day Julia stopped in my office just to visit. She talked about a learning-in-retirement class she taught on Tuesday nights. She has fifty-four retirees who wanted to learn about Shakespeare. "They don't want to do anything demanding, just something they can enjoy. They chose to discuss Shakespeare's characters. They first enjoyed talking about Othello during their two-hour class session. Next week they will talk about Cleopatra. The preparation is energizing." Appreciation renews her desire to teach even during what might be leisure hours. Signs that students, old or young, are enjoying the class or independent study give Julia the inspiration to keep working and planning. She wants them to value the class, which brings appreciation, a form of feedback that recognizes her efforts. In turn, she is stimulated to praise her students: "I feel fortunate to be working with you." "You should repeat what you said, for I want everyone to hear it." Students want validation that they are doing well. The feedback creates a bond between Julia and her students, regardless of age, and they also want to please each other. She looks forward to classes charged with these special relationships, and students look forward to class. Any butterflies flutter away while Julia considers how to engage her students.

Conclusion

Julia's diverse teaching commitments extend beyond traditional students, beyond the campus buildings, into the schools, the community, and across the ocean. I found myself in awe of her ability to touch the lives of others—to make a difference. She sets her own pace and her own standards with her emphasis on thoughtful responses rather than mechanical comments. She plans her classes to focus on her students' minds, not the number of assignments. Yet she does not work in isolation. She stresses that only through connections with other professionals can teachers develop a sense of what to use and how to develop students into articulate thinkers, capable of resisting mindless obedience to others' opinions.

Through helping others find meaning in literature, Julia gives significance to her own life. The harmony between her teaching and professional activities culminates in recognition, public awards, and feedback. Julia's sensitivity to the students' feedback—and her own willingness to give feedback, including sighs, "ah's," smiles, written messages, or body language—encourages students to keep working. Students in the process of developing insights keep the class fresh and new. Feedback keeps Julia striving to improve their minds. Feedback keeps renewing her. Csikszentmihalyi's research found that people usually mention that work demands concentration, clear goals, and immediate feedback (1991, 49). If we are absorbed in our work, we are less aware of problems, which gives us a sense of control, which in turn removes concern for the self, allowing the self to emerge stronger. This makes us willing to expend lots of energy in order to experience such pleasurable feelings. This process aptly describes Julia's engagement with teaching.

After thirty-five years, Julia still reports experiencing spontaneous feelings of joy in teaching. A colleague of hers writes, "If she has ever been 'burned out,' her students have not known it." At this point in their careers, many teachers are thinking only about retirement. But Julia is thinking about her Hopkins presentation in Ireland and ways to improve her courses.

"Logic and Sermons Never Convince": Maternal Thinking as Renewal

MARILYN RICHARDSON
Lincoln University

Implement new ways to improve high school students' reading—that was our committee's charge. We were trailblazers, setting out to gain a better understanding of reading theory, to explore new classroom strategies, and to serve as faculty resources. The principal and I quietly talked to the workshop participants about our personal transformations, from teachers who lectured and were praised for effective teaching into teachers who know that students learn best in a language-rich, diverse community in which feelings, values, and new ideas are essential to learning—in all, a less understood view of student learning.

While the workshop had been congenial, in my heart I knew that these teachers lacked the passion to change their teaching, either because they had never experienced that passion for teaching in the first place or because they feared that with change, content and rigor would suffer. Earnest in his desire to improve education, the principal wondered, "Just how do I get teachers to improve what they do in the classroom?" Instead of focusing on students, he asked the teachers to reflect on their teaching practices. He urged them to consider possibilities, take risks, make mistakes, and try again. He offered them the freedom they wanted, yet they resisted. Why?

When we describe those great teachers who ignited our love for history or psychology or some other subject, we often say that they love their subject and teaching. But how do we know? Why do some teachers have this drive and passion while others do not? Educational reform often focuses on how to change the students, the content, the techniques, or the assessment procedures. But we rarely identify and explain the teacher's internal transformation. What causes teachers to become reflective practitioners? What creates a desire to radically change teaching practice in a profession dominated by tradition? What gives teachers the internal strength to withstand criticism from peers and administrators? And finally, what can we learn from their transformations that will support preservice and graduate teachers?

I knew there had to be a way to help educators discover how to inspire in students a love for learning. So I chose to study Pat, a colleague of mine in literacy education. We teach courses in the teaching of reading and writing, as well as a general education course on cultural diversity, at a state university. I conducted personal interviews, collected written questionnaires, and observed her class as she worked with students preparing for a psychology test. As I read her words and the words of others, I felt the need to ask more questions.

Inspired

> I can honestly say I had a transforming experience. In the methods of teaching reading class, I felt compelled to learn for the first time. Before that, I had only felt obliged to learn, at best.

Pat and I had met ten years earlier in a reading methods class at the university. I arrived early on the first day, but I was not the first student in Room 318. Pat sat in the front row. She immediately introduced herself and we politely talked. I don't remember the substance of our conversation except that we both dreaded taking the course. We expected tedium, unaware that the content and the instructor would grab our attention and move us beyond our immediate goal of elementary certification. As two former high school teachers who had left positions to raise our children, we didn't know that we could be transformed as learners and as teachers. Nor did we dream that we would seek graduate degrees and immerse ourselves in endless talks about learning. But in this class, we became the passionate ones—the ones whose idea of a good time included burying ourselves in the works of Paulo Friere. Today, we are college instructors, colleagues teaching daily in Room 318, where we met. The tattered, dusty old school books that lined the shelves remain, but the mechanical readers and controlled-vocabulary texts have been replaced by books spanning every genre, as well as by students actively posing problems and sharing possibilities as they make sense of their world.

Our first assignment in that long-ago class was to write about how we thought reading should be taught. Cautiously I wrote, "Reading cannot be taught," and hoped the instructor wouldn't react too strongly. Pat had also been forthright in her views. "I remember writing about my perception of teaching reading on the first day of that class, and boldly stated that I had no intention of teaching reading because I found it tedious and boring. I had tired of listening to first graders in my son's class 'sounding it out.'"

Our instructor, Leslie, was a doctoral student studying under Dr. Dorothy Watson, an advocate of whole language. Leslie was cute, perky, half our age—the stereotypical primary teacher. The first day she introduced us to a strategy she called, "What's in the Sack?" After reading Shel Silverstein's poem "What's in the Sack?" she produced a brown bag containing three items. She pulled them out one at a time, beginning with a Coca Cola can, and talked about how each symbolized her life. After demonstrating the strategy, she asked us to bring our own sacks with three artifacts to represent who we were.

After many in the class shared awards and pictures of their families, it was Pat's turn. She had swept the stairway in her turn-of-the century home and dumped the resulting contents into a plastic baggy. Lint, dust, crumbs, and bits of unimaginable things that had fallen from the hands of three kids told us exactly who she was. Her second item was a photo of the family's johnboat, complete with a homemade cabin slapped together with discarded lumber, which they navigated on the Osage River. Her last item was a picture that still hangs on her bedroom wall—a hand holding a red rose which has been thrust up through a pile of manure. Pat's irreverence exposed a refreshing, rebellious nature. The rebel in me connected.

Transforming

It shocked me that respected educators and theorists agreed with me that kids shouldn't "sound it out." The more I heard about the whole language approach, the more questions I had. I found myself reading everything I could find on the subject and looking for people to discuss it with. That wasn't easy, and that's when I met you. Not many people were open to whole language theory. Most of our classmates were threatened and hostile. This only added to my attraction, rebel that I am. I went from not wanting to teach reading at all, to wanting to be one of these rebel teachers.

As the semester progressed, Pat and I shared more of our mutual values and beliefs as we sought to understand the educational philosophy being introduced to us—whole language. But Pat didn't find activities and projects and fun things. Rather, she found a philosophy that reflected what she sought, but outside the traditional paradigm. Pat was excited about the whole language approach because it was more in line with how she felt children actually learn. Whole language education nurtures children and rejects competition; it views real learning as social; it challenges authorities who advocate drilling kids with knowledge and plying them with rewards to motivate them. She was hooked.

Csikszentmihalyi (1991) describes the common transformational process that Pat was experiencing. He defines self as containing "all the memories, actions, desires, pleasures and pains . . . . [T]he self represents the hierarchy of goals we have built up, bit by bit over the years" (34), and he defines attention as the psychic energy needed to "retrieve appropriate references from memory, to evaluate the event [incoming information], and then to choose the right thing to do" (31). Pat's past experiences and internalized goals found a match in the educational philosophy (incoming information) of whole language, creating a challenge that spurred her attention (needs and desires) in exciting and enjoyable ways. As an older, returning student, Pat was the mother described by Ruddick (1980) who could see the effects of "injurious stratification, competitiveness, gender stereotyping, hypocrisy, and conscription to war. Damage to a child is as clear to her as the effect of a hurricane on a young tree" (355).

Pat's experience as a high school physical education teacher had not prepared her for the emerging world of girls' sports in the early seventies. When Pat's school told her to develop girls' teams, she had reservations.

> It's that competition thing. I just didn't accept the rationale for it in education, but they needed a coach. I enjoyed starting a track team, a basketball team, and a tennis team for girls, although there was no support from the athletic department or the administration, nor funding, and of course, no extra pay. All this would have been worth the effort except I had no talent for inspiring victory in my young players. In fact, I didn't care if they won or lost. I didn't even like interscholastic sports, so I must have been in the wrong field entirely.

When Pat left high school teaching, she often served as a volunteer in her son's first-grade classroom. Just as she questioned the value of sports competition, she saw the negative effects that competition could have on six-year-olds. During reading instruction, students were asked to sound out the words, and they received smiley faces and dinosaur stickers for their efforts, while matters such as students' comprehension and aesthetic responses to literature never surfaced. Pat was disgusted.

> I dared to question some of the common classroom practices. I saw children under pressure to compete for stars on a chart. Six-year-olds just don't need to learn under stressful conditions.
> The teacher was sure his way was best, but I was convinced I could do a better job. I was looking for activities and projects and individualized instructional strategies. I was hoping to motivate kids and make learning fun. I was well on my way to being prepared when I enrolled in the methods of teaching reading course.

According to Csikszentmihalyi (1991), the relationship between self and attention is circular: "Attention shapes the self, and is in turn shaped by it" (34), thus creating a dynamic, progressively absorbing process, a passion for learning.

> For the first time in my life, I was actively seeking answers to my own professional questions. It became a natural and compelling

process, much like the one I had experienced as a new mother wanting to know everything possible about my child and the ideals of mothering. I soon abandoned my interest in *activities* and *individualization* as my understanding of learning increased. I accepted that children's naturally arising questions created a demand for experience, and that most of what I had been taught about designing curriculum would result in stilted, contrived, irrelevant, meaningless exercise.

Pat soon accepted a position teaching seventh grade. No longer thwarted in her desire to modify traditional teaching methods as she had been as a high school phys ed teacher, Pat searched for ways to implement the whole language approach. While still teaching seventh grade, Pat began a master's program. She engaged in hours of conversation about ideas and practices, oblivious to the outside world. Csikszentmihalyi calls this a flow experience, one in which an individual is so engaged that it is the activity itself which is valuable, not the product, resulting in a more complex self (1991, 41). Pat describes her growth toward complexity:

> I used to think the teacher provided all the information and materials and directed all the experiences, and that a good teacher was clever and creative, organized and dynamic. I also thought she was in control of learning. The change in my notion of a good teacher was dramatic. I now wanted to be a facilitator rather than a performer or an orchestrator. In the class, I began to see that children can take a lot more responsibility for learning than most teachers allow. I had a sense of how it worked, but no clue as to how to implement it. That's when we visited whole language classrooms and talked to the students about their learning.

Pat reveled in ideas rather than in methods and techniques. She realized that she and her students could create their own learning experiences. Her desire to understand more about whole language led to her growth of self, which in turn fed her desire to know more, creating the circular process that Csikszentmihalyi (1991) describes as transforming.

When Pat returned to teaching after being a full-time mother, she visualized a room full of junior high students "with a door that would close out the rest of the world and in which I could engage young readers and writers in stimulating inquiry." Pat's principal embraced her practices. He loved what Pat was doing with students and encouraged her to become a researcher in the classroom.

During graduate school, Pat and I carpooled to evening classes. We would talk about learning theory during the entire ninety-minute round-trip. Then we would stand at the car and talk for another hour after the road trip, continuing what Pat called The Great Conversation. We were obsessed. Pat left her seventh-grade position when her fourth child was born, stayed home with him for a while, and then began teaching at the university where I taught. We were set to continue our great conversation. Together we researched and presented our findings at conferences.

The Teacher

> Logic and sermons never convince. The damp of the night drives deeper into my soul.
>
> WALT WHITMAN

When I asked Pat to tell me about her experiences that were totally absorbing, she replied, "Making costumes for school plays, writing scholarly treatises with a colleague, learning a new function on my computer, wallpapering, stimulating conversation, and teaching." All of these satisfy Csikszentmihalyi's (1991) criteria for a flow experience. Pat said they were "enjoyable, had some intended outcome, and required a certain amount of mental gymnastics." Pat's most enjoyable flow experience is teaching. She is totally absorbed in it.

> The questions and discoveries seem endless. Teaching is totally absorbing when I'm in the classroom, or when I'm planning the next learning experience. I have never repeated something exactly as it was done the previous semester. That's what keeps the job interesting—the inquiry aspect of teaching—being a co-learner as well as a researcher in the classroom. If I simply dispensed knowledge or repeated past performances, I would soon tire of the whole thing.

Teaching is most enjoyable for Pat when she experiences something new, such as when students take topics in new directions, or give new twists to ideas, or identify unique problems to solve, or when they are so engaged that they take control, especially when they challenge her authority. Csikszentmihalyi refers to such a stance as a "paradox of control" (1991, 59). That is, even though Pat has given up actual control, she still has a sense of control. She is confident that the spontaneity needed for active learning will occur, even though she knows it is only a possibility: "A flow experience definitely has an element of surprise. I feel good when everything comes together, but in surprising ways." Deci, Kasser, and Ryan's (1997) ideas about intrinsically motivated teaching are similar to Csikszentmihalyi's flow experiences. They state that such behaviors are "performed for the spontaneous experience that accompanies them (i.e., the reward is inherent in the doing of the activity itself)" (59).

One afternoon while visiting with Pat at the university where we were teaching, one of her students rushed in: "Mrs. Pollock, our group wants to tour the public TV station's studio. We called and got a time, four o'clock Tuesday afternoon—that way anyone who wants to can go. Will that work out?"

"Sure, but be sure that students know when and where, and let the station know about how many are coming." The students had taken control of the class, going beyond the requirement. They viewed Pat as a resource and as a guide rather than as an authority figure, as Pat explains:

> That group invited a guest speaker, then told me about it. They even arranged to videotape the presentation and televise it on public-access TV. They met in small groups outside of class to tour radio and TV stations. Then they reported about these outings to the rest of the class. The research took on a life of its own as they engaged in a lot of things that weren't required for a grade. The irony is that the more this group became engaged, the less involved I was.

I asked Pat, "Was this enjoyable for you?" She responded, "Because it was working." Her goal is for students to engage in learning for its own sake, and that is what was happening. She had provided the opportunity and the impetus. The result made Pat feel good. When I shared this information with other teachers, they couldn't imagine how Pat created an environment in which students became actively engaged with their learning. Although we might suspect that introducing an interesting topic or making learning relevant creates interest, the answer is more complex. Allowing students to select a topic makes the task easier, but Pat's students also became engaged with topics she had selected. In both situations, Pat created a learning environment in which students adopted a researcher's stance, branched out into their own inquiry, explored, and made decisions.

Classroom Inquiry

> When I walk in the classroom, I have something in mind and some means of initiating this experience. I'm kind of the captain of the ship. And everybody's got to do their share to keep us navigating. Often we brainstorm, such as when we decide on a topic. I write on the board and ideas emerge. It's magic what comes off the board. That's the lesson plan. There's a lot of spur-of-the-moment stuff. My plan is to release this control as the class starts doing what's expected of them. I provide the opportunity for them to be actively engaged, but for the most part they're motivated because they're wanting answers to their own questions or they're wanting to share their insight. If they have a thought, they share it; in fact, often they're eager.

Pat's medical ethics unit exemplified her approach. She prepared sets of related, published articles for several specific real-life events. She also prepared a written survey with statements such as, "If there was only one donor heart, a mother of three children should receive it rather than a seventy-year-old male alcoholic." She asked her students to mark "agree," "disagree," or "undecided" by each statement. Other survey items focused on medically assisted suicide, euthanasia, medical research, living wills, and decisions to separate Siamese twins. The students' responses brought their values, beliefs, and feelings to a conscious level and exposed conflicts in their thinking. For example, in addition to the preceding statement about the donor heart, Pat wrote, "No one's life is more valuable than another's life." Those students who agreed with both statements were forced to deal with the resulting conflict.

After completing the survey, students jotted a quick note next to those statements which stirred a reaction or posed a question for them. In small groups, they discussed the survey, their thinking, and their questions. Next, the students wrote again for a few minutes and were asked to conclude their writing with questions for the group to discuss later.

Students then read a brief article that might answer some of their questions but might also lead to new dilemmas. The one-page article from *The New England Journal of Medicine*, "It's Over, Debbie," is a story of a terminally ill young woman's request to die, written anonymously by the doctor who responded to her plea. Students met in small groups again to make sense of the story and debate whether the doctor committed an act of murder. The article contained sufficient ambiguity for students to consider several interpretations. Again they were asked to write briefly and pose questions. Pat viewed this medical ethics project like others—as a varied experience that began with students' knowledge, beliefs, and values. The secret was getting students to explore, to question, to evaluate. As Pat noted, students had personally conflicting views on the issues. They couldn't help but express their beliefs, and because they relied on themselves as experts, they explored new ground:

> One group tried to compare abortion and euthanasia. Following the students' discussion, I heard an expert on NPR [National Public Radio] note that the commonalities of abortion and euthanasia issues were finally being considered. But the dialogue had already taken place—in one of the medical ethics groups in my class when students were trying to make sense of the likenesses and the differences of abortion and euthanasia.

Pat focused on the intellectual, on allowing inquiry to grow out of the questions students were asking—on inviting and allowing rather than demanding or coercing. As a result, students recognized the relevance of the topic in their lives.

Rebel and Maternal Thinker

Pat's teaching transformation paralleled her change in understanding how we learn, especially how transmission compares to social interaction. What brought about this change? Pat attributed her transformation to her rebellious nature. Yet as I analyzed her words, I recognized something else—maternal consciousness. According to Ruddick (1980), "The passions of maternity are so sudden, intense, and confusing that we ourselves often remain ignorant of the perspective, the thought that has developed from mothering" (342).

As a mother of four children, Pat embraced parenting, investigating alternative birth experiences, and other forms of parenting that seemed natural and nurturing to her. According to Ruddick, not all mothers are able to do what is best for their children. But those who do, in spite of social conditions or pressures they cannot control, become reflective mothers.

> Along with my desire for a naturalistic birth experience, I intended to breast-feed . . . not just token breast-feeding, but entirely without the use of bottles. I had heard stories about my grandmother nursing her babies for two years and I wondered why that had become unfashionable. Since I wasn't a bit concerned about what people would think, I figured I'd do what was best for my child and emulate Grandma.

Ruddick (1980) describes three interests which can be seen at work in Pat's classroom: protecting the child; fostering the child's physical, emotional, and intellectual growth; and helping children grow in socially accepted ways (348). Pat's thinking focused on all three interests. She especially believed in protecting children from stress, an extension of her disapproval of competition in the academic setting. In her opinion, schools should begin by helping children develop confidence in their abilities: "No frustration. No competition. We provide them with a bed of roses and if they have nothing but good experiences in the beginning, then they will have the strength to deal with the bad things when they do occur. We're supposed to give them positive experiences—nothing detrimental to their egos."

In Pat's opinion, most college classes inadequately prepare teachers to meet those needs of children that Ruddick considers the second focus of maternal thinking—their physical, emotional, and intellectual growth. "Within a single survey course, the expected outcome is unrealistic. There, learning a little about a lot is the goal, but no one can pull it off. The courses need to be constructed so students explore topics, ask questions, seek answers, debate, dialogue, and so on, about some aspects of the content."

Pat's pedagogical approach is student driven and inquiry based. She views knowledge as the integration of process and content and believes that if students are allowed to make choices, decide how they will learn, and decide how to demonstrate what they have learned, they will speak with their own voices. Belenky et al. (1986) note that such practice is typical of a midwife teacher, one who focuses on students' knowledge rather than the teacher's knowledge, as a lecturer does: "They [midwife teachers] contribute when needed, but it is always clear that the baby is not theirs, but the student's" (218). When we discussed how Pat decided when to tell students something and when not to, she explained,

> The difference is, when I'm telling students what to do, it's part of an ongoing dialogue with them. It's not that I have the same plan for six semesters and I'm going to tell this student to do what I told another one to do in the past. It all evolves in the process. Students don't always have the answers. To give the student the answer to a process question is legitimate.

Such a stance is central to caring maternal relationships that support the development of self (Belenky et al. 1986).

> Many mothers interview their children, rather than lecture, possibly because they are genuinely fascinated by the child's thoughts and feelings and enjoy drawing the child out. Also, mothers may intuit that drawing out the child's ideas helps him or her articulate and develop emotions and thoughts. Ultimately, it is the receiving of the child and hearing what he or she has to say that develops the child's mind and personhood. (189)

Central to the idea of a child's growth is the development of autonomy, which Deci, Kasser, and Ryan (1997) describe as essential to self-determination. Without it an individual is incapable of developing a "more elaborated, refined, and adaptive self" (58). Zebroski (1989) explains how this occurs through dialogue with others: "People are ontologically social. That is, the self only comes into existence through community. The self is made of social stuff, put together in social ways, by communities, at least at first. Vygotsky views the self as developing from shared activity to individual processes" (151).

Although independent learning and social learning may *seem* paradoxical, Pat understands how the unique construction of self is supported through interaction with others. In her classes, students step into a community in which members can nurture each other and support the maturity of each person's ideas. All are expected to learn, but knowledge is not massed produced.

Ruddick's third quality of maternal thinking, the desire for children to grow in ways acceptable to society, presents a dilemma for mothers. They must decide whether to raise children in ways that dehumanize them by teaching them accepted norms (e.g., competition), or to think independently, even when their values and beliefs do not reflect the current norms. Like many mothers, Pat's decision depends on the situation. Mothers intuitively decide when to reject the norm, when to play the game, when to alter the game, or when to change the system. As a graduate student working with student study groups for history and psychology majors, Pat did not change the system, but she did alter the game by shifting the focus away from a class that relies on the lecture mode of teaching and multiple-choice tests.

About all the students are introduced to in this textbook is a vocabulary that they can apply to further learning down the road if they take another class. It's difficult to study vocabulary in psychology out of context, so if they can get together with others and talk and try to attach some meaning to the concepts, they're learning; they're likely to score better on the tests. That's what the students want. And in the meantime, they're learning more about psychology than they would otherwise.

Even though the learning of vocabulary the students would not use seemed meaningless, Pat was able to find a way for them to apply it and make meaning. By altering the game, Pat made learning more social—more authentic—and thus remained true to her maternal thinking.

Whole Language and Rebellion

> He violated all the rules of rational transmission of information; he was the exact antithesis of a well-designed teaching machine. Yet what a professor he was!
> MIHALY CSIKSZENTMIHALYI, "Intrinsic Motivation and Effective Teaching"

The qualities of maternal thinking are compatible with the basic tenets of whole language philosophy, and therefore Pat was drawn to whole language. "It was easy to embrace what the instructor had to offer in the methods of teaching reading class. 'Hey, this is going to make students feel good. They're going to be engaged. They're going to be successful.' That was my starting point." Pat was right. When she first returned to college, that class was her starting point. As Pat said, "I went from not wanting to teach reading at all to wanting to be one of those rebel teachers."

Intertwined with Pat's maternal instincts is her joy in challenging authority. When Pat returned to school, however, she did not intend to challenge the transmission model of learning—just the accepted methods of teaching within that model, a form of accommodation. Pat would likely not have had a transforming experience if the teaching reading class had been based on a skills model. In fact, she had already taken many courses emphasizing a skills approach in which she eagerly created games and designed activities to motivate students. She wanted to be the very best at implementing the material she had developed. As Belenky et al. (1986) suggest, Pat operated within an "I can do it better" mode of systematic thinking:

> Women who rely on procedural knowledge are systematic thinkers in more than one sense of the term. Their thinking is encapsulated within systems. They can criticize a system, but only in

the system's terms, only according to the system's standards. Women at this position may be liberals or conservatives, but they cannot be radicals. . . . [T]hey do not question the premise of the structure. When these women speak of "beating the system," they do not mean violating its expectations but rather exceeding them. (127)

It became obvious early in the teaching reading course that many students held strong beliefs about traditional teaching. This led to tension within the class, including an outburst by one student. Such reactions made it evident that instituting whole language practices in the classroom would be more of a challenge than the ideas that had previously fueled Pat's rebelliousness. But Pat was ready: "Not many people were open to whole language theory. Most of our classmates were threatened or hostile. This only added to my attraction, rebel that I am." But Pat was not challenging authority just for the sake of being a rebel. Rather, as she states, "the new discoveries about teaching and learning excited the rebel in me." And it was her maternal thinking that helped determine what was "right." Thus the relationship between rebelliousness and maternal thinking appears both circular and mutually supporting. The result created in Pat a passionate commitment to teaching and learning. Her teaching is about supporting students' cognitive, emotional, and moral development— the kind that empowers students in the same ways that Pat's transformation empowered her.

Two years ago, Pat initiated a new course on cultural diversity designed to engage students in becoming aware of institutionalized inequalities and challenging the status quo. And as an outgrowth of the course, she and a colleague launched Barrier Breakers, a campus organization of students, staff, and faculty dedicated to celebrating diversity and working to improve dialogue among all people on campus. Pat's view on teaching also applies to working for social change: "We rebels are often challenged by the rest of the world. Being revolutionaries, visionaries, we know we are right, but we have to work hard to appeal to an unreceptive audience. Maybe that's the number one reason for collaboration. It allows us to take greater risks—to challenge authority and the status quo."

Pat and I have had intense discussions about why we rebelled against traditional modes of teaching. We delved into our personal histories, looking for commonalities that might explain why two individuals who questioned everything did not question the philosophy of whole language presented in the teaching reading course (although we posed many problems about how to implement it). We concluded that we believed in what was natural, and to alter a natural event in any way other than to enhance it conflicted with our beliefs about growth and development. That was whole language. But the belief alone—that natural was synonymous with good—did not create our rebellious stance. Much literature focuses on gender, power, and women's resistance to authority. Although we were not exposed to these ideas during our discussions (even though we are conscious of them now), somehow resistance to authority was instilled in us. Maybe it was as Ruddick (1980) suggests: "It is because we are daughters that we early receive maternal love with special attention to its implications for our bodies, our passions, and our ambitions. We are alert to the values and costs of maternal practices whether we are determined to engage in them or avoid them" (346).

Perhaps it was our mothers who gave us the strength to resist outside authorities—to resist those who would place our babies on feeding schedules or insist that we raise our children for the competitive world, to be better than others at everyone else's expense. Perhaps it was our mothers who gave us the strength to resist the inauthentic, who taught us that everyone needs to have choice, to feel connected to others, and to feel successful for the self to grow in humanistic and empowering ways. Perhaps it was our mothers who taught us to be rebels.

WHIRLWINDS

Whirlwinds spin upward in unpredictable directions. The motions appear chaotic. The teachers in this section find themselves swept up in renewal, to the point that the volatile nature of change itself becomes the defining experience. In Chapter 7, Patrick Shaw's "Finding Her Way: Searching as Renewal," Tish Spenser encounters just as many obstacles in her professional life as she does in her personal life, riding a roller coaster to "find her way." Roy Fox's first-person account in Chapter 8, "Chaos and Renewal," also describes numerous obstacles he faced when his professional and personal selves split apart. The following sections summarize how the major processes of renewal—social contexts, passion and flow, voice, and dual identities—affected the teachers described in Part III, Whirlwinds.

Social Contexts

The teachers in the following chapters operate within a range of social contexts in their quests for renewal. In Chapter 7, Tish, fearing her small town's response toward her lesbian relationship, isolates herself from her colleagues and sublimates her emotions through intense work. When this relationship fails, she tries to cushion her personal loss with professional renewal. Later, a new relationship helps lead her again to a more balanced renewal. Also, a larger social context—the cultural issues of literacy, media, and gender—help Tish not only to sustain her renewal but also to further develop her professional and personal selves. In Chapter 8, Roy seems to move through increasingly larger rings of social context—from that of his immediate family, to his students, to generations of people caught up in the throes of cultural change—as he tries to understand his own journey toward renewal. Like Tish, Roy feels isolated from others when his professional and personal selves do battle.

Passion and Flow

Passion and flow experiences account for much of the volatility in the lives of these teachers, who throw heart and soul into work but then must extricate them when larger issues of survival and renewal suddenly surface. In Chapter 7, Tish Spenser's own words ring with pride as she speaks of how hard she worked on her school's yearbook, noting that even the school coach was impressed with its stellar quality. When Tish "burns out" because of a failed relationship, however, she puts aside her huge investments and moves on. In Chapter 8, Roy Fox's passions for teaching, language, and other symbols drive him to leave a job, people, and place to which he feels deeply tied, resulting in a rupture between his professional and personal selves.

Voice

Both teachers profiled in Whirlwinds experience a loss of voice but regain it. In Chapter 7, Tish does not confide in anyone during an intense, personal trauma. She is also temporarily silenced when a student writes her a bigoted message. But she refuses to accept this label and finds her voice more powerful than ever when she begins writing about issues of gender and literacy. On the other hand, in Chapter 8, Roy does not so much lose his voice as it abandons him. Language fails so many consecutive times that it temporarily clouds his perception of those times when language *does indeed* work effectively. When voice or language does not work for teachers, we can become disoriented. Then we have little choice but to create meaning for ourselves in nontraditional ways, such as raising horses or raising consciousness.

Dual Identities

The adult and childlike selves function clearly in both of the teachers described in this section. In Chapter 7, Tish's childlike self wants to ride horseback deep into the woods and glory in nature. Her adult self wants to be the demanding instructor who resists any intrusions into her personal life. Tish finally reconciles these two selves by becoming the successful teacher who raises horses—one who harbors no fears and explores through public discourse the larger issues embedded in her personal life. In Chapter 8, Roy's childlike self wants to remain in the Northwest, continue to nurture relationships, and fish for cutthroat trout. The adult self, though, craves a challenging new job. The two become more reconciled when the childlike self revels in the freedom of the new job.

Finding Her Way:
Searching as Renewal

PATRICK SHAW
Lincoln University

Success in your work, the finding of a better method, the better understanding that insures the better performing is hat and coat, is food and wine, is fire and horse and health and holiday. At least, I find that any success in my work has effect on my spirits of all these.

RALPH WALDO EMERSON, *Emerson's Journals*

A s teachers, we are given to see our work in this peculiar institution as the place where our public and private lives collide. We manipulate solitary acts of thinking into social acts of teaching and learning while constantly on display in the busy, negotiated, communal classroom space. For Tish Spenser—an eleven-year veteran of private and public secondary and higher education who continually functions as a participant and learner while teaching—negotiating a balance between private and public has been an arduous yet compelling journey. For Tish and all teachers, our histories, our stories, become part of the hours, the days, and then the years that become careers making up the substance of our public lives. Tish now teaches at a small university in the Midwest where we are colleagues. An hour before my class, I walk by the small cluttered room, stand a few yards from the door, watch, and listen.

"Mr. Jones, you have yet to type up your summary? With more than seventy work stations at your disposal, Mr. Jones, surely you can find time to type up your assignment and place it in my mail box." Poor Mr. Jones slumps in his seat in obvious distress that his negotiation for an extension has become decidedly public.

"Ms. Spenser, it's like this. I have my rough draft here." For his colleagues, he displays the evidence: four bedraggled sheets torn from a spiral notebook.

She raises her hands. "Mr. Jones, I have a blank disk you can borrow. Contrary to popular belief, I am not here solely to oppress you."

Although slight laughter surfaces, students rarely outmaneuver Ms. Spenser. In the back, leaning against the wall, young men unconsciously arranged in a rainbow coalition sprawl in their seats. Mr. Jones shakes his head and declares to the class:

"Ms. Spenser, you're too rough on us."

"Well, that's why they call it college."

She moves through the ten o'clock Cultural Diversity class with the good-natured assurance of a teacher who has found success and happiness in her work. But for a time, some years back, this was not the case.

Later in the afternoon, we sit on the front porch of Tish and June's tall wood house and watch the sun go down. Tish has just finished putting up the horses. Her half-finished Miller High Life bottle sits by her worn, muddy boots. She has that far-off, determined look, like someone who is pulling a notion out of the past and is determined to make these comments right when finally ready for public hearing. For a woman who sits in her faded Carhart jacket, nursing a beer after a hard day of wrangling with students and horses, what she has to say is revelatory.

You know, it's hard for me to articulate how far, how detached back then I became from my teaching. I had never felt so much love in my life—I couldn't concentrate! But I got over that stage of just total infatuation. I knew it couldn't last forever. And then Dyna dumped me. And when I was going through my rough times, I felt like I lost my moorings. I had invested so much of my "self" in this relationship, I had no idea who I was anymore. And when she broke it off, I didn't have anything to fall back on. All of those things that made meaning in my life had lost their meaning. And one of those things was teaching. I didn't want to teach high school kids anymore; I didn't want to live in Smithville anymore—I wanted out. And I became the burnout queen—they still talk about how burnt out I was.

Tish sits talking about a past life that for me, her friend and colleague, seems so far removed it sounds like fiction. In the growing darkness, an orange coal glows on the horizon. I try to picture this other time, this other person, through the made-up, pastel haze of a classroom in the past. The Tish I know commands students the same way George C. Scott commanded tanks in *Patton*. I've heard her troops in the halls, coming out of her class: "That Ms. Spenser, she's rough, tough, and hard to bluff."

Tish has gone inside to answer the phone. I hear her voice getting faster, louder. She reappears, growling a complaint. "That was Dyna." Dyna, I have learned, is the ex-lover—the one who brought Tish's personal and professional life to a shuddering halt.

"She's calling up about our new chain saw. Our brand-new Husqvarna. June told me, 'Don't let her touch that chain saw, she doesn't know how to use it, she'll bring it back in a million pieces.' And you should see the condition she brought it back— ugh!" It's the all-purpose grunt of disgust I've grown used to. When I drove in earlier, I'd seen on an overturned oil drum the once bright-orange chain saw, now muddied and abused by the same woman who ten years ago nearly broke Tish's life.

The Search

Tish's story is of a search that most individuals, if asked to bare to the world, would find agonizingly personal. And then layer into this search where and how it unfolded—in front of her students, in the classroom, in the teacher's lounge, and at home grading papers. What Tish searched for is both simple and profound —what Csikszentmihalyi (1991) would call the struggle to find happiness: "Yet we cannot reach happiness by consciously searching for it. 'Ask yourself whether you are happy,' said J. S. Mill, 'and you cease to be so.' It is by being fully involved with every detail of our lives, whether good or bad, that we find happiness, not by trying to look for it directly" (2).

I had chosen Tish as the subject of this project to explore teacher renewal because she was a dynamic individual and teacher, and I was intrigued by her personal history. In searching for happiness, Tish, like most of us, had to begin with the "everyday"— the moments that pass in the classroom, at home, with those we find important, and in that time we spend alone. As a teacher, I also know the isolations and struggles that come precariously close to symbolizing a life of quiet desperation rather than success and happiness. Tish is a master teacher. When I chaired the search committee that interviewed her, I was struck by her combination of high school teaching experience and academic credentials. She was—and still is—a remarkable mixture of candor, confidence, and good humor. As Tish often says, "I know what needs to get done in the classroom." At the top of my notes from that first interview, one word is written: HIRE. So I admit my biases in my admiration for Tish.

Accordingly, I viewed this project in many ways as a self-reflective, dual search. First, I was delving into the private and public selves of someone who, as both friend and colleague, I knew on a fairly personal level. I knew her to be an incredibly hard worker who accepted a variety of academic responsibilities, such as creating and implementing a new course, chairing various committees, and teaching a full load. In her Cultural Diversity class, for example, Tish brought together a remarkably diverse student body of both rural and urban as well as African American, white, nontraditional, and international individuals. Her classes explore important yet difficult issues of race, class, and gender. She manages all of this while fostering goodwill in the class, preventing the discussion of these sometimes contentious problems from lapsing into brawls reminiscent of *The Jerry Springer Show.*

We also have attended conferences together, enrolled in similar graduate programs, shared writing assignments, and discussed, at length, our views of learning, pedagogy, and theory. Consequently, my stance as researcher cannot easily be separated from my stance as friend. I would learn about myself as much as I learned about Tish. Many times during this project, when sitting on the front porch after helping Tish put up bails in the barn, I felt a little chagrined about intruding into her private life, fearing that I had neither the right nor the bravery to uncover such information. Yet our friendship helped the entire experience from becoming, as Tish would say, "too morbidly introspective." Because we are friends, many of our interviews were a rich yet peculiar combination of deep thought and one-liners. For example, both Tish and her partner, June, are intense horsewomen who have invested an immense amount of time, effort, and money in these creatures. I asked her if horse riding was meaningful.

> TISH: Well, my god, of course it is! There is something about a horse that is different from any other animal. A horse is very majestic, beautiful. They can do what I wish I could do. They can run so effortlessly, they smell good, they are the most beautiful creatures.
>
> PATRICK: . . . and they have cheekbones to die for. But you know, to me, horses seem big, dumb, and expensive.
>
> TISH: Shuddup! Horses are profoundly sensitive, and my Champion is the most sensitive of all. But there are times, I must tell you, I drive by the house I used to own in my "other life" when I taught high school. It had a beautiful deck, hardwood floors, a big backyard—and sometimes I do think about how much money we are putting down gullets and on their hooves.

So how could I, as participant/observer in this process, bring a semblance of objectivity or trustworthiness to this inquiry? Together we would delve into burnout and renewal. I would learn secrets that Tish felt were crucial in telling her story, drawing me in closer to the rich, complex mind—the private self—of this person with a public livelihood. As she began to share her history, we made connections that many in education likely share. We both discovered, for example, that in the beginning neither of us had any idea what we wanted to do with our lives:

> Well, I didn't go to school with the desire to become a teacher. I went to school and majored in mass communications with an English minor. I then went back and changed my major to business education. Then I quit school, came home, and worked at mind-numbing clerical jobs. So then I went back to good old CSMU and began taking all those education classes, and wouldn't

you know it, I was signed, sealed, and delivered to St. Andrews High School in the April of my senior year. So I really didn't want to be a teacher. I kind of backed into it.

Tish shares photos of herself from the St. Andrews yearbook, for which she was faculty sponsor. An onerous, extracurricular task always foisted on a new teacher, it became her own *Bridge on the River Kwai*. Being the sponsor for the yearbook becomes a telling symbol of Tish's first teaching job and the evolution of how she saw her professional life. For teachers, old yearbooks are artifacts documenting our public and private selves. When we look at these frozen moments, sometimes in blurred, off-center photographs, most of us cringe at the images of what we once were. For Tish, the yearbook and the first teaching job at a small Catholic high school represent another life.

> TISH: I taught at St. Andrews for five years. My first contract was for $9,500. It was a pittance, but remarkably, I made a living. I had a furnished upstairs apartment in downtown Smithville.
>
> PATRICK: Was salary an issue?
>
> TISH: Isn't salary always an issue? We're teachers, remember? And I was hired in the full knowledge that I was going to work in servitude to do the yearbook. I got paid a whopping one hundred dollars in my contract—it literally added up to pennies an hour. I finally got Billy-Bob Dimwittie, the principal, to get my stipend up to six hundred dollars. He actually tried to shame me for asking for so much money. "Six hundred dollars, Tish? That's as much as some coaches make!" So every spring, every Sunday, I spent working on the yearbook. I did all the typing because I couldn't trust my kids to do it. I had a lot of my self invested in it. I even got snotty about it. In fact, after my yearbook came out (and I did call it *my* yearbook), the wrestling coach said it was the best yearbook he had ever seen at St. Andrews.

Tish stops talking and begins her habitual, long, straight-ahead stare. I look at these photos that show another person—yet they do not. When I have gone to conferences with Tish, she has dressed in upscale western wear, complete with denim shirt and bolo tie. As colleagues, we have joined a few others in quietly and deliberately subverting the university's aged dress code policy by wearing blue jeans, flannel shirts, and ties. When I recently asked what she was going to wear to the Arts and Sciences faculty banquet, Tish growled, "Well, I won't like hell be wearing a dress." But in these seventeen-year-old photos, surrounded by her students, Tish wears flowered sundresses and polyester pantsuits. Looking into this other world, I see common threads connecting Tish, the first-time teacher at St. Andrews High School in 1980 obsessing over the yearbook, with the Tish who stares and shakes her head at the images she sees: "I finally gave most of the yearbooks to my folks to keep. I don't look at them much anymore."

The Work We Do

Teaching (along with many other professions) means investing much of one's happiness in work. To articulate everything that constitutes what creates happiness in work is to delve into unquestioned assumptions and rituals that make up living.

> In the lives of many people it is possible to find a unifying purpose that justifies the things they do day in, day out—a goal that like a magnetic field attracts their psychic energy, a goal upon which all lesser goals depend. This goal will define the challenges that a person needs to face in order to transform his or her life into a flow activity. Without such a purpose, even the best-ordered consciousness lacks meaning. (Csikszentmihalyi 1991, 218)

At our university, Tish and I attend the monthly faculty senate meetings—one of the many things we do every day as part of our academic responsibilities. Although we take our senate responsibilities seriously, some of our co-workers obsess over every jot and tittle of senate business. Tish and I usually sit in the back row and pass notes. At every meeting, there are four individuals who, on nearly every issue, will stand to make a contentious or tedious point concerning some particle of bureaucratic minutiae. One colleague, known as "Professor Hedgecock," has become famous for picking an obscure point, standing up, and pontificating upon it until his large round head turns crimson. At committee and department meetings, when the conversation becomes overbearing, the phrase "Hedgecocking something to death" is affectionately used. I wonder how much of our own public displays—from the way we dress and talk to how we conduct our classes and interact with our students—is part of that internal drive that makes teaching meaningful. Teachers constantly struggle to balance time spent effectively teaching with negotiating the bureaucratic details of academic life. We continually and inwardly work to maintain idealism while being evaluated and undertaking such activities as hallway monitoring, yearbook publishing, and grading—endless grading.

Tish's particular journey has taken her from a small Catholic high school to a huge public high school to a small university. She clearly and simply states that at St. Andrews, the amount of work far exceeded the salary and was the primary reason for the second job search.

> So I knew there were going to be some openings at Smithville High School, which is huge. And I went through their arcane, labyrinthine, and rigorous interview process. I got hired and got stuck with four freshman classes in a row. I knew I had to pay my dues! I also missed the sense of community I felt at St. Andrews, and that was missing at Smithville because it was so big. I don't know how to describe it, but at St. Andrews, as opposed to Smithville, there really was a sense of parental input—it was a Catholic school, and that sense of Catholic mission was very evident.

Tish's first job change represents a universal truth many teachers face—being overworked and underpaid: "I liked teaching at St. Andrews, I could tolerate the yearbook, but I just got tired of living in penury." With changing schools came a new set of obstacles. On the one hand, Tish was freed from the overburdened drudgery of coerced extracurricular activities, and she received a raise in salary. On the other, Tish wanted to teach senior composition and literature courses, but the reality of "paying one's dues" by teaching four composition classes made finding an optimal teaching experience difficult. Tish stoically faced the daily burden of teaching classes she frankly disliked and soldiered through the everyday grind.

In her second teaching position, Tish acquired the experience and self-reflection to realize that she wanted more. At the same time, her gnawing question, "Is this all there is?", relates directly to Csikszentmihalyi's (1991) definition of what brings renewal to our lives: "In normal life, we keep interrupting what we do with doubts and questions. 'Why am I doing this? Should I be doing something else?'" (54).

Tish's professional history is a remarkable story, especially when juxtaposed with the struggle between her public and private lives that would begin to make teaching unbearable. At first she experienced a "little" burnout, caused by professional and economic issues. Then came what Tish calls the "big, big burnout" when Dyna entered her life, dwarfing her teaching concerns. But Tish's big burnout was more complex than that she fell madly in love and was dumped. As the interviews unfolded, I rediscovered how this confident, articulate teacher went through several waves of burnout and renewal, each one helping to create the person I know. In her first burnout, Tish began questioning her career choices:

> I just began to feel trapped. I kept asking, "Is this it? Is this it?" I looked around and I looked around at all those career teachers, those "thirty and outers," and I thought, "Ugh, man!" Some were just there, didn't care, but many did and could just keep happily teaching. There was Mrs. Hortense, who was my world novels teacher when I was in high school, and she helped during my two burnouts—my little one and my big one. She is in it for the long haul, and her heart pumps blue and white blood. She's a very caring teacher, but she'll keep going until she dies in Smithville.

Tish's first realization of burnout and her own views as an educator took a decidedly public stance. Throughout those days of making copies, filling out forms, and taking roll, she felt the need to answer the question, "Is this all there is?" Tish wanted to find significant ways to excise the drudgery and doubt from the everyday and make teaching meaningful. She became an activist and leader in her National Education Association chapter and the Student Teacher Association. She began and completed a master's degree in English education, and she enrolled in the Missouri Writing Project. Tish wanted these pursuits to be outward symbols of professionalism and renewal. But while these activities had intrinsic value and provided renewal, certain core questions still needed answers.

These questions revolved around how Tish saw herself as a human being and around elemental issues of identity and sexuality. To claim that she worked through these questions by taking on the mantle of "superprofessional teacher" is an oversimplification. As Britzman (1994) articulates, teacher identity is part of a complex social construction that is constantly negotiated, and the contradictions, struggles, and creation of teacher identity continually evolve. Through this complex evolution of creating a public, professional identity, there must also be intrinsic connections with the private self, providing satisfactory answers to the "Why am I here?" question. Tish's plunge into intense professionalism was a way to add meaning to her life, but the inner conflicts remained.

Tish describes how the outward symbols of renewal that represented the inner need to find happiness could no longer stop the inevitable private "big burnout." In her public persona, she received professional and public acclaim. But all the trappings of professional success could not stop the inner psychic meltdown.

> I went to the Writing Project in 1988, my third year at Smithville, which was not my big burnout. I was closing in on my master's degree, and our school went through this wrenching change in political affiliation. The NEA got a hold of us and we went radical! I ran for office and became the third vice president of the [local teaching association]. I started to go to NEA conferences and conventions. I was elected to become a delegate to the statewide NEA convention. I even started wearing business suits; you should see the pictures—jacket, skirt, high heels! Could you imagine me, every day, wearing these suits and dresses, because I thought it was all part of my new image as a professional? And I wanted to look as professional as I possibly could. My principal stopped me one day and said, "Tish, you're just a different person!" And with the Missouri Writing Project, I started networking, man. I finally found colleagues who were as interested in teaching writing as I was. We would sit around and talk about how we could make the teaching of writing relevant and real. It

was the first time I felt I could be a writer. I had the power suits, I was in control, had gotten my master's degree, done the writing project. But when Dyna entered my life, it all turned to ashes.

The "Big, Big Burnout"

If one wants a ready-made symbol of the teaching life, study a teacher's desk or an instructor's office. On Tish's wall is the photo of a young sandy-haired woman running in a crowded marathon under the shadow of the St. Louis Gateway Arch. The same woman appears in another photo, but she's older, mugging with the huge, quizzical, cinnamon-colored head of a horse. On the desk, cluttered with journals, is another photo of a fat, rather annoyed cat being forced to pose for the camera. Steam rises from a small white coffeemaker as it sputters and rattles. Tish sits and slowly turns in her chair, gazing out at the rain-splattered window, drumming a green felt-tip pen against the papers in her lap.

"Look at this grading! Every semester I tell myself I'm not going to get behind. But these journals."

I point out that, even though journals are a useful tool in helping students explore their ideas through expressive writing, if one does not assign journals, then one does not have to grade journals. With a sharp look, Tish answers, "As opposed to you, Mr. Shaw, I just don't hand out B's like candy on Halloween."

Even before I intruded into her life, I was impressed by Tish's quiet, instinctive resoluteness toward what matters and makes her happy: her partner, June; their farm and horses; her degree program; and her teaching and her students. "It all turned to ashes" for Tish when the big burnout culminated in irreconcilable differences between her public and private lives. Tish had to hide her first relationship and eventual breakup with Dyna ("my first relationship with a woman") while appearing as the super professional. Quite simply, a conservative rural high school and community would not tolerate an openly lesbian teacher. The public and private were on a collision course. As teachers, we all know the importance of having a support system. Many of us live in solitary confinement in our homerooms or offices. Tish was surrounded by students and responsibilities but hiding the most important elements and decisions of her life. She fell into a depression, which Deren (1997) describes as "like being dead. It is like being a ghost . . . . You float through your days feeling insubstantial, cut off from warmth, light, and all feeling. Sometimes it feels like you're in a coffin buried alive. You're screaming inside your head, but no one can hear you" (1). And while this description at first sounds melodramatic, the sense of despair and helplessness that can grow to the point at which a person feels unable to live mirrors Tish's own description of what she calls her "big, big burnout":

> I sort of hate revealing this about myself. It showed me to be such a weak, sniveling person. I was so pathetic! I literally couldn't teach my classes anymore. I'd have to leave between classes and cry my eyes out. Most other teachers thought I had just been doing so much with becoming the "superprofessional teacher" that I worked myself into this state. Only a few really knew what was going on. And one of the most awful parts of the "big burnout" was how much I was letting down my students. I got to the point where one of the things that meant most to me—teaching—didn't even matter anymore.

Tish stops talking for a moment. Unopened boxes of textbooks are stacked precariously next to the overfilled bookshelves. Student journals are splayed open, thrown in a messy pile, and have begun to migrate toward the door. The coffeemaker rattles in the background. Beyond the closed door is the muffled world of the university. I look at Tish and reflect on her story; I know she has not and will not tell me everything. Only she knows the depths of the depression that drove her out of high school teaching. Once I asked if she had sought professional help for burnout and depression, and Tish flatly replied, "More than you will ever know." As a friend and colleague, I have trouble envisioning these "others"—the Tish at St. Andrews and Smithville High Schools who wore power suits, ran marathons, and finally faced such despair in reconciling a shattered private life with her public life that it all but effectively ended a ten-year teaching career. Tish is still wary about going into the details of falling in love and then breaking up with a woman while teaching in a conservative high school not known for its tolerance toward race and gender: "I knew my old life was over."

As I learned more about this ordeal in her past, I tried to figure out a tactful way to ask how Dyna—someone who has caused such suffering and change in Tish's life—could now be good friends with both Tish and June, so much so that she was allowed to borrow and abuse their new chain saw.

Tish and I sit for a couple of minutes and complain about our department chair, who has sent out a memo about the upcoming Christmas office party and is asking for specific suggestions about "how to make the affair more sparkly." In fifteen minutes, we will be sitting in the back row of another senate meeting, passing notes and critiquing the grandiloquent monologues. Tish talks about the struggle to get young male students, regardless of ethnicity, to trust her enough to open up and communicate in her cultural diversity course. At the same time, she continually keeps me apprised of the obsession in both her and June's life—horses. One of their three horses, "Yah-boy," a twenty-two-year-old gelding, has again turned up lame, even though he's been fitted with hard-plastic orthopedic shoes. As I listen to Tish's description of the pain and suffering a human must endure to force a pill down a horse's throat, or the time and patience needed to clip properly all four hooves, I compare this Tish now at peace to the other Tish who had lost a sense of life's meaning. The latest step in the evolution of Tish's search for personal and professional satisfaction is her relationship with June and their love for horses. When Tish talks about her own horse, Champion, she loses all sense of time:

> Don't get me started about my horses. Good lord, sometimes I stop and think of the time, effort, and expense these creatures are—but my beloved horse. It's weird, it's incredible. When I came home Sunday, I came in the door and started talking to June. I had been at my folks' house over the weekend, so we went out to give the horses some carrots. And he didn't know I was home, so I stepped out onto the porch and called, "Champy, Champy, Howizyou, Champy?" He threw his head up, trotted toward the fence, and took the carrot. June said, "Well, he never does that for me!"

I think about Tish's beginnings as a teacher and how her search for fulfillment in both her personal and private lives remained a struggle for so long. As teachers, we occasionally share in this struggle, applying the "Is this all there is?" question to our own personal and private lives. Even during my early experiences as a student and substitute teacher, I remember seeing those "lifers" who had become so institutionalized that they had become caricatures of teachers. At the university level, there are tenured faculty, such as poor Professor Hedgecock with his stream-of-consciousness filibusters, whose lecture notes have faded yellow and who find lunch the highlight of the day. But for Tish today, the complaints about horses and the complaints about workload are a world away from the obstacles she faced in teaching high school. Although Tish deals daily with the problems and responsibilities endemic to college teaching, she no longer faces the psychic meltdown between personal and private. She does not keep horses in the vague pursuit of "something else," some unarticulated sense of fulfillment—she keeps horses because she loves them, and there is a real challenge and complexity in this devotion to her animal companions. Tish no longer must hide her sexual identity and personal life. Ms. Spenser's identity in the classroom is the one she wants to portray. And our "portrayed" identity is made up of the everyday social construction we continually negotiate through our interactions with students, colleagues, administration, and ourselves. Consciously or subconsciously, master teachers continually reevaluate their public teaching selves, habitually monitoring the person walking into the classroom each day. Tish finally found the balance between her own identity and how she wants to present it to the world. She has found happiness in her work, avocations, and private life, all of which have led to who she is now.

Tish Now

"Ms. Spenser's a dyke." The note, folded in quarters, was left by a student, stuffed into my literature book. He had meant to hurt, to insult, to belittle and demean. He didn't know, couldn't understand, that his supposedly insulting statement was my simple truth.

He meant to use the word as a club, to bloody my sense of self. All he did was state a reality, using a word I had taken for myself as a source of power.

It had been a rough year. The last ten years as a high school teacher had been interminable. I knew in early September that I could no longer be the teacher I had been, I could no longer live in the city I grew up in, or walk the hall I had walked as a student. Burned out. Bitter. But my students and most of my colleagues only knew the half of it. Broken-hearted. That's what was killing me, leeching my energy, my connections to my old life, right out of me.

Glancing up, seeing Tish standing by the window, I realize we are both at a place we have never been before. She reaches up and pulls aside the light-beige curtains. Before us stretches the patrician skyline of downtown Philadelphia, twinkling in the gray haze. Tish dresses for professional conferences in the same blue jeans and cotton shirts she wears for classes. She stares out the thirty-second-story picture window and declares:

"There she is, Patrick. The big city—big mama town. This is the biggest city, the most eastern city I've ever been in. We're going to find us a cheese steak."

While Tish is thinking cheese steak, I have just read one of the most brutally honest, compelling, severe narratives I've ever read. As graduate students, Tish and I have shared interests in popular culture and, luckily, we are both presenting papers at a conference in Philadelphia. Through some peculiar work of fate, we have ended up sharing a five-room suite larger than my apartment. Tish's paper is part of a session titled "Through the Lens of Male Desire." Her paper, "Lesbians in This House: *Sister My Sister* and Lesbian Subjectivity," focuses on how gender affects an individual's reading of the film *Sister My Sister*, the lurid yet true story of two French sisters forced into domestic servitude in the 1920s. The sisters fall in love with each other and murder the domineering mistress of the house.

Tish ended up being an informant in my own research project on the television program *Star Trek: Voyager*. In return, I got to be the official male viewer for *Sister My Sister*. My contribution to the study through my decidedly male gaze was that even though the film does portray a patriarchal, heterosexist, capitalistic society in early twentieth-century France, I found the ending of lesbian incest and multiple murder rather troubling. I also suggested that maybe re-releasing the film with the new title of *Twisted Sisters* might be a way of gaining a wider male audience. Tish was thrilled that I validated a "typical male reading of the film."

As Tish continued to tell me her stories, I was intrigued with the way she had evolved by piecing together the past and using her depression and burnout to create the confident, integrated person she is now. Considering the despair that caused her to jettison ten years of her life—the Tish of power suits and professional activism who simultaneously weathered the relationship and breakup with Dyna—the Tish of today proves to be an individual who not only endured great change but also was actually strengthened by those days she describes as "too dark to bear." Without those days, the Tish I know would not exist. The life of the past, both public and private, no longer worked for Tish. Her description of this past ("a private hell . . . you could not imagine what was going through my mind . . . I was a mess") compared to the Tish of the here-and-now answers the question, "How can teachers renew themselves, even when the worst things imaginable happen to them?" For teachers to be happy with their work, the classroom has to provide some sense of community and inner comfort to teachers, even when they are battling principals and collecting milk money. The daily skirmishes must become part of the complexity and richness of a job we want to do well, not daily symbols of a burden we must endure. On the plus side for Tish, she was generally happy most of the time in her early teaching career. "I don't want people to think I spent every waking moment at St. Andrews's or Smithville in the fetal position, weeping." Tish did have a certain stability when she was "hooked into the social life of St. Andrews." And at Smithville, her personal experiences with the Missouri Writing Project and other professional organizations brought her "to do wonderful things inside and outside the classroom." Yet Tish's deliberate, outward efforts that transformed her into a superprofessional teacher could only partially answer that inner search for meaning in her private, gnawing, "Is this all there is?" life.

Finally accepting the truth that she was a lesbian in a community intolerant of such truth, "falling head over heels in love," and subsequently breaking up with Dyna while simultaneously carrying on as what had become a shell of her former self, Tish realized that in the collision of her two worlds, the former Tish could not survive: "I was letting down my students, I was letting down myself. I was becoming a rotten teacher—and I didn't even care anymore!"

To varying degrees, we can share in Tish's brutal assessment of her own burnout. But unless we have experienced it, we can only approximate understanding the abyss of depression. Many of the public symbols of her former life—everything that made up the world of high school teaching, including her former sexual identity—had to be transformed if Tish were to survive without also killing her burning desire to teach. Now teaching at the university level, Tish's refusal to hide her sexuality, her writing and scholarship in lesbian folklore and popular culture, her beloved partner, and her horses have all helped to bring stability to and between the public and private selves that were once in conflict.

> I must admit that teaching at the university level finally offers what I've always wanted from teaching. I like schmoozing with colleagues, checking my e-mail, even department meetings. And I must admit I'm thrilled at how supportive the dean has been about the cultural diversity class. And teaching is still a big ego booster for me. I like the time and freedom of college teaching that gives me the chance to be in the woods and be with my horses. And let's face it, I like being the center of attention. Horse riding and teaching can sometimes just happen. When we are in class, discussing these issues with my students, challenging students to tell their stories, their prejudices and biases, it's amazing how quickly the time goes.

Finding Her Way

The fact that Tish shared with me the first page of her autobiography and complained about "not being a writer" demonstrates how her private and public selves are still gaining complexity. Even after all of her disclosures, Tish is chagrined about her own expressive writing. She makes fun of herself, calls her writing "smarmy," and lampoons terms such as "empowering" by substituting her own "shazzamin." Self-deprecation illustrates the way Tish deals with the uncomfortable process of making her personal thoughts visible. Her standards for writing differ little from the standards she held for herself when publishing the St. Andrews yearbook or teaching first-year composition at Smithville. As a writing teacher, she believes that her own writing, especially writing about the most personal and heartfelt experiences, can still be poor.

> I know my limitations! If I could write profoundly moving essays, then I would be doing it. Like the death of my cat, Asia. I wish I had the ability to put this commonplace event in terms that [would allow] people [to] recognize some beautifully written, universal truth. But I know it's going to come out like, "boo-hoo-hoo, my cat died!" What pathetic, melodramatic bathos. It'll suck!

In the academic sphere, Tish writes with authority. What was once the deepest secret Tish held ("the secret, the simple truth I used as a club to bloody myself") has now given her an assured voice to explore the issues most important to her as a lesbian and scholar. While she cringes at the notion of writing down her feelings about the death of her cat, her writing about film and feminist theory rings clear and strong. For example, the social phenomenon of Ellen Degeneres's "outing as television text" was an issue of debate in the gay community long before the straight community became aware. Tish foreshadowed the event in her own writing and demonstrated her authoritative, insightful voice. "Ellen has been on the air for three years now, and has a large following among lesbians and heterosexuals alike. She has their sympathy to a large degree already. The door to Ellen's TV closet is open; we may assume that she will walk through it and out of the closet as the season progresses." Academic writing provides Tish a bridge, allowing what was private to become public in a manner that affirms her social, political, and cultural beliefs. She no longer closets herself or her ideas.

In fact, through both teaching and writing, Tish now openly challenges assumptions held by her students concerning race, class, and gender without beating them over the head with ideology.

I could tell my students recognized the secret that "Ms. Spenser's a dyke." And I couldn't teach there [at Smithville] with one of the most important aspects of my being not only hidden but used against me. I wasn't going to keep my sexuality a secret anymore, because the secrecy was making me sick. And I really believe you are only as sick as your biggest secret. I wasn't going to let them "out" me as a way of manipulating or getting back. I was going to take the power of the secret away.

For Tish the writing process remains onerous and self-monitoring. She will stalk around her computer or pace the office trying to get started. Working at home, Tish forsakes writing for the chance to saddle Champion for a long ride deep into the woods. Writing for Tish is usually a hard-won optimal experience.

There's some flow in writing, but I rarely feel like I've lost myself for hours. In fact, I usually write a paragraph, get up, walk around, drink some coffee. It takes so much effort to think about what I'm trying to do, and I'm often impatient with that effort. You know that memoir I gave you? Do you know how far I got? One typed page! And you know why? I'm too damned busy writing and thinking about writing and thinking about teaching to even think about writing for pleasure.

Even as a chore, however, writing has become much more meaningful in that the once private person has found not only a voice but also an audience. The personal for Tish is profoundly serious, and "writing for pleasure"—expressive, personal writing—demonstrates how sharing her private self remains difficult. After all these events and the discussion of her history, Tish—like most of us—still feels strongly about keeping part of the self where she believes it should be kept—in private.

Keeping a Horse

On our third day in Philadelphia, conference fatigue sets in. We decide to eschew "Commerce in the Islamic World in the 11th Century" in favor of walking around the city. As we pass narrow, well-scrubbed brownstones, Tish shakes her head and states, "Couldn't live here, couldn't keep a horse." If any avocation holds Tish in a true flow experience, it is horses. Csikszentmihalyi (1991) notes that one of the key elements of the optimal experience is that it must be an end in itself. While we walk the city streets, Tish complains, "Man, I'm ready to go. Five days in the city is too much." I understand, because Tish and June have built their own world in the woods that revolves around their three horses, Champion, Challenger, and Yah-Boy.

> They are such beautiful creatures, and you go on these trail rides, crossing creeks, bluffs, open plains, and you think, yes, there is something, in the poetic sense, very romantic about the whole thing. . . . I love being in the woods. Talk about a flow experience; it's hard to put into words. You form a relationship with your horse that is very unique. The horse knows you and you know your horse—it's almost like a lover relationship.

Tish finds the joy of keeping horses to be one of her strongest flow experiences. Weaving in and out of our discussions about the struggle between Tish's public and private selves and the difficulty of maintaining a teaching as well as a personal identity, the continual talk about horses seemed almost superfluous to the actual flow experiences with them. It was as if talking about horse riding somehow diminished the actual experience. Tish called herself a "horsewoman" and struggled for words to describe an activity that borders on the transcendent. But when the right words came, her talk about horses was intense and introspective and, for nonhorse people like myself, fascinating. When Tish did offer statements, she frequently wanted to refute and explore her own thinking about what draws her toward keeping horses. She also shared how this fervor connected with the stability and happiness she found in her personal life.

> Ever since I can remember, I was drawn to these beautiful, mysterious creatures. There are no other creatures on earth like them. They can do things I wish I could do—run like the wind, forever! Think about it. And when I ride Champion—talk about a flow experience—horse riding and keeping horses. It's like Carter's Little Liver pills—it gave me a new lease on life. When I first got

my horse—and you talk about my own symbol system or sense of renewal—when I bought Champion, I thought, who do I know who could possibly share the joy and excitement of this animal the same way I do? And it was June.

Two days after our return from Philadelphia, I have a chance to experience what Tish was trying to put into words. It is a cold November early evening. At Tish and June's house in the woods, the lights of the city gone, you become aware of the dark, quiet sky. Their small farm sits on the edge of a state forest where the neighbors' houses are only identifiable by the thin streams of chimney smoke rising behind the creeks and fields. Getting out of my car, I feel the cold, wet gloom of the woods at night in winter. At the barn, I hear Tish's familiar, sharp "Patrick!" which means "Come quick and keep quiet." Tish is a shadow leaning against the fence, a square of hay the size of second base in her hand.

"Listen."

Out in the dark field, I hear a rumbling snort. Then something I remember hearing in my youth on television—rumbling hooves. These were getting louder, and they were real! I wonder if horses can see well in the dark and if they are going to jump the fence like they do in the beer commercials. Slowly yet suddenly, through the gloaming these huge, breathing, snorting, ornate creatures sidle up against the fence. I wonder how you possibly coerce these huge things into giving you a ride.

"Here, take this hay down about fifteen yards and feed Challenger."

As I grab the hay, a huge, hide-covered head bumps into mine, and the earthy, leathery horse smell is everywhere. I can make out a large, annoyed eye peering down at me. As I walk the fence to drop the hay, I look back at Tish, who has turned on the soft glow of the barn light and grabbed Champion by the bridle, quietly talking to him. I can't hear the conversation. Both are slowly walking toward the stall, finding their way.

CHAPTER EIGHT

Chaos and Renewal

ROY F. FOX

University of Missouri–Columbia

I have always believed in language—not just in how it communicates but how it shapes thinking. I also invite students to discover for themselves how nonlinguistic representations of reality are valuable in and of themselves, as well as how they can affect language and thinking. One night during an experiment in a graduate course on Writing and Knowing, the students and I switched senses while we sketched and wrote. We drew any unusual yet common object, such as a condenser from a radio, which we were only allowed to feel with our hands while surrounded in total darkness. While drawing, we first listened to slow tempo and then upbeat music. Next, we wrote about the object we had just sketched. Finally, we discussed what happened to our meaning-making processes when one sense modality was altered or deprived.

This activity clearly showed us the wide range of "mental" experiences that we all have, how we should think of language as just another fish in the pool of knowing. "Sure," I told myself at the time, with confidence, "I *know* that language is only a single way of knowing." I have researched it, read it, taught it, lived it, been there, got the T-shirt. I also know that language cannot be trusted. Hayakawa and Hayakawa (1990) and countless others taught me that. So did serving twenty-three years on NCTE's Public Doublespeak Committee. I knew these things.

The synesthesia experiment we conducted in class also revealed the role of background knowledge and context in think-

---

An earlier version of this chapter appeared as an essay titled "Dog Day Literacy" in *English Education* (Vol. 29, No. 3, October 1997, pp. 202–15).

ing: students who had mechanical and technical experience knew the radio condenser when they felt it (or made a good guess). The writings they did about this object differed considerably from those of the other students. E. H. Gombrich (1984) calls this "the beholder's share" of meaning. It can range from extensive background knowledge to something that happened to us an hour earlier.

In another activity with this class, on the same night, the grad student conducting the experiment instructed us to draw the dominant image that entered our minds while we listened to music in total darkness. I had no choice that night about what to draw. It had to be a Dalmatian. As hard as I tried, that was all I could think about. My beholder's share that night consisted of one thing—a madly running spotted dog.

Earlier that afternoon, a Dalmatian streaked wildly out of nowhere, crossed four lanes of traffic, and materialized directly in front of my car. I squealed my brakes and skidded. The front bumper thumped. Then I glimpsed the dog roll over, land on its feet, and scamper away. I was shaken. More so than I normally would have been, because my family owns a Dalmatian. We had bought her for our children a year earlier to replace their cat, Jennifer, who likely perished in Pine Bluff, Wyoming, because of my belief and trust in words.

Yes, words were a conspirator in the death of my children's pet. My family was traveling from Idaho to Missouri because I had taken a new job, one I couldn't refuse because it allowed me new opportunities to play with words—to write more, to teach more graduate courses in literacy. As much as I hated to leave Idaho, the promise of deep professional renewal, rooted in the lure of words, had us on the highway that dog-day afternoon.

And words influenced what was to happen in other ways, too. I drove the largest moving van that U-Haul offered. And the fullest. This massive truck was also pulling our old Dodge van, itself packed to the gills with books. My wife drove our car, which pulled a trailer. A hundred miles out, when we hit the scorched Idaho desert, we knew that both vehicles were greatly slowed by the weight. With steep mountain roads ahead of us, we stopped to repack. We got rid of the trailer on the back of the car, since we wanted our children to be in the lightest, hence safest, vehicle. In a white-hot parking lot, we unloaded furniture from the trailer, carted it to a transport service, and shipped it to Missouri, before returning the trailer to a nearby dealer. Next, we carefully wedged the books from the trailer into the van hooked to the moving truck. Of course, we knew that the truck might now be too heavy, but at least our children were safer. After several hours, we were back on the road.

Then, periodically, while humming down the highway, the truck's engine, with no warning whatsoever, would shut down. Click off in midstream. Just like that. I would frantically glance into the mirror and coast the truck to a stop along the shoulder. The ignition would never turn right back on, so we'd wait forty minutes until it would crank up again. During these waits, in between silent curses and scanning through all the possible causes and effects for the truck's lack of cooperation, I would pause, gaze out the windshield, and utter a pathetic thank you to God for seeing to it that a full logging truck was not tailgating me when the engine decided to quit. Language was no help. Neither my curses nor my frenzied scanning for solutions made a shred of difference. Even my prayers of gratitude for not having been run over seemed lame, for they were reactive—not proactive— and I doubted that a truly controlling God would approve.

But the periodically dying engine wasn't my main problem. Even more irritating was not being able to shift out of second gear. Once in a great while, the stick shift somehow mysteriously slipped into third. But most of the time it refused, grinding insanely until I gave up and slowed down. Of course, I could never reach anybody at U-Haul on the phone. By the evening we crossed into Utah, I somehow deduced that if the truck were lighter, the engine wouldn't suddenly stop, and I would be able to shift out of second gear. Near midnight, exhausted, I steered the big rig with van attached into what appeared to be a normal motel parking lot. I drove around a building and up a driveway, and then found myself wedged within a tiny lane, atop what must have been a converted ski slope. Fearing for my physical safety, I devoted the next half hour to cursing, squinting my eyes, and straining my neck as I inched the truck back down the seventy-degree incline. Finally inside Ogden's Red Barron Motel, our small children had become more energized, gaining momentum after a long, passive day cooped up in the car. Their activity level was intensified by the motel's black and red decor. So, in order to sleep for a few hours that night, I ingested something artificial. When language fails and the god of renewal doesn't show up for work, reality itself sags. When that happens, take drugs.

The next morning, with throbbing headache, I decided to chuck language right there at the motel. To hell with books. I unloaded nine boxes of Norton literature anthologies, technical writing textbooks, and "concise" grammar handbooks. As I nodded toward the neatly stacked cartons, I solemnly assured the maid, "You should be able to sell them." I left the maid with her mountain of books on the sidewalk in front of our room and climbed into my truck. What, I now ask, was I thinking? Has anyone but college bookstores ever made money on used textbooks? Was there a lucrative market in Ogden, Utah, for Prentice-Hall's *Handbook for Writers*? I had deluded myself into deluding an innocent hotel employee.

Once again we headed out. Once again the engine died. Words seesawed in my head as I weighed an unsavory option: demand a new truck, wait God knows how long for it, unload the full one, and reload the replacement. This could easily take four days of hard labor in August heat, with small kids and a cat at loose ends, to boot.

While battling the halting truck and thinking about the possibility of this extra time, labor, and expense, I somehow pieced together—from a few patchy conversations with fellow Grapes-of-Wrathers at rest stops—why the truck's gearshift wouldn't shift. I gleaned that perhaps a governor had been placed on the gears that prohibited me from shifting into third unless I was traveling at precisely thirty-six miles per hour. Not thirty-five, not thirty-seven, but exactly thirty-six. The speedometer had to read thirty-six on the nose. That's why sometimes it worked and most of the time it didn't. Everything had been perfect during a scant few and random split seconds when I just *happened* to be moving at 36 mph—and *simultaneously* decided to shift gears. These precise conditions had occurred in the past few days about as often as planetary alignment.

How could I have missed such a basic piece of information about driving a big dumb truck? For starters, I expected speed to be a *variable* thing, not for a single, exact speed to be necessary to perform a particular driving maneuver. (I had driven other trucks with governors that shifted gears within a *range* of speeds.) In other words, I assumed that simple driving, like speaking or writing, could be accomplished in multiple ways. Silly me. As a knee-jerk English educator, I applied the language paradigm of multiplicity to driving. It didn't hold true. I mistakenly thought that, well, since language can generate an infinite number of sentences and meanings, then so should moving vans function at any speed.

Okay, okay. So I operated with the wrong schema, with an inappropriate set of assumptions. A big ol' slippery language-and-knowing thing got by me. It happens. But somehow, some smaller language-and-knowing things also eluded me, which contributed to my ignorance about the truck's governor. Distrusting words in the first place (not to mention being a responsible person and fine citizen), I had dutifully read all the manuals for the truck and listened attentively and asked questions when the truck-rental manager gave me my orientation. That pesky little governor was never mentioned, never exposed in any form, to the light of language. I don't know why. About the only reason for such secrecy is that the governor on *this* truck must have been a piece of pivotal evidence in the JFK assassination—some mechanism bearing fingerprints which linked mobster Johnny Roselli to a spent shell recovered from the grassy knoll in Dallas.

At any rate, when I finally learned about the governor, I gained power, or at least a semblance of feeling more in control. I was so relieved that I forgave the world for keeping the gearshift gizmo a secret. That was okay, I reasoned. After all, words don't always come through when they're supposed to; they are just as fleeting and unpredictable as images or the faint echoes of never-before-played melodies. I knew that. *At the same time,* I relished the fact that language, those several abbreviated conversations with strangers, had led me out of ignorant darkness and into the celestial light of knowledge. Now that I was shifting into higher gear at *the* correct speed, the truck's engine stopped playing sudden death with me. Life was perfect. Here, I applied the same generative principle of language: if I talked with several people, a solution would emerge from the options or coalesce into an answer.

This generative principle of language that had failed me in the previous days now succeeded. Such is the elusive nature of language and other symbols in a postmodern world: meanings evaporate at the same time that they appear. Sussman (1989) and others echo what Korzybski warned us about decades ago: "If the works we read point to any world, it is one in a constant state of flux and reversal, where structures and meanings supplant one another as they proliferate" (1933, 1). However, this never occurred to me while I was on the road.

With the gears now shifting, the engine never halting, all was well . . . but not quite. Language struck again, this time embodied in the form of my computer and printer. I had insisted that my new hardware be safely enthroned in the car driven by my wife. These word-tool gods had to be air-conditioned, since my life depended on them. They had to be protected at all costs throughout the long days of highway heat. Therefore, my children, aged seven and four, nested in the back seat, on either side of the huge computer boxes. "Just as well," I thought. "It will keep them out of each other's hair." As Emmy and Joel listened to their tapes and read books, they happily shared their space with Jennifer, our little black-and-white cat. There had been no room for the cat carrier. For the first three days, Jennifer napped and quietly explored the car. At night, she silently crept about motel rooms, sniffing out musty closets, eating her Science Diet crunchies, coping far better than the rest of us. I secretly envied her equanimity. At the same time I'd been stranded on highways, cursing the weighty old furniture and books, hissing at the halting engine, I had also madly entertained increasingly drastic solutions, including this most dreaded one: "Go straight to the nearest airport, fly the rest of the way, and pay a crazed hitchhiker (one who looks like Bruce Dern or Jack Nicholson) to drive the damn truck."

So, the engine purred perfectly. Silken gears shifted silently. After a few hours of this bliss, we encountered our steepest grade, the monumentally vertical road out of Laramie. For forty-five minutes, my free right hand pushed mightily down on my right knee so that I could keep the accelerator floored—all desperately needed to keep the truck chugging at ten miles per hour. I was moving as fast as I could. My wife followed in the car behind me, blinkers flashing, fending off traffic. As I crept up the steep grade, inch by inch, I feared that the engine would gurgle and die at this slow speed. If that happened, I didn't expect the brakes to hold that much weight on the steep incline. The whole rig would slip back downhill, my old van in tow, leading the way to my dusty, fiery death. At this point, language was not doing me in. Instead, it was my mental imagery: the rapid-fire edited scenes of my truck, van, and car careening backward down the steep road, floating off the edge in slow motion, crashing into the hard rock far below, exploding into metal fragments mixed with slivers of bone and flesh. Somehow, though, we made it to the top.

After this trauma and a night in Cheyenne, we were off again, secure in our unshakeable belief that the worst was now behind us. Total renewal: a fresh morning shimmered before us, with no fears of unpacking, no fears of extra days teeming with hot labor and massive expenses. We happily hummed along the highway for, oh, forty minutes. Then, in my calm and blissful state, I happened to notice that my wife had pulled over onto the shoulder of Interstate 80. Still glowing in my hard-won relief, I cheerfully waved at them as I passed, assuming that she had merely paused to fill their water glasses and retrieve a cookie for our fortunate children. After a short time, she caught up with me, passed, and turned into a truck stop. I followed her because I needed gas anyway. A pleasant little stop would be good for all of us.

Few stress-racked parents (we had been on the road each day until dark for four days) could imagine a more unsettling sight than that which awaited me. Under the fiberglass canopy towering over the diesel gas pumps, my darling little girl, her tear-stained face contorted in agony, steadied herself against the car fender.

"Mommy killed Jennifer!" she sobbed.

Her small body convulsed in grief. I glanced up at my wife. Her hand was wrapped in layers of bloody Kleenex. My son was also bleeding. Jennifer had exploded in the car. The frenzied cat—teeth and claws extended—screeched, whirled, and careened from front to back, back to front, side to side. Fearing for her children, my wife pulled off the highway and rolled down the window, letting Jennifer dart into the sagebrush, finalizing her divorce from us. At this very moment, my wife had glanced up to see me glide by, surreal in my big, smooth-running rig, smiling and waving smugly—Chevy Chase, oblivious, in his National Lampoon moving truck, heading for another "adventures in moving" disaster. With no help and two hysterical, confused children, my wife rolled up her window and drove off after me.

After six days on the road, we arrived, benumbed, in Missouri. No crew was available to help us unload the truck. But that was okay, because we had decided to leave it parked in front of our rental house and drive another two hundred miles to buy a Dalmatian to replace Jennifer, who, I assured our kids, had been adopted by a kindly rancher (the only symbolic Band-Aid I could muster). With our children starting a new grade in a new school and city, with no friends, we wanted their minds focused on something positive. We all craved something positive.

So we bought Patty, the Dalmatian puppy my daughter had always pined for. Ever careful about who she entrusted her puppies to, the dog breeder grilled us for two hours to make sure that her puppy would thrive in a safe, healthy, loving environment. (We did not volunteer the details of our most recent trip.) Then we drove home to unload the truck ourselves. Patty—the wild, streaking, openhearted puppy—provided the explosion of optimism we sorely needed. We had never even touched a Dalmatian, and her thick silky coat assured us that life could be good, after all. She has turned out to be the gentlest dog we have ever known.

That was then. A year later, I was driving the same van I'd towed from Idaho when I thumped into the Dalmatian that I described at the beginning of this story—the one that came darting madly out of nowhere. That's why I was shaken. Even though I had seen the dog bounce up and run madly away, hitting it was like experiencing a Vietnam flashback. I told my family what happened. All through dinner and on my way to class, I bore the heavy baggage of my whole convoluted history of trucks and dogs and cats and kids and words and images.

That night in class, a graduate student was conducting the synesthesia experiment. After listening to somber instrumental music in pitch-blackness, I could do nothing except begin sketching a Dalmatian. More depressed than ever, I slowly outlined the dog's head and back. At this point, our teacher abruptly switched the music to rollicking Dixieland.

My black, heavy balloon of depression popped. Just like that.

I suddenly realized that the dog I'd hit earlier *was* very much alive, since it had landed on its feet and dashed away in a single fluid motion. My hand began quickly sweeping across the large sheet of butcher paper. I soon completed a Dalmatian with wild, happy eyes, its panting tongue streaming madly out of its mouth, trailing back behind its head, with all four legs outstretched, in crazed, very-much-alive flight. Its energy uplifted me as much as our own Dalmatian's spirit had elevated us after the road trip the year before.

Although these quicksilver changes in perception are hard to pin down, I do know that the new music altered or refocused my image. In this situation, words were irrelevant, but I was of course still thinking. In addition to the role of background and context, I was thinking musically, imagistically, or both, becoming absorbed in representations of reality that differ from language. Other symbol systems—in this case, images and music—had influenced *what* it was I chose to think about in language in the first place, as well as *how* I chose to cast those thoughts.

The changes wrought by shifting modalities that night in class were so uplifting that a week later I drew another, larger picture of this darting Dalmatian in full color—her legs fully outstretched, long tongue flapping, eyes wild in raw freedom. Above and below the soaring Patty, I drew my son and daughter flying right along after her, as they often did, visually linking my children's rebound with that provided by the dog. We framed the drawing and hung it in our home as a reminder that words are only one way of knowing—that language cannot always be counted on. Indeed, no symbol system can always be counted on; the meanings and structures of literacy—be they words, images, numbers, or music—are like my soaring dog: they never stand still. They never have and never will. It's just that sometimes we're more keenly aware of their flight, their seamless cycle of appearance and disappearance.

So that's the story. Rescued from my verbal doldrums by images and music, I felt lucky and relieved. Other modalities got me back on track. This experience became another stone in my "Hurray-for-Alternative-Symbol-Systems" pile—another rock placed in the wall against language, a wall which I have long championed. A wall built by Coleridge, Keats, van Gogh, Whitman, William Carlos Williams, Ingmar Bergman, Steven Spielberg, and countless other diviners of imagery. A wall fortified by Gardner's (1985) notion of multiple intelligences and Arnheim's (1986) lucid essays on the primacy of visual thinking.

Before I celebrate too hard, however, I am obligated to remind myself of a few things. First, nobody can completely avoid language, at least not for long. When I was sketching the Dalmatian during class, it's true that I was submerged in visual and aural imagery. But this question keeps surfacing: To what degree do nonlinguistic symbols alter our thinking—and to what degree is such change due to *the simple absence or displacement of language?* I have had similar epiphanies when I was not engaged in alternative symbol systems, but rather, when I was merely distracted from verbal thinking—when its volume was lowered or switched off as I hiked up a trail or washed dishes.

Second, I must remember that, even though language seemed to fail so many times on that trip, it also succeeded. For one, those brief talks with other drivers made a significant difference, helping me tame the truck from hell's garage. And again, telling my children that a kindly rancher would soon adopt Jennifer helped for a little while, when their grief burned hottest. Conversely, I must also remember that, while sketching the dog reshaped my verbal thinking in positive ways, images also worked against me on that trip, such as when I imagined the truck rolling backward off the mountain road.

Third, I have to remind myself that we often think of imagery and language as separate things. They are not. Visual and verbal thinking are more accurately characterized as interdependent processes. For example, both language and images are generative: words may elicit other words—or images; and images may elicit other images—or words (Paivio 1990; Begg 1983). Additionally, as a teacher I must remember that in the long run any type of symbol is neither better nor worse than any other. Imagery, like language, can giveth at the same time that it taketh away.

Finally, I have developed another perspective on my excruciating excursion. But before I explore this view and expose my amateur Jungian psychologizing, a little background about our move to Missouri is in order. During the four months before hitting the road, my psyche was split asunder, right down the middle. My professional self wanted to work in Missouri; my personal self wanted to live in Idaho. Just that simple. My professional need for renewal was locked in brutal battle with my personal needs for family, friends, and place. Unfortunately, forsaking the familiar has long been the wrenching price teachers must often pay to take advantage of new professional opportunities. (And, like imagery and language, our personal and professional selves continually merge and separate.) In Jungian terms, my self was "individuating"—pulling apart to become something other than what it was. We grow and change, often whether it agrees with us or not. So, while I was listening to and following my professional self, I was denying and battling my personal self. I was disconnected, not whole. Several times during this period, I crept within inches of dialing the phone, backing out of my new job, and yanking the **For Sale** sign out of the front yard of the home I so loved. This internal wrenching occurred even after an exhaustive period of careful deliberation with all parties about all possible issues.

Such battles with the self, such disregard for instincts, means—again according to Jung—that I was ripe for "synchronicity," an ancient way of knowing, which he defines as

> a meaningful coincidence of two or more events, where something other than the probability of chance is involved. . . . When coincidences pile up in this way, one cannot help being impressed by them—for the greater the number of terms in such a series, or the more unusual its character, the more improbable it becomes. (1969, 520–21)

Synchronicity explains the improbable events of my trip as well as any other explanation I have tried to muster. The trip's events may have occurred because I ignored my deep identity—my surface structure fell out of sync with my deep structure. Indeed, too many unrelated events piled up, which made uncanny sense to my ongoing internal struggle. In several ways, the truck seemed to work hard at *not* helping us. My professional reasons for moving (language, symbols) seemed to flare up at me every inch of the way, assuming different forms. Even our innocent cat refused the move. And, of course, there are those running dogs. I am constructing meaning out of these unrelated events, out of this chaos, through my private, idiosyncratic signs and symbols. And this is what I think Jung means when he states that synchronicity is an "*acausal* connecting principle" (418; emphasis added). As I understand Jung, the unconscious can only respond to such ruptures of the self through signs and symbols, such as synchronicity or dreams. The weird events which plagued me seem born from the battle between my professional and personal lives, yes, but also from the conflict between the conscious and unconscious. So—that's the best I can do with those August days of chaos. If you have an explanation that fits better, please send it to me, typed and double-spaced. (You could win a small appliance.)

While these events were happening, there seemed to be no order upon experience—no rhyme or reason for the weirdness. When that happens, life (or our perception of it) seemingly unravels. Since that trip, I've wondered how others fare in such situations, when little or nothing in life seems to work. I especially wonder about those people whose situations are far more extreme, more disorienting, more frightening than mine. I especially worry about my own students. In their early twenties, my students are academically accomplished, achievement oriented, bright, hardworking, polite, and seemingly secure and happy. Nonetheless, I cannot help but notice their extreme wariness about life, their obsessive caution about so many things, large and small. Almost like spooked cats, their watchfulness transcends the normal apprehension that most of us would expect from people their age. I wonder if my students have sensed more chaos in their experiences than I have perceived in mine. I wonder if my students have grown up surrounded by more chaos than I have— more frequent and intense episodes, when synchronicity had to kick in because there was no other way to make sense of their world.

The twenty-five years which separate me from my students' age have been filled with fundamental, radical changes in our culture, only a few of which I will mention here. First, since I was their age the family unit has shifted and redefined itself. Most of my students are children of separations, divorces, and remarriages. I know from their writing that it was invariably hard on them, especially at the time, and that its effects still rattle their identity and security.

Second, in the past few decades our collective perception of institutions, especially government, continues to erode. We live in a time when every government news story, deservedly or not, is christened with a name ending in "gate"—from Watergate to, at this writing, Monica-gate. By the time you read this, I suspect a few other gates will have swung open. Our students, then, have never had the luxury of sensing that their government stood steady behind them, a decent anchor to reality.

Third, our students have grown up in a country overloaded with information, which has helped make their lives fragmented and overspecialized. Whereas we formerly used one technician or one bureaucratic form or one brand of cereal or one department or one TV station, we now have 36—or 82 or 98 or 256. When overspecialization, fragmentation, and the volume and speed of information all run amok, we are forced to devote more of our lives to simply managing, to merely manipulating such things just to get through the day. We respond by training and educating people for increasingly specialized roles in narrowly defined jobs. What gets shortchanged (or completely ignored) is the individual's humanness and uniqueness—mainly, the unconscious—the deeply internal side of our selves. And, as my travelogue from hell suggests, when that side finds no expression, something else will make itself heard.

Fourth, American life may be more disorienting today due to the nature of the heavily saturated media/technology environment in which people are now bred. The world is dense with layers upon layers of signs and symbols—verbal, visual, musical, numerical, you name it. And the greater the number of messages, the more frequently any given message must be understood in terms of *other* messages, across time and space. And the greater this intertextuality, the more slippage occurs between signs and their referents. All of this creates uncertainty, makes it harder to figure out exactly what a message really means.

Further, the frequency and intensity of media messages help create a kind of symbolic vertigo (or vacuum) in which everything is simultaneously true and not true: O. J. Simpson is innocent in one media trial but guilty in another; Marshall Applewhite and his Heaven's Gate brethren embrace the hard logic of computers but drink poison cocktails to materialize at the next spiritual level. Our hot-wired world continually generates such instant media gods, reconfiguring or blotting up many other more grounded concerns. Such disorientation not only distances us from reality, but it also makes us less certain of who we are; how we connect to other people, places, and things; what our place in the world should be. In short, these shifting relationships between symbols and the things to which they refer, in addition to forcing individuals to live with truth and nontruth simultaneously, all mean less stable ground for students to stand on. And when the ground beneath us shakes, we move about warily, much like Jennifer the cat crept about our moving car. And occasionally, also like Jennifer, we take leave.

This catalog of contemporary American dilemmas could go on, of course, but my point is that such an incessantly shifting, unanchored culture necessarily generates chaos, or at least unpredictability, uncertainty, doubt, confusion—considerably more than I experienced growing up. Generally, when we find ourselves on shifting terrain, we try to negotiate meaning as we gingerly make our way, assuming of course that we have the time, ability, money, and inclination. This is the best-case scenario, although few of us have these resources instantly available when we need them. More likely, when we realize we are in chaos, we will impose our own structure—our own, more idiosyncratic meaning—on an experience, as I have done in the aftermath of my trip. Others may respond in less socially acceptable ways, through crime, violence, alcohol, drugs, or withdrawal.

So, because postmodern America seems so fragmented and ever shifting, I can advise nothing about teaching and renewal with absolute certainty. But even the most chaotic world imaginable automatically warrants that we try. So here goes. For starters, in an unstable world, teachers and students must become literate in as many symbol systems as possible, because these systems (and their conduits, electronic and otherwise) largely establish the codes by which we live and construct meaning out of life. Even our traditional definition of rationality is changing, due mainly (again) to our strong nurturance of technology and, especially, visual media. As Postman (1985), Purves (1994), Karl (1994), and others suggest, the temporal, detached, classificatory structures of print literacy are becoming subsumed by (and often replaced by) the structures of electronic and visual media, which are characterized by juxtaposition, contradiction, incongruity, immediacy, multiple contexts, hyperintertextuality, ambiguity, and emotion. Teachers and students must learn to accept, define, and understand this emerging form of rationality. Doing so will help us realize that such a basis of reality is neither inherently bad nor chaotic, just different.

Finally, regardless of our culture's chaos and mutations (or evolutions), what is most important is not technology, not representations of people, not language *about* people—but people themselves. Everything depends on our ring of students and colleagues, friends and family. For teaching, learning, and renewal to take place, our connections with people have to unfold on a level playing field of acceptance and trust. Only then can the heart assume more command.

What put me on the highway toward renewal during those August dog days was not *just* my love of language and symbols,

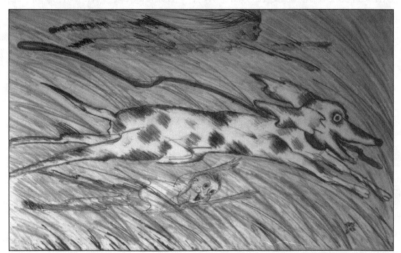

"Patty." Graphite, colored pencil, and ink on matte board, 15" x 24".

but also the sharing of them, within a context of equality, with other people. In my old job, which was more administrating than teaching, I didn't have enough of that. Moving remains the hardest thing I have ever done, but I have never regretted it. Every day, the power and beauty of symbols and the good people surrounding me reaffirm my decision. As for Patty, all of these issues—making meaning, renewing ourselves—remain irrelevant. Never running low on heart, she never doubts the wisdom of motion.

Toward a New Model for Teacher Renewal

ROY F. FOX

University of Missouri–Columbia

The purpose of this final chapter is twofold. First, I will speculate about how this study's four major themes or processes—social contexts, passion/flow experiences, voice, and dual identities—work together to generate the larger processes of *differentiation* and *integration*, which lead to a more complex and renewed self (see Figure 9.1). Then I will provide some recommendations for anyone concerned with teacher renewal, a light which illuminates far beyond the classroom.

Notes toward a New Model for Teacher Renewal

The four main processes operating in this study appear in the model depicted in Figure 9.1: social contexts, passion and flow experiences, voice, and the dual identities of professional/personal selves and adult/childlike selves. In this model, the two sets of selves (professional/personal and adult/childlike), as well as passion/flow and voice, surround the psychological processes of differentiation and integration, which comprise the self's "core." Working outward from the center of the model, differentiation and integration appear first, since they are responsible for reshaping the self. Simply put, differentiation means accepting or learning how one's self diverges from others, while integration means learning how one's self is akin to other people or ideas.

Next, in the ring surrounding differentiation and integration, you will find the more observable, concrete processes of passion/

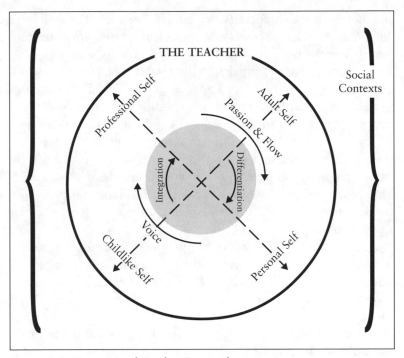

Figure 9.1. *Processes of Teacher Renewal*

flow and voice. That is, with some guidance and knowledge, we can often *see* these processes occur, as in Julia's questioning and conversing with students (Chapter 5) and in Kate's poetry writing (Chapter 1). Passion/flow and voice appear in the same circle because they can influence each other; one can lead to the other. Alex's energizing and highly positive experiences in a peer writing group—her episodes of passion and flow—helped to galvanize and extend her voice (Chapter 2). Stronger voices are typically the result of passion/flow experiences because we want to make sense of them for ourselves and others—which we accomplish through language.

Passion/flow and voice constitute the actions, words, images, feelings, and attitudes which lead to differentiation and integration. Hence, the passion, flow, and voice experienced by Julia, Kate, and Alex enabled them to differentiate or *separate* themselves from one element in their lives, as well as to integrate or *align* themselves more closely with other elements. These activities increased the complexity of each teacher's self. For example, Julia learned what she was *not*—a lecturer, thus *differentiating* herself from others, such as her own professors who relied on lectures and published criticism. Julia also learned what she *was*— a more equal conversation partner with students. Thus she *integrated* herself with others who were more like her. And these processes included flow experiences, which in turn helped to strengthen her voice. As Csikszentmihalyi (1991) and others argue, differentiation and integration create growth of the self by making it more complex. In other words, Julia became renewed. Differentiation and integration are two fundamental processes of identification which often work together, or at least one can lead to another.

Surrounding the first two rings in the center of Figure 9.1 you will see the dual identities: the professional/personal selves and the adult/childlike selves. Like the other elements of this model, these selves can interact with each other. It is most likely, however, that the two selves at the top of the model, the professional and adult selves, will interact with the two at the bottom, the childlike and personal selves, simply because these pairs differ so much from each other. That is, the professional and adult selves are similar to each other, as are the childlike and personal selves. For example, matters relevant to the professional self (e.g., participating in a state teachers' organization) roughly parallel concerns of the adult self (e.g., responsibility, consistency). By the same token, concerns of the personal self (e.g., relationships with family and friends, hobbies) are overall more compatible with concerns of the childlike self, such as play, pleasure, and freedom.

Also, each pair of identities appears on either end of a continuum or line to indicate their "opposing" relationship with each other. While most teachers usually function somewhere between these polarities, sometimes one type of self may dominate, as in the period when Tish focused exclusively on participating in professional organizations, even dressing the part. At other times—though much more rarely—a teacher's childlike self will dominate, as when Kim's principal visited her classroom and, just for fun, she asked her students to get down on their knees and chant, "Hail Mrs. Stover!" The four selves (two pairs) also interact with all of the other elements within the model. At the same time, they can function as *products* of all the "inner" processes. Overall, these dual identities oppose *and* complement each other, reflecting one of civilization's most elemental dichotomies (or complementarities).[1]

Finally, surrounding the teacher's self are social contexts, which range from family or colleagues to the community and larger culture. These social contexts also interact with the other elements of the teacher's selfhood, and they can help or hinder teacher renewal. For instance, school bureaucracy greatly distracted Kim from her teaching (Chapter 4). On the other hand, Kate's mentoring group helped her survive a traumatic first year in the classroom.

I should emphasize that each component of this model operates as an equal and reciprocal process. Each may affect the others. For example, the more a teacher's personal and/or childlike self operates in his or her teaching, the greater the chances that the teacher will engage in flow experiences and develop a professional voice and identity. Julia's professional and adult selves suffered when, early in her career, she panicked because she could not teach literature without depending on the ideas of professional critics and former professors. She felt like a failure as an adult and a professional expert. Julia eventually developed a more egalitarian and process approach by engaging students in questions and conversations about the literature—in essence, restoring balance by allowing her personal and childlike selves to attain more power. Consequently, Julia enjoyed teaching more and received positive feedback from her students, resulting in more frequent and intense flow experiences. These successes helped her to develop a stronger, more confident voice.

Although the major parts of this model are of equal importance, they are fluid and dynamic, constantly shifting, one expanding as another shrinks, as a teaching life evolves. As the cases in *UpDrafts* demonstrate, a teacher's selfhood is *relational*. It is therefore likely that one part will sometimes dominate the others. For example, Tish recalled that her professional and adult selves dominated her life during a period when she became active in teachers' organizations (Chapter 7). Change and growth occur when these approximately equal forces become skewed, as one force dominates the others, creating tension. Eventually, balance is restored, but not in the exact proportions as before. Tish reduced tension and regained some balance by changing her teaching focus and discovering a new personal relationship. Likewise, Kate restored equanimity by delving into poetry and pottery, and Alex decided to help teachers. Through the changes that contention and discord generate, conflicting selves become better integrated, rifts are healed, and fragmentation yields to a new kind of wholeness.

The components of this model are highly interactive because they overlap. For instance, an intense flow experience is often made concrete or visible by a teacher writing or talking about it. Such discourse is naturally going to be more grounded and anchored in detail, more emphatic and powerful, than the language produced about more humdrum experiences. Another reason these components are interactive is that one experience with flow, or with gaining voice, or with defining what we are or are not, often leads to another such experience. As to the question, "What, exactly, gets the model going in the first place—what ignites one of these components of renewal?," I have to answer, "That depends on the individual." The teachers profiled here had very different experiences and preferences. No single size of renewal fits all. Nor should we expect it to. Before I return to this central notion of uniqueness, let me venture some recommendations for the future of teacher renewal.

Recommendations

The following recommendations are suggested by the patterns observed in these case studies, as well as other sources, including the literature of professional development, self-actualization, technology, and culture.

1. *Demystify teacher renewal.* The most obvious conclusion of this study is that each teacher's route to renewal will be highly idiosyncratic. The second most obvious conclusion is that, while teachers are engaged in the processes of renewal, most will feel isolated. These two simple conclusions expose an irony for the

teaching profession: Something as desirable as renewal too often makes teachers feel like freaks, alienated from their profession and colleagues. Teachers feel alienated because they consider themselves somehow inferior or abnormal. The truth is that it is quite natural to question the status quo and look for something we perceive as better. Renewal is a natural part of a teacher's evolution. If we can accept this, then we can plan for it.

Renewal also needs to be demystified because it is invariably linked to "burnout"—a term which only perpetuates ignorance, exacting a heavy toll in time, energy, and expense. "Burnout" is a term which oversimplifies the complex phenomena of renewal because it locates the causes and effects within a single entity— the teacher himself or herself. This label elicits images of teachers who no longer care, or worse, who are somehow incapable of caring. In short, we tend to view burnout as something like leprosy, its scabbed victims slinking off to sell insurance.

This view of teachers, however, is inaccurate for the teacher-subjects in this study. (It is likely wrong for other teachers, as well, including those who never experience renewal.) In this project, teachers sought renewal for many reasons beyond the individual's control, as Kate does in Stanovick's chapter, "Making Myself Visible." In short, renewal seems *natural*—something that happens to most teachers, sooner or later, more than once. But we don't think of it this way.

Teacher renewal also remains a confusing concept because it is often thought of as "professional development": lectures about classroom management, outcomes-based assessment, or state department of education guidelines and bandwagons. And if it is not defined this way, it may be regarded as further training in one's specialized discipline—lectures about Shakespeare or recent research in cold fusion processes. While both areas are important, they usually ignore teachers' personal responses and lives—that vital main trunk which supports these branches.

In teaching and other professions, grapevine wisdom posits that anything "personal" is automatically disqualified from *also* being "professional." Whether one is a police officer, surgeon, or teacher, an unwritten rule prescribes that a "pro" never lets emotion get in the way of work—never lets anything on the job spill over into private life. It would all be too messy, the reasoning goes. In many people's minds, the terms "professional" and "personal" function as opposites.

Teachers are highly sensitive to being thought of as unprofessional because most have grown up in the throes of public criticism of education—from government reports to media hysteria about "declining standards" and "Why Johnny Can't Read"—or write or do math or chew gum. Additionally, these teachers focus narrowly on professionalism because they have grown up surrounded by media which depict teachers as anything *but* professional: from the befuddled Fred MacMurray as the absentminded professor to Eddie Murphy (and the manic Jerry Lewis before him) as the nutty professor; from the crazed professor in the *Back to the Future* films to the mean law professor in *The Paper Chase*; from the soused teacher in *Educating Rita* to the uninhibited one from *Beverly Hills 90210*. And, lest we forget, Jack Nicholson's character in *The Shining* was a teacher. In such contexts, it is little wonder that we divorce the professional from the personal.

Because teachers have been defined for us as inferior, and because "burnout" carries misconceived, ugly baggage, it therefore makes more sense to speak of "teacher renewal." This—the heart of teaching and learning—can no longer remain untended or ill-treated. It can no longer remain something mysterious, ill-planned, or not planned at all. Teachers, school systems, colleges of education, and the general public should accept teacher renewal as a normal and recurring stage of every teacher's work. We should plan for periodic renewal opportunities, such as scholarly sabbaticals, leaves without pay, role switching ("trying out" another grade level, class, or administrative position), internships in related and unrelated disciplines, and other nourishments. Also, when teachers are in training they need to learn that renewal is to be expected periodically throughout everyone's career. This can be achieved by having students read about famous teachers' highs and lows (e.g., Anne Sullivan), as well as by interviewing teachers in the field.

Finally, to help us demystify the nature of the term "renewal," we should resist our habit of looking for similarities across cases, of looking for patterns or commonalities in teachers' paths to renewal. In some ways, it is an inappropriate, even damaging, strategy because it denies or trivializes the profound uniqueness that we have to respect when people engage in renewal. It is like asking for common threads in each person's DNA. If we do not expect common routes in the first place, we will more effectively help teachers locate their own routes to renewal.

2. Reimburse teachers for the costs of professional development. Six teachers in this study cited their experience in writing projects as professionally energizing. Another teacher benefited from the whole language movement, and another from the National Education Association. Professional development helps teachers cultivate their personal and professional voices and thereby better define their identities and gain more independence. Teachers have a profound need to communicate with one another outside of their own schools. To accomplish this, teachers must receive financial support from their schools. Even internally motivated teachers will think twice before driving a hundred miles to attend a professional event if they also must pay for their own substitute teachers. Teaching seems to be one of the few professions in which people pay for their own professional development. Because professional development really works, it should be supported—but not from the teacher's paycheck.

3. Provide teachers with career/psychological counseling. When police officers experience trauma, their employer routinely sees that they receive the assistance they need. While teachers and law officers do not engage in the same type of work, and while many workplaces do sponsor employee "wellness" programs, the fact remains that teachers must usually fend for themselves. Given the constant, often volatile negotiation that occurs between teachers' professional/adult selves and their personal/childlike selves, it seems likely that counselors specifically trained for this dual focus could help—that, at the very least, they could contain some of the damage. Students will benefit the most—from more effective instruction and enhanced relationships with teachers and others—only when we tend to the *whole* of teacher renewal.

4. Provide participatory and flexible options for teacher renewal. Much of teachers' professional development work consists of relatively similar and passive experiences. Consider, however, that the highly effective teachers in this study were learners and students *first*—and teachers second. They valued participating in learning far more than serving as expert sources of information. Therefore, teachers should engage actively in other types of direct work experience, such as editing newspapers or magazines or coordinating community service organizations. Such experiences could include alternative internships in radically different content areas, with students of different cultures, environments, ages, and levels. After such experiences, teachers could either leave or return, invigorated with new perspectives. At the least, a mandatory wait period for people who decide to quit would be preferable to losing good teachers from the profession forever. Of course, most other professions do not tell their members to "Get another, completely different job, and then come back." But alive and good teaching differs from many other professions because it demands constant change and growth.

Further, teachers should have more freedom to decide *when* they should do these things. Some renewal projects may need to occur in many brief phases over a long period of time, while others may require a single, sustained activity. Teachers need to go elsewhere and do other things, much like college and university teachers do. In this study, all but two of the teachers somehow changed their jobs: they switched to new age and grade levels, new schools, similar disciplines, and even entirely new disciplines. These teachers had little or no flexibility in the timing of their renewal activities. However, *when* such activities occur is crucial and, again, one plan will not fit each teacher's highly unique needs for renewal.

The value of teacher renewal resides in teacher growth—not sheer consistency or longevity in any role or place. According to Bateson (1990), in order to grow, we must challenge the assumption that continuity in life is an unbroken thread of commitment, that consistency is a good thing. Alex and Pat changed disciplines, while Kate and Tish switched to teaching students of radically different age levels. Our research team agreed that these teachers changed and/or left their positions primarily because they cared so much, not because they didn't care at all. Leaving one's position is a serious, traumatic, and complex matter and should not be held against the teacher. Renewal is not something that only "other teachers" need. We should expect this natural and recurring stage.

When it comes to reinventing ourselves, we may be more like rock stars than doctors or lawyers. Bob Dylan could not spend his entire life singing "Blowin' in the Wind" again and again in exactly the same way. Instead, he felt the need to reinterpret this song as he changed. Even more, he felt the need to write new songs—to continue growing, to be alive.

5. Integrate teachers' personal development with professional development. We all need to anchor external ideas to personal matters. Only then will such ideas take on a life of their own. Some professional development programs recognize the value of not divorcing teachers' professional lives from their personal lives. For instance, it is common practice for National Writing Project sites to encourage teachers to explore personal issues and themes in their own writing, since "ownership" of one's writing is crucial for later response and revision. Teachers also collaborate on group projects which demand personal investment, as well as schedule working lunches together. Indeed, integrating a teacher's professional self with his or her personal self accounts for a large measure of this program's success. For the teachers explored here, one professional or personal renewal experience quickly led to another. It seems logical, then, that if teachers focused on professional and personal growth simultaneously, they would discover initial positive experiences earlier, thereby helping the renewal process to snowball more quickly.

Finally, the entire concept of professional/personal development needs to be better understood. Most of us are not good at translating our passion for our discipline into our own, more personal, uses. We even have a hard time translating teacher stories, like the ones in this book, into material for our own use. Instead, we tend to view them as museum artifacts residing behind glass cases, as fine pottery to be admired from a distance— not as canteens to hold the water we will drink from this morning. We are unskilled at these things because we view them as outside the boundaries of "professionalism."

6. Create environments which enable teachers to demonstrate their passion for content—for exploring it and for communicating it. Sadly, teachers' passion for their content—for inquiring into it and for communicating it with others—often gets cut off at the pass by the glitzy distractions of popular culture. In other words, our daily lives (and especially those of our students) are akin to a microwave oven that produces hot bits in a flash, but with damaged texture, poor taste, and less nutrition. Conditioned to expect the shock of "jolts per minute" delivered by electronic media, students and teachers become too conscious of keeping the class moving. Many of us fear becoming bored and boring. Conversely, if we ignore pacing, we lose students at the outset.

While we must provide variety and find middle ground here, the fact remains that flow experiences and demonstrations of passion cannot be predicted or prescribed in minute detail. Sorry, wrong paradigm. The environment conducive for teachers to demonstrate their passion is more like that of a Crock-Pot—a slow cook over time. For example, immersion in flow experiences demands that we *forget* about time. The same holds true for developing voice or for defining identity—for all the big, important things.

Although there is no magic recipe which fits all teacher and student needs, this kind of environment must be physically safe for everyone, of course, and psychologically safe as well, so that people will take risks. At the same time that teachers demonstrate their own passions, students must search for theirs—which means they must experiment with many activities which will *not* elicit their passion. We must define the classroom as a kind of laboratory for learning about learning—a place for reflective experimentation. Again, experiencing genuine, long-lasting enthusiasm demands much time. This calls into question our current gaggle of competitions and distractions in the classroom—from meaningless bureaucratic tasks, to the assigning of grades, to the arbitrary starting and stopping times of classes, to the prescribed movements of teachers and students, to the high value we place on students knowing bits of jargon. Teachers demonstrating passion and flow experiences, students comprehending and learning from them and then doing the same things themselves—all of this demands (indeed, has *always* demanded) deep context and deeper time, the two qualities most foreign to a technological, media-driven culture.

7. *Create environments which enable teachers to demonstrate how their passions connect to students' larger cultures.* Students who grow up in our hot-wired environment will also need to know how these passions—their teachers' as well as their own—connect to their larger culture, especially those media which resonate most powerfully with them, such as television, music, film, and computers. If passion, flow, and voice dominate instruction and teacher renewal, as they should, students must still understand how and why they intersect with the larger culture. After all, haven't students *always* needed to know how and why their classroom lesson links to the world outside? How the dots connect? Isn't this just a simple human need for context? Isn't this notion foundational for other educational movements, such as student-centered learning, or relevance in education, or whole language, or cultural studies, or experiential learning, or constructivism? Just as social context is the province of destructive forces, such as bureaucracy and teacher isolation, it is also home to saving graces—the fertile fields surrounding disciplines, the larger pictures of true knowledge.

Conclusion

The study presented in *UpDrafts* did not directly focus on the usual elements of teacher stress such as class size, job insecurity, school management, staff shortages, low salaries, classroom discipline, and time management. Nor did this study focus on the usual elements of relieving teacher stress such as exercise, biofeedback, and relaxation training. While these topics are useful and important, this study explored the larger, more abstract processes of teacher renewal: the development of teacher voice, the nature of passion and flow experiences, the integration of professional/adult selves with personal/childlike selves, and the roles of social context. These dynamic processes seem to encompass all else. However invisible and slippery these concepts are, I remain convinced that they constitute the root issues of what we are as teachers, of what we want to become.

Let me now reiterate the primary conclusion of this study: each teacher's route to renewal is highly unique. Similarly, the preceding seven recommendations for teacher renewal—and indeed this entire study—focus on the individual. Why is it so important to focus on teachers as individuals, especially for the future of teaching as a discipline? Let me answer by returning for a moment to the larger culture. Every time humans make a major shift—from being a hunter-gatherer society to becoming an agricultural one; then from agricultural to industrial; and now from industrial to informational—our social order is ruptured. It is logical that nations, regions, neighborhoods, and families become torn, because the larger culture is in the throes of change, shifting from one type of job and human relationship and educational system and way of thinking to new ones.

After the initial jolts of change, humans invariably gravitate toward cohesion and social order. We reorganize and reconstruct our lives, collectively and individually. Fukuyama (1999) reminds us that in the past, especially in the Industrial Age, we achieved social order through a "top-down mandate by hierarchical authority," such as that embodied in politics and religion (56). As many have argued, however, our age of technology and information is anything *but* hierarchical. Institutions can no longer impose sets of external rules on people who are now decentralized, who often live and work and think apart from centralized authority.

Instead, these days social order arises out of the "self-organization of de-centralized individuals"—an observation which has been empirically supported by, as Fukuyama further notes, a huge amount of research "coming out of the life sciences in recent years, in fields as diverse as neurophysiology, behavioral genetics, evolutionary biology, ethology, and biologically-informed approaches to psychology and anthropology" (56). The teachers in this study and others are the decentralized individuals of the Information Age who are creating a new social order—in their classrooms and beyond—by first imposing order in their own lives. By reconstructing and renewing *themselves*, they more effectively renew others. Tomorrow too there will be no external authority to do it for us, or even to help much. In the future, renewal must come primarily from within.

Note

1. This basic dichotomy or complementarity is reflected in the following pairs of elements: night and day; light and dark; yin and yang; emotion and reason; tension and equilibrium; complexity and simplicity; life and death.

WORKS CITED

Arnheim, Rudolf. 1986. *New Essays on the Psychology of Art*. Berkeley: University of California Press.

Atwell, Nancie. 1987. *In the Middle: Writing, Reading, and Learning with Adolescents*. Upper Montclair, NJ: Boynton/Cook.

Ayers, William, and William H. Schubert. 1994. "Teacher Lore: Learning about Teaching from Teachers." Pp. 105–21 in *Teachers Thinking, Teachers Knowing: Reflections on Literacy and Language Education*, ed. Timothy Shanahan. Urbana, IL: National Council of Teachers of English.

Bakhtin, Mikhail. 1981. "Discourse in the Novel." Pp. 259–422 in *The Dialogic Imagination: Four Essays*, ed. Michael Holquist, trans. Caryl Emerson and Michael Holquist. Austin: University of Texas Press.

Bateson, Catharine. 1990. *Composing a Life*. New York: Plume Books.

Bateson, Gregory. 1978. "The Birth of a Double Bind." Pp. 39–65 in *Beyond the Double Bind: Communication and Family Systems, Theories, and Techniques with Schizophrenics*, ed. M. Berger. New York: Brunner/Mazel.

Begg, Ian. 1983. "Imagery and Language." Pp. 288–309 in *Imagery: Current Research, Theory, and Application*, ed. A. Sheikh. New York: John Wiley.

Belenky, Mary Field, Blythe McVicker Clinchy, Nancy Rule Goldberger, and Jill Mattuck Tarule. 1986. *Women's Ways of Knowing: The Development of Self, Voice, and Mind*. New York: Basic Books.

Bissex, Glenda L. 1994. "Teacher Research: Seeing What We Are Doing." Pp. 88–104 in *Teachers Thinking, Teachers Knowing: Reflections on Literacy and Language Education*, ed. Timothy Shanahan. Urbana, IL: National Council of Teachers of English.

Britzman, Deborah. 1994. "Is There a Problem with Knowing Thyself? Toward a Poststructuralist View of Teacher Identity." Pp. 53–75 in

Teachers Thinking, Teachers Knowing: Reflections on Literacy and Language Education, ed. Timothy Shanahan. Urbana, IL: National Council of Teachers of English.

Carter, Kathy. 1993. "The Place of Story in the Study of Teaching and Teacher Education." *Educational Researcher* 22 (January–February): 5–18.

Cohen, Rosetta Marantz, and Samuel Scheer, eds. 1997. *The Work of Teachers in America: A Social History through Stories*. Mahwah, NJ: Lawrence Erlbaum.

Csikszentmihalyi, Mihaly. 1991. *Flow: The Psychology of Optimal Experience*. New York: HarperPerennial.

————. 1997. "Intrinsic Motivation and Effective Teaching." Pp. 72–81 in *Teaching Well and Liking It: A Flow Analysis*, ed. James L. Bess. Baltimore: Johns Hopkins University Press.

Csikszentmihalyi, Mihaly, and J. W. Getzels. 1988. "Creativity and Problem Finding." Pp. 91–116 in *The Foundations of Aesthetics*, ed. F. H. Farley and R. W. Neperud. New York: Praeger.

Csikszentmihalyi, Mihaly, J. W. Getzels, and S. Kahn. 1984. *Talent and Achievement: A Longitudinal Study of Artists*. Report to the Spencer Foundation and to the MacArthur Foundation. Chicago: University of Chicago.

Dana, Nancy Fichtman. 1995. "Action Research, School Change, and the Silencing of Teacher Voice." *Action in Teacher Education: The Journal of the Association of Teacher Educators*, 16(4): 59–70.

Deci, Edward L., Tim Kasser, and Richard M. Ryan. 1997. "Self-Determined Teaching: Opportunities and Obstacles." Pp. 57–75 in *Teaching Well and Liking It: Motivating Faculty to Teach Effectively*, ed. James L. Bess. Baltimore: Johns Hopkins University Press.

Deren, Deborah. 1997. "Wings of Madness: What Does Clinical Depression Feel Like?" Homepage. 4 May 1997 <http://members. aol.com.depress>.

Dodson, Susan. 1998. "An Examination of the Sources and Practices of Art as Transformation: A Case Study of Peter London's Philosophy and Teaching Process." Ph.D. diss., University of Missouri–Columbia. Quotes from: London, P. 1995. "Transforming the Art of Art Education." Paper presented at Colorado Art Education Conference, October, in Breckenridge, Colorado.

Drake, S. M., A. E. Elliot, and J. Castle. 1993. "Collaborative Reflection through Story: Towards a Deeper Understanding of Ourselves as Women Researchers." *Qualitative Studies in Education* 6(4): 291–301.

Elbow, Peter. 1990. *What Is English?* New York: Modern Language Association.

———, ed. 1994. *Landmark Essays on Voice and Writing*. Davis, CA.: Hermagoras Press.

Fine, Michelle. 1987. "Silencing in Public Schools." *Language Arts* 64(2): 157–74.

Frankl, Victor. 1963. *Man's Search for Meaning*. New York: Washington Square.

Freire, Paulo. 1993. *Pedagogy of the Oppressed*. NY: Continuum.

Fried, Robert. 1995. *The Passionate Teacher: A Practical Guide*. Boston: Beacon Press.

Frymier, Jack. 1987. "Bureaucracy and the Neutering of Teachers." *Phi Delta Kappan* 69 (September): 9–15.

Fukuyama, Francis. 1999. "The Great Disruption: Human Nature and the Reconstitution of Social Order." *Atlantic Monthly,* May, 55–80.

Gardner, Howard. 1985. *Frames of Mind: The Theory of Multiple Intelligences*. New York: Basic Books.

Gilligan, Carol. 1994. "Letter to Readers, 1993." Pp. 177–85 in *Landmark Essays on Voice and Writing*, ed. Peter Elbow. Davis, CA: Hermagoras Press.

Goldberg, Natalie. 1984. *Writing Down the Bones: Freeing the Writer Within*. Boston: Shambhala Publications.

Gombrich, E. H. 1982. *The Sense of Order: A Study in the Psychology of Decorative Art*. 2d ed. Ithaca, NY: Cornell University Press.

Guggenbuhl-Craig, Adolf. 1979. *Power in the Helping Professions*. Irving, TX: Spring Publications.

Hayakawa, S. I., and Alan Hayakawa. 1990. *Language in Thought and Action*. 5th ed. San Diego: Harcourt Brace.

Heilbrun, Carolyn G. 1988. *Writing a Woman's Life*. New York: Norton.

hooks, bell. 1994. *Teaching to Transgress: Education as the Practice of Freedom*. New York: Routledge.

———. 1994. "When I Was a Young Soldier for the Revolution: Coming to Voice." Pp. 51–58 in *Landmark Essays on Voice and Writing*, ed. Peter Elbow. Davis, CA: Hermagoras Press.

Inchausti, Robert. 1993. *Spitwad Sutras: Classroom Teaching as Sublime Vocation*. Westport, CT: Bergin and Garvey.

Jung, Carl. 1969. *The Structure and Dynamics of the Psyche*. Vol. 8 of *The Collected Works of C. J. Jung*. 2d ed. Translated by R. F. Hall. Bollinger Series XX. Princeton: Princeton University.

———, ed. 1976. *Man and His Symbols*. Garden City, NY: Doubleday.

Karl, Herb. 1994. "The Image Is Not the Thing." Pp. 193–203 in *Images in Language, Media, and Mind*, ed. Roy Fox. Urbana, IL: National Council of Teachers of English.

Korzybski, Alfred. 1933. *Science and Sanity: An Introduction to Non-Aristotelian Systems and General Semantics*. Lancaster, PA: Science Press Printing.

Lamott, Anne. 1994. *Bird by Bird: Some Instructions on Writing and Life*. New York: Random House.

Lieberman, Ann, and Lynne Miller. 1992. *Teachers—Their World and Their Work: Implications for School Improvement*. New York: Teachers College Press.

Lindley, Daniel A. 1993. *This Rough Magic: The Life of Teaching*. Westport, CT: Bergin and Garvey.

Maslow, Abraham. 1954. *Motivation and Personality*. New York: Harper.

Murray, Donald. 1990. "Teaching the Other Self: The Writer's First Reader." Pp. 33–43 in *To Compose: Teaching Writing in High School and College*, ed. Thomas Newkirk. 2d ed. Upper Montclair, NJ: Boynton/Cook.

North, Stephen. 1987. *The Making of Knowledge in Composition: Portrait of an Emerging Field*. Portsmouth, NH: Heinemann.

Paivio, Allan. 1990. *Mental Representations: A Dual Coding Approach*. New York: Oxford University Press.

Postman, Neil. 1985. *Amusing Ourselves to Death: Public Discourse in the Age of Show Business*. New York: Viking.

Purves, Alan. 1994. "People Prose." Pp. 21–28 in *Images in Language, Media, and Mind,* ed. Roy Fox. Urbana, IL: National Council of Teachers of English.

Ruddick, Sara. 1980. "Maternal Thinking." *Feminist Studies* 6 (Summer): 342–67.

Stake, Robert E. 1995. *The Art of Case Study Research: Perspectives on Practice*. Thousand Oaks, CA: Sage Publications.

Sussman, Henry. 1989. *High Resolution: Critical Theory and the Problem of Literacy*. New York: Oxford University Press.

Zebroski, James T. 1989. "The Social Construction of Self in the Work of Lev Vygotsky." *Writing Instructor* (Summer): 149–56.

Zeichner, Kenneth, and Daniel Liston. 1996. *Reflective Teaching: An Introduction*. Mahwah, NJ: Lawrence Erlbaum.

INDEX

Abortion, 116
Acausality, 159
Adult/childlike selves, xxxvii–xli, 3–4, 64, 125, 166, 167
Alex, xxvi, xxx, 1–4, 24–42
Alsup, Janet, xxvii, 61, 65, 189
Applewhite, Marshall, 161
Arnheim, Rudolph, 157
Art, 20–22, 35–36
Assignments. *See also* Classroom practices
  hero paper, 74
  poetry, 75–77
  research projects, 69–70, 114
  wasting of time with, 28–30, 42, 80
Attention, 111–12
Atwell, Nancie, 80
Ayers, William, xix

Bakhtin, Mikhail, xxxiv
Barrier Breakers, 121
Baruffi, Susan, xxvi, 24, 189
Basketball, 6–8
Bateson, Catharine, xxi
Bateson, Gregory, 172
Begg, Ian, 157
Belenky, Mary Field, 81, 118, 120
Block scheduling, 73, 75
Britzman, Deborah, xxi, xxxiv–xxxv, 136
Bureaucracy, xxvii–xxviii, 62, 70, 78, 82, 134, 167
Burnout, 128–29, 131, 135, 137–40, 143, 169

Carole, xxvi, xxxiii, xl, 1–4, 44–59
Carter, Kathy, 5, 66, 180
Castle, J., 23
Change agents, 80
Chaos, 148–63
  synchronicity and, 158–59
Childhood experiences, 56–59
Chuang Tzu, xxxii
Classroom practices, 28–30, 80, 96–100, 119–20, 174. *See also* Assignments
  content and, 174
  outside world and, 175
  pacing and, 174
  student-centered classroom, 85–106, 118
Cognitive processes, 81–82
Cohen, Rosetta Marantz, xx
Collaboration
  student, 62
  teacher, 26, 77–78, 121
Community, 9–10, 137, 162–63. *See also* Collaboration; Mentoring
Competition versus cooperation, 63, 111, 117
Complementarity, 177
Complexity, xxxi–xxxii, 82, 112, 143–44
Computer-assisted teaching, xii
Connections. *See* Community
Control, paradox of, 114
Council for Advancement and Support of Education (CASE), 85

Creativity, 35–36, 75–77
Crosswinds (metaphor), 61–64
Csikszentmihalyi, Mihaly, xi, xx,
    xxxi, xxxii, 13, 49, 50, 51,
    74, 78, 82, 89, 100, 105,
    110–14, 120, 129, 135,
    146, 166
Cultural diversity classes, 121,
    128, 130, 143
Cultural health, xxviii
Curriculum, xi, xviii, xxxvi, 69.
    See also Assignments;
    Classroom practices
    medical ethics, 115–16
Cynicism, xxvi

Dana, Nancy Fitchman, 180
Daydreaming, 49. *See also*
    Visualization
Deci, Edward L., 114, 119
Deren, Deborah, 138
Dialogue, 62–63, 86–89
Differentiation, xxxi–xxxii,
    164–66
Disciplinary knowledge, xviii,
    90–92, 174
Drake, S. M., 23
Drama, 2, 3, 50–56
Dual identities, xxxv–xli, 3–4,
    64, 125, 136, 140, 166–67.
    See also Adult/childlike
    selves; Professional/
    personal selves
Du Bois, W. E. B., xx
Dunnington, Esther, xxii

Editing, 101–2
Elbow, Peter, xxxiv, 95–96, 97
Eliot, T. S., xxvii
Elliot, A. E., 23
Emerson, Ralph Waldo, 127
Emotional health, xxviii
English Journal, 102

Euthanasia, 116
Extracurricular activities,
    132–34

Faculty senate meetings, 133, 139
Family as institution, 160
Feedback, 4, 26, 31
    comments, 94
    freshmen and, 97–100
    loop, 94
    as renewal, 85–106
Fine, Michelle, 18
Flow experiences, 164–65
    concentration and, 51
    cooperation as, 63
    definition of, 51
    dialogue as, 62–63
    horseback riding as, 145–47
    hypothesizing and, 62
    poetry and, 2
    reflection as, 74–75, 78
    surprise and, 114
    talking as, 14–15, 18–19
    time and, 174
    visualizing and, 2
    volatility and, 124
    writing as, 13
Fox, Roy F., xvii, 123–25, 148–63,
    164, 187
Frankl, Victor, xxi
Freire, Paulo, 82, 109
Fried, Robert, xxi, xxvix, xxx
Frymier, Jack, xxvi, xxvii, xxviii
Fukuyama, Francis, 176

Gardner, Howard, 157
Getzels, J. W., xx
Gilligan, Carol, 7
Goldberg, Natalie, 34
Gombrich, E. H., 149
Government, 160
Grammar, 68, 79–80
Guggenbuhl, Craig, xl

Happiness
  ownership and, 59
  work and, 133
Hayakawa, Alan, 148
Hayakawa, S. I., 148
Health, xxviii
Heilburn, Carolyn, xxiv
Homosexuality, 1, 3, 137–41
hooks, bell, 16, 18
Hopkins, Gerard Manley, xl,
  102–4
Horseback riding, 131, 139,
  145–47
Humor, 64, 77–78, 81

Identity. *See* Dual identities
Imagery, 157
Imagination, 43–59. *See also*
  Creativity
Inchausti, Robert, xxxix, xxxviii
Independent learning, 119
Individuation, 158
Information, 160
Inner child. *See* Adult/childlike
  selves
Inquiry. *See also* Dialogue
  teaching and, 113, 115–20
Integration, xxxi–xxxii, xxxvi,
  164–66
Internal versus external stimula-
  tion, 50–51
Isolation, xix, xxv–xxvi, 8–10,
  123–24

Journal writing, 10–15
Jung, Carl, xxi, 158, 159

Kahn, S., xx
Karl, Herb, 162
Kasser, Tim, 114, 119
Kate, xviii–xix, xxv–xxvi, xxxiii,
  xxxvi, xl, 1–4, 5–23
Keats, John, 88

Korzybski, Alfred, 153
Kozol, Jonathan, xvii

Lamott, Anne, 33
Language
  as communication, 148
  generative principle of,
    152–53, 157
  imagery and, 157
  paradigm of multiplicity, 152
  powerlessness of, 150, 157
  as a shaper of thinking, 148
  voice and, 165
Learning-in-retirement classes,
  104
Lieberman, Ann, xx
Lindley, Daniel A., xl, xxi, xxxix
Liston, Daniel, 71
Literacy, xi, 161–62
Literature, 72, 90
  division between literature and
    writing, 95–96
London, Peter, xxxix, xxxviii
Lying, 54–55

Marx, Karl, xxxii
Maslow, Abraham, xxi
Mass production, applied to
  schools, xi
Maternal thinking
  characteristics of, 117–20
  as renewal, 107–22
Meaning
  "beholder's share," 149
  socially constructed, 97, 140
  in teaching, 134, 135, 140
  in texts, 95
Media. *See* Popular culture and
  media
Media expert, 36–39
Medical ethics, 115–16
Mental imagery, 2, 4. *See also*
  Visualization
Mentaya College, 8

Mentoring, xl, 1, 9–10
Mill, J. S., 129
Miller, Lynne, xx
Missouri Writing Project, 25, 27–28, 30–31, 71, 136, 142
Modern Language Association (MLA), 100
Multiple intelligences, 157
Murray, Donald, xxxii
Music, 155–56

Narrative
  as inquiry, xxiv–xxv
  personal, 65–66, 72
  as retelling story, 22–23
National Council for the Accreditation of Teacher Education (NCATE), 85
National Council of Teachers of English (NCTE), 85, 100–101
NCTE's Public Doublespeak Committee, 148
National Education Association, 135, 136
National Writing Project, xxxiv, 29, 173
NCTE's Double Speak Committee, 148
New England Journal of Medicine, The, 116
Noise, xxvii
North, Stephen, 73

Optimism, 50, 52

Paivio, Allan, 157
Passion. *See* Flow experiences
Pedagogy, xxxvi, 69, 71, 91, 118
  change and, 80
  dialogue and, 86–89
Pep assemblies, 48–49

"Perfect Picture, The," 32–33
Physical education, 111
Physical health, xxviii
Poetry, 2, 12–15, 25, 75–77
Pollack, Pat, xxvi, 61–64, 108–22, 172
Popular culture and media, xxviii–xvix, 160–61, 176
  health and, xxviii
Postman, Neil, 162
Pottery, 20–22
Professionalism, xxxvi, 97, 169–70
  costs of professional development, 171
  organizations, 100–105, 135–37
Professional/personal selves, xxxv–xxxvii, 3–4, 5, 15–18, 135–37, 158–59, 166, 167, 169–70
  integrating, 173
Psychology, 119–20
Purves, Alan, 162

Reader-response theory, 97
Reading methods, 107–10
Rebellion, 117–22
Reflection, 65–84
  learning how to reflect, 70–77
  reflective teaching, 71, 174
Renewal, teacher
  chaos as, 148–63
  definition, xviii
  demystifying, 168–69
  doubts and, 135, 140
  feedback as, 85–106
  flexible options for, 171–72
  imagination as, 43–59
  individual nature of, 176
  maternal thinking as, 107–22
  model for, 164–77
  periodic opportunities for, 170
  processes. *See also* Social context
  dual identities, xxxv–xli. *See also* Dual identities

flow experiences,
xxx–xxxiii. *See also*
Flow experiences
social contexts and,
xxv–xxix. *See also*
Social context
voice, xxxiii–xxxv. *See also*
Voice
recommendations for, 168–75
as reflection, 65–84
searching as, 127–47
voice as, 5–23
writing as, 24–42
Research. *See also* Study design
action, 79–82
research projects, 69–70, 114
teacher as researcher, 72–74,
79–82, 113
Richardson, Marilyn, xxvi, 61,
107, 189
Risk taking, 75–77, 174
Rofes, Eric, xx
Ruddick, Sara, 110, 117, 119, 122
Ryan, Richard M., 114, 119

Scheer, Samuel, xx
Schubert, William H., xix
Schultz, Marilyn, xxvi, 61, 85, 189
Searching as renewal, 127–47
Seeing scenarios. *See* Visualization
Self, 111–12, 119
reinventing, 173
as relational, 167
Self-exile, xix, 8–9. *See also*
Isolation
Shaw, Patrick, xviii, 123, 127, 189
Silencing. *See* Voice
Silverstein, Shel, 109
Simpson, O. J., 161
Social context, xxv–xxix, 1–2,
62, 123–24, 164, 167,
176. *See also* Bureaucracy;
Isolation; Popular culture
and media
Social health, xxviii

Social learning, 119
Socratic questioning, 86–87. *See
also* Dialogue; Inquiry
Spenser, Tish, xviii–xix, xxxvi,
123–25, 127–47, 172
Stake, Robert E., xix, xxiv
Stanovick, Lucy, xviii, xxv, 5, 189
Story. *See* Narrative
Stover, Kim, xxvii, xxx, xl,
61–64, 66–84, 166
Stress, 51
Stuart, Jesse, xx
Students
collaboration among, 62. *See
also* Teacher-student
relationship
freshmen, 97–100
giving books to, 46
high school students, 68–69
lying and, 54–55
middle school students, 69–77
student-centered classroom,
85–106, 118
wasting time of, 28–30, 42
Student Teacher Association, 135
Student-teacher relationship
student-centered classroom,
85–106, 118
Study design, xix–xxv
case study selection, xxi–xxiii
emergent approach, xix
narrative as inquiry, xxiv–xxv
procedures, xxiii–xxiv
theoretical framework, xx–xxi
Sullivan, Anne, xx, 170
Support system. *See* Community
Sussman, Henry, 153
Symbols, xviii, 157, 162–63
Synchronicity, 158–59
Synesthesia experiment, 148–49,
155–56

T. S. Eliot Society, 100–101
Tailwinds (metaphor), 1–4
Talking workshop, 10

Teachers
  as co-learners, 113
  counseling for, 171
  identity. *See* Dual identities
  institutionalized, 140
  public discomfort with, xxvi
  rebellion, 117–22
  as researchers, 72–74, 79–82, 113
  roles of, xvii, xviii
  in Roman Empire, xi
  slaves as, xi
  successful, xxi–xxiii, xxx
Teacher's lounge, 26, 43
Teacher-student relationship
  equality and, xl, 167
  fear and, xl
Teaching
  context, xviii, xxix. *See also* Social context
  doubts and, 135, 140
  learning how to, 67–70
  leaving, 36–39, 82–84
  liberating teaching, 18
  methodology, 90–92, 119. *See also* Classroom practices
  pressures, xii, xviii
  proactive approach, 45
  renewal. *See* Renewal, teacher
  as sacred task, xi
  student-centered, 85–106, 118
  technology and, xii, xxviii
  time away from, 22
  trial-and-error approach, 71
Teaching awards, 85
Technology, xii, xxviii
Text
  classroom as, 80
  fragmentation, xxix
  location of meaning in, 95
Therapy, 3, 16–17, 19
"To Autumn" (Keats), 88
To Kill a Mockingbird, 72
Transformation, 110–13

Visualization, 2, 4, 46–49. *See also* Drama
Voice, xxxiii–xxxv, 2–3, 63–64, 124, 165
  bureaucracy and, 78
  as renewal, 5–23
Vygotsky, Lev, 119

Watson, Dorothy, 109
Weisner, Jill, xxvi, 43, 190
"What's in the Sack?" (Silverstein), 109
Whirlwinds (metaphor), 123–25
White, Julia, xxvi, xxix, xxxiii, xl, 61–64, 85–106, 166, 167
Whitman, Walt, xx, 113
Whole language, 109, 110, 112, 120–22
Wilcox, Dorothy, 44
Willard, Emma Hart, xx
Work, 89, 133
Writing
  academic, 144
  division between literature and writing, 95–96
  every day, 30–31
  inspiration, 34
  as a means of coping, 10–15
  mythology of, 34
  ownership, 28, 173
  personal narrative, 65–66
  practice, 34
  process, 145
  as renewal, 24–42
  teaching, 26, 28–30, 93–96, 136–37
  truth and, 31–34

Yearbook, 132

Zebroski, James T., 119
Zeichner, Kenneth, 71

EDITOR

Roy F. Fox teaches courses in language, literacy, and culture at the University of Missouri–Columbia, where he also directs the Missouri Writing Project. His book-length study of how in-school television commercials affect students, *Harvesting Minds* (1996), received second place for the 1998 George Orwell Award for Distinguished Contribution to Clarity and Honesty in Public Discourse. Fox's other books include *Images in Language, Media, and Mind* (1994), *Technical Communication: Problems and Solutions* (1994), and *MediaSpeak: Three American Voices* (forthcoming). From the University of Missouri–Columbia, Fox received the Maxine Christopher Schutz Award for Distinguished Teaching and the William T. Kemper Fellowship for Teaching Excellence.

CONTRIBUTORS

Janet Alsup teaches English education courses at Purdue University, West Lafayette, Indiana. She received her Ph.D. from the University of Missouri–Columbia and taught high school English for seven years in central Missouri schools. Alsup has worked in several summer institutes for practicing teachers and serves as co-assistant director of the Missouri Writing Project.

Susan Baruffi, a native Chicagoan, received her B.A. from the University of Illinois at Urbana-Champaign in 1989. In 1992 she received her master's in English at the University of Missouri–Columbia. Since then she has taught high school Spanish and English in rural Missouri and in St. Louis. She now serves as a Missouri Writing Project co-assistant director.

Marilyn Richardson is assistant professor at Lincoln University in Jefferson City, Missouri, where she teaches basic writing and cultural diversity courses. Her focus of study is rhetoric and composition, writing to learn, and the pedagogy of diverse learners.

Marilyn Schultz teaches English and educational psychology at Lincoln University in Jefferson City, Missouri. She has been involved in teaching since 1969, a career disrupted for several years when she became a social worker. Schultz is also pursuing a doctorate in English education.

Patrick Shaw teaches writing in the developmental studies department at Lincoln University in Jefferson City, Missouri, where he has taught since 1990. His research interests include basic writing instruction, popular culture, and visual literacy. He is currently pursuing a Ph.D. in English education at the University of Missouri–Columbia.

Lucy Stanovick teaches courses in English education and freshman rhetoric and composition at the University of Missouri–Columbia, where she is also a doctoral candidate in English education. Stanovick serves as co-assistant director of the Missouri Writing Project. She previously served as literacy coordinator for the Columbia Adult Basic Education Program and taught high school in southwest Virginia.

Contributors

Jill Weisner, an Oregon native, received her Ph.D. in English education from the University of Missouri–Columbia. She is currently assistant professor of literacy education at Wilamette University in Oregon. Her research interests include the role of autobiography in reflective practice and feminist pedagogy.

This book was typeset in Adobe Sabon by Electronic Imaging.
Typefaces used on the cover include Giovanni and Latin Extra Condensed.
The book was printed on 50-lb. Williamsburg Offset by Versa Press.